EAST GERMAN HISTORIANS SINCE REUNIFICATION

EAST GERMAN HISTORIANS SINCE REUNIFICATION

A DISCIPLINE TRANSFORMED

Edited by

AXEL FAIR-SCHULZ AND MARIO KESSLER

SUNY PRESS

Cover photo of Brandenburg Gate from iStockphoto.

Published by State University of New York Press, Albany

Printed in the United States of America

For information, contact State University of New York Press, Albany, NY
www.sunypress.edu

Production, Diane Ganeles
Marketing, Michael Campochiaro

Library of Congress Cataloging-in-Publication Data

Names: Fair-Schulz, Axel, 1969– editor of compilation. | Kessler, Mario, 1955– editor of compilation.
Title: East German historians since reunification : a discipline transformed / edited by Axel Fair-Schulz and Mario Kessler.
Description: Albany : State University of New York Press, [2017] | Includes bibliographical references and index.
Identifiers: LCCN 2016031464 (print) | LCCN 2016034510 (ebook) | ISBN 9781438465371 (hardcover : alk. paper) | ISBN 9781438465364 (pbk. : alk. paper) | ISBN 9781438465388 (ebook)
Subjects: LCSH: Germany (East)—Historiography. | Germany (East)—History—Study and teaching. | Historians—Germany (East)
Classification: LCC DD281.6 .E19 2017 (print) | LCC DD281.6 (ebook) | DDC 907.2/0431—dc23
LC record available at https://lccn.loc.gov/2016031464

10 9 8 7 6 5 4 3 2 1

In memoriam.

Georg G. Iggers (1926–2017) and

William A. Pelz (1946–2017)

Contents

Introduction

AXEL FAIR-SCHULZ AND MARIO KESSLER

Two and a half decades have passed since the collapse of the former German Democratic Republic, the GDR, and its absorption into the Federal Republic of Germany. With the end of the East German state, its historians and traditions of historiography have also reached a critical point where they were removed from the once dominant mainstream discourse and relegated to the periphery of historical reflection. As early as by the mid-1990s, only around forty historians were still in their old posts. Twenty-two had been offered temporary positions within the Wissenschaftlerintegrations-Programm (WiP), a scheme set up to allow them to continue researching and teaching. Less than a handful succeeded to be appointed by universities after their WiP contract had expired. Today, less than a dozen GDR-trained historians are employed by universities or various research institutions, such as the Zentrum für Zeithistorische Forschung, the Center for Contemporary History, at Potsdam (Germany).[1] Others established a network of alternative research activities primarily around the Party of Democratic Socialism (now Die Linke), the renewed successor of GDR's old ruling party, the SED (Socialist Unity Party of Germany).[2]

A conference entitled "The Transformation of Historical Scholarship in Eastern Germany Since 1990" that was held at the State University of New York at Potsdam (USA) on September 1–2, 2008, sought to understand and assess what has been gained and lost in this process of transformation and dissolution of practically all former GDR historical institutions. The conference was co-organized by Initiative Sozialwissenschaftler Ost, an informal network of East Germans that lobbied on behalf of scholars from the former

GDR.[3] The conference participants were keenly aware of the human costs involved in this complex and contradictory process.

Scholars from the former GDR and the United States responded to the call for this conference and delivered papers, while invited West German scholars did not. The conference organizers were very interested in including papers from East German historians who could not attend the symposium and accepted, therefore, delay of publication. Some of the contributors finished their papers despite serious health problems. Several papers are more panoramic in scope, while others offer detailed studies of particular institutions or subdisciplines in the East German historical profession. In addition, our authors vary greatly by age and background. While some historians, like Marcus P. Aurin and Axel Fair-Schulz, came of age after the transition of 1989–1990, others, like Ludwig Elm and Werner Röhr, lived through much of the East German experience and were socialized within its academic culture. Again, other participants, like Georg G. Iggers and Konrad H. Jarausch, have observed East Germany and its historians largely from the outside, while having visited East German institutions and colleagues many times over the decades. Other contributing scholars, like Stefan Bollinger and Mario Kessler, represent the generation of East German historians who came of age during the 1980s. The editors of this book come from two locations that bear the same name: Potsdam (New York), USA, and Potsdam, Germany.

In the following paragraphs, the basic ideas of the different contributions are briefly presented.

Mario Kessler: *A Different Starting Point, a Different End: East and West German Historiography After 1945* gives an overview of historical scholarship in both German states during the beginnings of the Cold War. The impact of Western political culture upon German society after 1945 was substantial. Within West German universities, however, the process of democratization occurred very late. A fundamental de-Nazification was not carried out, and a critical reflection of history's methodological and theoretical traditions did not take place until the late 1960s. The key West German decision makers behind historical scholarship, as in the other disciplines within the humanities, did not make much of an effort to reintegrate the scholars who had been driven into exile since 1933. In East Germany, returnees were welcome, yet they had to adapt to immense pressures of ideological conformity. They were indebted, as some gradually came to realize, to a regime whose practices had little to do with the overly optimistic expectations that those in exile had envisioned for a socialist society.

Georg G. Iggers: *Where Did Historical Studies in the German Democratic Republic Stand at the Eve of Unification?* is devoted to the ideological patterns under which East German historical scholarship existed. After a brief period of transition until about the mid-1950s, when so-called bourgeois, i.e., non-Marxist, historians coexisted with historians who represented the viewpoint of the Socialist Unity Party (SED), the latter, once cadres of professionally trained historians were available, assumed a monopoly in the universities, research institutions, and schools. The ideological guidelines were closely integrated into a system of political control and discipline of the historical profession. But within this highly centralized system of control with its prescribed conceptions of history and society, there nevertheless existed at all times a degree of diversity and broad areas in which independent work was possible, although more so in the last two decades of GDR's existence than in the previous twenty years after the consolidation of power by the SED in the 1950s.

William A. Pelz: *The Revenge of the Krupps? Reflections on the End of GDR Historiography* points out that after unification approximately three-quarters of East German university academics lost their jobs. Between 1994 and 1998, of the 1,878 professors employed in the Eastern states only slightly over a hundred came from the East. Pelz argues that the elimination (or at very least the marginalization) of Marxism, socialism, and any type of critical anticapitalist historical research was a priority. This aim was pushed by right-wing ideologies that attempted to reduce the entire complex experience of the German Democratic Republic to a story of villains and heroes. In this narrative, East German historians become nothing more than jaded pens put to paper to serve the totalitarian state.

Helmut Meier: *"Once Upon a Time . . . :" Losses in Scholarly Competence as a Result of German Unification* investigates the closing of the Institute for the History of the German Working-Class Movement at the Academy of Social Sciences, attached to the Central Committee of the Socialist Unity Party of Germany. This institute was part of the system of research and political education of the SED and was thus dissolved. However, its most committed scholars were, from the very beginning, aware of the fact that a profound and self-critical probing into the standpoints they had hitherto held was indispensable for all further investigation. They gave up outdated positions, openly admitted errors, as well as the wrong judgments and deficits of their own work, and bravely turned to new ways of coping with the problems. A great number of publications since 1990 attests to this argument.

Stefan Bollinger: *German Unification and the Debate of the West German Social Sciences* points out that dismissed East German experts could have contributed much to historical research and teaching in united Germany, especially in fields that were strong in the GDR, such as Eastern

European, Arab, African, Latin American, and Asian studies. In addition many East German scholars have considerable expertise on the formerly Soviet, Central-Asian region, which remains a hot spot in today's political, economic, and military affairs. Bollinger states that the exclusion of East German scholars went hand in hand with the retirement of more critical West German scholars who belong to the generation of 1968.

Konrad H. Jarausch: *Anticommunist Purge or Democratic Renewal? The Transformation of the Humboldt University, 1985–2000* contrasts two narratives. One view, propagated mostly by dismissed scholars, alleges an "anticommunist purge" of personnel as well as a restoration of "capitalist conditions." This victimization narrative emphasizes the drastic reduction of the professoriate, which threw a large number of GDR academics out of work. Moreover, the critical version claims that internal reform efforts were shunted aside and Western structures imported instead, which amounted to a kind of academic *Anschluss,* invoking the notorious term for Hitler's conquest of Austria. In contrast, the leading proponents of the transformation tell a success story of a fundamental renewal of Eastern universities. He argues that the transformation during unification sought to apply academic standards of discipline structure, scholarly achievement and personal integrity, since only those who did not fit the new profiles, were unproductive, or had collaborated with the Stasi were to be excluded.

Kurt Pätzold: *Research on Fascism and Antifascism in the GDR: A Retrospective* gives an overview on the substantial research on Nazism and the Holocaust in East Germany. He emphasizes that surviving antifascists, who belonged to the GDR's political leadership and had taken part in intellectual and other conflicts, themselves became the initiators and guardians of a historiography that can be described, in the words of Karl Marx, as "without eyes, without ears or teeth." For all its undeniable accomplishments, which are substantiated in public research, East Germany's antifascist scholarship served above all to legitimize this group's authority.

Manfred Weissbecker: *Painful Transition and New Research on the History of Political Parties in Germany* writes about his personal experiences during and after 1989, when he was dismissed from his professorship at the University of Jena. He argues against the assertion that the science and scholarship in the GDR was monolithic and uniform. This judgment was, as he writes, particularly misleading with regard to his own topic of research: political parties in the Weimar Republic outside the labor movement. He mentions numerous contemporary debates and also controversies that may show a different picture in the field of research on the Weimar Republic and Nazism—his special fields of expertise.

Ludwig Elm: *Research on Conservatism in Jena: The Beginning and the End of an Inter-disciplinary Research Project* discusses the interdisciplinary "Research Group on Conservatism" that he founded in 1978 at the University of Jena, from which he was dismissed in 1992. The group's network included mainly historians, philosophers, economists, and legal experts from the universities of Jena, Halle, and Berlin, and also from the Academy of Sciences, the Academy of State and Law at Potsdam-Babelsberg, and the Academy of Social Sciences. Three international conferences were organized in Jena in May 1981, June 1986, and June 1990. The main theoretical issues that were discussed in all of these conferences and workshops included: social and economic foundations of modern conservatism, conservatism and neoliberalism, political and intellectual traditions of conservatism since the eighteenth century in international perspective, and also notions of progress, as well as the concept of humankind in conservative thought.

Jörg Roesler: *The Dissolution of East German Economic History at the Economic University in Berlin-Karlshorst: A Typical Anschluss Procedure* looks first at what happened to a group of economic historians, who taught at the GDR Economic University in Berlin-Karlshorst. Then he makes some comparisons about their fate, which was typical for GDR academics after the *Wende* [turnaround], with other university personnel in different countries and at other times, namely academics who were in similar situations. He discusses the *Abwicklung* [dismantling] of East German scholars in an international and comparative perspective.

Axel Fair-Schulz: *The Dissolution of the Institute for Economic History at the Academy of Sciences* argues that the Institute for Economic History that was very much linked with its founder Jürgen Kuczynski, was one of the most innovative places of research in East Germany. It had a pronounced research profile on a very broad spectrum of topics, including the history of everyday life, everyday life in the agricultural sphere, foreign trade, banking, population demographics, the economic elites, capital exports, the transfer of technologies urban centers, and the development of territorial structures. Research on the history of economic crises, economic booms, as well as ecology and statistics were part and parcel of its areas of special focus. In addition, the Institute for Economic History also researched themes like environmental history, industrial archeology, the history of technological innovations, as well as the social and economic history of industrialization, the social history of the poor and marginalized, the social history of elites, the comparative economic history of East and West Germany, and the economic history of rural areas. All these merits did not prevent the institute from being dissolved in December 1991, and less than a handful of its former members were able to find new positions in German academia.

Werner Röhr: *Dismantling the GDR's Historical Scholarship: A Case Study of the University of Leipzig* selects the Department of History at the Karl Marx University in Leipzig for three main reasons, in order to illustrate some of the key problems and processes associated with the dismantling of the GDR's historical scholarship after 1990: (1) The university-based historical research institutions in the GDR, the Department of History at the University of Leipzig was the largest, the most productive, and the most innovative; (2) Nowhere else did the transformation of the department structures, its teaching, as well as scholarship programs proceed as far as in Leipzig; (3) The developments in the University of Leipzig's Department of History showcases how the process of self-renewal was ultimately thwarted, when whole subsections were summarily dissolved (on the orders of the new ministries) as the GDR was incorporated into West Germany and its academic structure. After the dismissal of all but three former professors, Röhr concluded that what happened in Leipzig also happened elsewhere in the former GDR, in terms of the mechanisms and procedures that led to a "cleansing" of East German scholars. Röhr's chapter is part of his substantial two-volume study on the *Abwicklung* in East Germany.

Rainer Schnoor: *From "Imperialist Class Enemy" to "Partners in Leadership" in 365 Days? East German American Studies Since 1989* comes to a more positive judgment about the American Studies at the University of Potsdam. He concludes that despite the obvious "you won—we lost" situation, the transformation of East German American Studies after 1991 has had positive results: a long impasse had ended, and ideological fossilization was overcome. Fruitful exchange as well as mutual help and cooperation between the East and West, appeared, on the one hand, while condescension, attempts at domination, and arrogant behavior by the new powers, occurred on the other. Statements like the author's former, now deceased, colleague D.Sch.: "my East German colleagues are incompetent and lazy," have not promoted an atmosphere of collegiality for the academic cause. The price for all the progress, however, was the end of East German American Studies.

Ulrich van der Heyden: *Handling GDR Colonial Historiography* investigates East German historiography on the "Third World" and mainly Africa. After the *Wende*, some West German scholars have not simply refused to consider fairly the analyses of East German scholars of colonial and Africa studies but have quite often ignored them entirely, he writes. This colonial-like suppression of the East German historians and other scholars seems to be based on the assumption that all GDR scholars of the humanities *per se* would have clung to Marxist ideology, being by definition incapable of serious scholarly work. Such sweeping claims are still being routinely made despite substantial evidence to the contrary. Although more recent publications on German colonial history have quietly incorporated research findings from GDR historians, the almost entire eradication of GDR colonial historiography after the *Wende* is still justified, more or less directly, by dismissing it wholesale as dogmatically Marxist.

Marcus P. Aurin: *Obscuring East Germany: The Phantom Menace of East Germany to Social Scientific Understanding of Post-Reunified Germany* interprets that the exclusion of East Germans—and a specifically East German experience of reunification—from mainstream social scientific discourse, and can be interpreted as a rejection of the quintessentially German tradition of *Geisteswissenschaft* [Intellectual Science]. This tradition is, according to the author, grounded in a rigorous methodological emphasis on subjective experience and knowledge, systematically informing scientific understanding. Social scientific understanding is explicitly placed in a dialectical relationship with society and is grounded in *Bildung* [the education of mind and sensibility]. It is understood as a form of insight into society, based on the cultivated, self-conscious, and social empathy derived from lived experience, or *Erleben*. According to this methodological approach, Geisteswissenschaft plays an important formative role in modern society, where, as the sociologist Karl Mannheim puts it, "theorizing is a prerequisite of [social] cohesion." Ironically, as Aurin writes, the failure of East German Transformation Studies seems to demonstrate Mannheim's dictum in reverse: theories of transformation premised on the disappearance of East Germany presuppose a fundamental lack of social cohesion within reunified Germany.

The contributors' different backgrounds and generational experiences account for significant latitude of methodological and political sensibilities. Yet what ties all pieces together is a willingness to think critically and self-critically about the achievements and failures of GDR historiography as well as its fate after German unification.

This book also documents an appeal, undersigned by several scholars with an outstanding international reputation. This appeal, at first published on November 9, 2002, in the German daily *Frankfurter Rundschau*, called for a more even-handed evaluation and treatment of East German scholars, based on professional criteria instead of pure political and ideological maneuvering. All scholars who undersigned this appeal had been expelled from their countries of origin (Germany, Austria, and Czechoslovakia) after the Nazi seizure of power. Not one of them had been an apologist of the former official East German understanding of history, but they all were keenly aware of the necessity to be nuanced, discerning, and mindful of the conditions, restraints, and complexities of historical research and teaching in East Germany.

While the editors must be responsible for the shortcomings that readers may find in this book, they did not make any attempt to influence any author's position that was expressed in the submitted manuscripts. Every contributor is solely responsible for the views that he presented. With this volume, the authors and editors intend to provide material for further study and discussion, particularly among English-speaking readers.

We gratefully acknowledge the generous contributions and financial support of the State University of New York at Potsdam, particularly the Department of History, the School of Arts and Sciences, the International Education Program, the Office of the President, and the Office of the Provost. The Rosa Luxemburg Foundation, Berlin, generously offered a grant that enabled a number of scholars to participate in the conference. Our thanks are due to German authors Jörg Roesler and Rainer Schnoor who submitted their contributions in English. Thanks are especially due to Beate Schiller (Potsdam, Germany) and the late Diana Loeser and Dr. habil. Hanna Behrend for the translation of the texts of Ulrich van der Heyden, Kurt Pätzold, and Helmut Meier. We are likewise obliged to Douglass Hansen, JD, who translated the appeal from *Frankfurter Rundschau*. The editors of this book translated other texts. Special thanks are due to Waltraud Peters for the preparation of the index of names. Finally, we thank Professor Ellen Schrecker (Yeshiva University) and Adjunct Professor Laura Fair-Schulz (SUNY at Potsdam [USA]) for scholarly advice.

Potsdam, New York, United States; and Potsdam, Germany
May 2016

Notes

1. See the biographies of East German historians in Lothar Mertens's massive though partly biased *Lexikon der DDR-Historiker: Biographien und Bibliographien zu den Geschichtswissenschaftlern aus der Deutschen Demokraischen Republik* (Munich, 2006). See also the Internet reviews by Mario Kessler on *H-Soz-u-Kult*, August 14, 2007 (http://hsozkult.geschichte.hu-berlin.de/rezensionen/2007-3-115) and Matthew Stibbe on *H-German*, July 2008 (http://www.h-net.org/reviews/showrev.php?id=14779).

2. See Stefan Berger, "Former GDR Historians in Reunified Germany: An Alternative Historical Culture and Its Attempts to Come to Terms with the GDR Past," *Journal of Contemporary History*, 38 (2003), 1:63–83, and Marcus P. Aurin's contribution to this volume.

3. See the material in: Stefan Bollinger, Mario Kessler, and Ulrich van der Heyden (eds.), *Ausgrenzung oder Integration? Ostdeutsche Sozialwissenschaftler zwischen Isolierung und Selbstbehauptung* (Berlin, 2004).

1

A Different Starting Point, a Different End

East and West German Historiography After 1945

MARIO KESSLER

The German Marxist and refugee historian Arthur Rosenberg wrote in 1938 about "the mission of the historians during the Emigration," which depends on "breaking the mutual isolation of the so-called bourgeois and socialist historians." Socialists, Communists, bourgeois democrats, and socially progressive Catholics, according to Rosenberg, should reexamine their inherent views and tactics. "Through non-dogmatic and critical work, the emigrated historians must make a concerted and cooperative effort to develop, out of the negation of the Third Reich, positive new principles for the future of German historical studies."[1]

Rosenberg, who died in 1943, did not live to see the failure of his hopes. The political situation of postwar Germany worked to prohibit a dialogue between the historians of various schools. The democratic-parliamentary conditions, which the Western occupation forces set up, functioned in such a way as to inhibit every attempt at altering the existing social structure.

Any assessment of postwar German historical scholarship must take into consideration the relationship between the discipline and Nazism.[2] In the immediate years after 1945, much emphasis was placed on to what extent historians had been able to maintain their scholarly integrity and responsibility under Hitler. Since historiography had always been the spearhead of the ideology of the German *Sonderweg* (German Special Path), the need for a fundamental reorientation of historical scholarship was seen as an ultimate task in both parts of Germany.

The impact of Western political culture upon German society after 1945 was substantial. Within West German universities, however, the process of democratization took place very late. A fundamental de-Nazification was not carried out and a critical reflection of history's methodological and theoretical traditions did not take place until the late 1960s. Historical scholarship as well as other disciplines in the humanities did not take much effort to reintegrate the scholars who had been driven into exile since 1933.

In East Germany returnees were welcome if only at the price of adaptation. They were indebted, as some gradually came to realize, to a regime whose practices had little to do with the overly optimistic expectations that those in exile had envisioned for a socialist society. Whoever turned their back on the GDR would automatically be welcomed in the west. However, once in the Federal Republic, those who stood by their critical assessment of the society's development would then be effectively marginalized, if not actively persecuted. Critical questions were directed, even posthumously, at anyone who stayed in the GDR, regarding their personal responsibility for the failures of that state. Those who share this experience include a group of historians who built up the GDR historical sciences in the 1950s and early 1960s.[3]

Many of these historians not only had to leave their desks and lecture halls, but also the land of their birth. Others were put in the camps or sent to jail for many years. Upon their return to academic work, they seized the chance to carry out scholarly studies while maintaining their integrity, in their understanding, as political historians.

To this theme I would like to pose two concise questions/issues. First: What were the specific paradigmatic historical assumptions, within which historians in East and West Germany had to work? Second: I would make a comparison between of the historiography in both German states mainly as it had developed in the two or two and a half postwar decades. Basically, to address these questions I will limit the analysis to the years up until around 1961, at which time the construction of the Berlin Wall created a caesura and not only for historians. But first a short overview: who were the relevant historians in East and West Germany during this time?

Who Were the Historians?

These re-immigrating historians who belong to the founding generation of GDR historical scholarship include, in order of birth, Hermann Duncker (1874–1960), Albert Schreiner (1892–1979), Alfred Meusel (1896–1960), Leo Stern (1901–1982), Jürgen Kuczynski (1904–1997), Karl Obermann

(1905–1987), Ernst Engelberg (1909–2010), Hans Mottek (1910–1993), Josef Schleifstein (1915–1992), Heinz Kamnitzer (1917–2001), Helmuth Stoecker (1920–1994), Marion Einhorn (1921–1996), Erika Herzfeld (1921–2011), and Manfred Nussbaum (1922–1981). Arnold Reisberg (1904–1980) and Wolfgang Ruge (1917–2006) came from the Stalinist camps to the GDR after the 20th Congress of the Soviet Communist Party.

All of them entered, upon their return, the eastern part of Germany, a land that was neither a *terra incognita* nor an uninhabited island, even in regard to historical scholarship. Connected with the re-immigrants was a group of historians who survived Nazi concentration camps or prisons, such as Erich Paterna (1897–1982), Hedwig Voegt (1903–1988), Walter Bartel (1904–1992), Rudi Goguel (1908–1976), Walter Markov (1909–1993), Herwig Förder (1913–1974), Heinrich Scheel (1915–1996), and Joachim Streisand (1920–1980). The Catholic-born historian Hubert Mohr (1914–2011) was able to hide his Jewish background during Nazism. Soon after he was drafted to the *Wehrmacht* during the war, he defected to the Soviet side.

Together this founding generation built up Marxist historical scholarship in the GDR. A few non-Marxist historians, whose careers were held back during the Third Reich, or who had identified with the resistance, achieved university positions after 1945: Friedrich Schneider (1887–1962), Heinrich Sproemberg (1889–1966), Hans Haussherr (1898–1960), Karl Griewank (1900–1953), and Martin Lintzel (1901–1955). Other historians who were, to varying degrees, tainted by association with the Nazis were granted the chance of a fresh start in their careers: Fritz Rörig (1882–1952), Hellmut Kretzschmar (1893–1965), Eduard Winter (1896–1982), and Walter Eckermann (1898–1978). In addition, some former hard-core Nazis had been given a new academic life. Among them were Johannes Kühn (1887–1973) and Albrecht Thimm (1915–1981), who soon left the GDR for the west.[4]

In West Germany traditional historiography managed to retain and stabilize its dominant position. Among those historians who took key positions in the academia were not a few who had been connected with Nazism: Hermann Aubin (1885–1969), Percy Ernst Schramm (1894–1970), Egmont Zechlin (1896–1992), Otto Brunner (1898–1982), Hermann Heimpel (1901–1988), Reinhard Wittram (1902–1973), Günther Franz (1902–1992), Franz Petri (1903–1993), Helmut Krausnick (1905–1990), Fritz Wagner (1905–2001), Theodor Schieder (1908–1984), and Werner Conze (1910–1986), to name but a few. Karl Dietrich Erdmann (1910–1990) is a special case.[5] Only a handful remained permanently excluded from the university, such as Karl Alexander von Müller (1882–1964), probably the most gifted Nazi historian, and Ernst Anrich (1906–2001), who became a co-founder of the NPD, the German neo-Nazi party.[6]

Very few West German historians had been opponents of Hitler: Fritz Kern (1884–1950) to a degree, Franz Schnabel (1887–1996), and especially Gerhard Ritter (1888–1967). Hildegard Schaeder (1902–1984), who is too often neglected, was a resistance fighter and concentration camp inmate.[7] Some historians survived the twelve years in inner seclusion. Among them were Friedrich Meinecke (1862–1954), Ludwig Dehio (1888–1963), and Hans Herzfeld (1892–1982). Two of them, Dehio and Herzfeld, were classified under Nazi rule as "Half-Aryans" and suffered from anti-Jewish persecution. Eight refugees returned to West Germany: Hans Rothfels (1889–1976), Hans Joachim Schoeps (1909–1980), Ernst D. Fraenkel (1891–1971), Dietrich Gerhard (1896–1985), Franz Borkenau (1900–1957), Helmut Hirsch (1907–2009), Golo Mann (1909–1994), and Walter Mohr (1910–2001).

In place of the subsequent disempowerment of the classes and strata from whose ranks Hitler enjoyed the most comprehensive support, a formal de-Nazification process was instituted, through which judges and corporate managers, high- and low-level civil servants, as well as numerous Nazi historians were integrated into the Federal Republic. Therefore, those persons returning from exile—who were wary or critical of this policy—were not welcomed.

Paradigmatic Assumptions of GDR Historians

In its first proclamation the SED was still oriented completely toward cooperation between Marxist and so-called bourgeois historians. However as of 1946, the exclusive claim for the universal representation of Marxism-Leninism would become more clearly formulated. Nonetheless, there existed the opportunity for true cooperation.

In the Soviet Occupation Zone, the dispossession of large-scale real estate and the nationalization of industry, banking, and wholesale trade were enforced under the ambitious claim of constructing a democratic socialist society: a project which was fully in keeping with the programmatic vision of the KPD as well as the SPD at that time. Those who had been driven out of Germany by the Nazi regime were encouraged to return. "To all of you who were driven out of Germany; all German scientists, scholars, artists, and writers beyond the borders of your homeland, we send our greetings," was the official statement of the *Kulturbund* (Cultural Association) for the Democratic Renewal of Germany, proclaimed in November of 1945. "The time of emigration has ended within Germany and outside its borders. Let it be known that Germany needs you."[8] For the first time in their lives many of these refugees had the feeling of being indispensable.

However, the Soviet reparations policy, in which the Soviet authorities appropriated valuable production materials in order to at least alleviate some of the worst consequences of the Nazi total war in their own land, had a sobering effect even among those emigrants who returned. Some critics of the rigorous Soviet measures, including more than a few Communists and Social Democrats, were brutally persecuted. The SED leadership, which was completely dependent on Soviet goodwill, supported this action, and this foreshadowed the Stalinization and transformation of the SED into a "Party of a New Type."[9]

Some of those old Communists, who had returned from exile or had been liberated from Nazi camps and jails, ignored the contradiction between the socialist ideal and the dictatorial reality. Others hoped that through their efforts they would be able to bridge this developing schism. Already before the time of their exile, they were convinced that crises, war, and material suffering could be overcome only through socialism.

This premise was the deciding point for those who returned to the Soviet Occupation Zone or the GDR. In this sense, it is striking how little the writings of the historians returning from England and the United States—to mention Meusel, Kuczynski, Mottek, Schreiner, and Obermann—reveal about social relations within a parliamentary system; however, Obermann in the United States (writing about Joseph Weydemeyer), and Meusel in the GDR (writing on the German Revolution of 1848), do address important questions about bourgeois society in the nineteenth century.[10]

The works on German history which were already being formulated during the time of exile, especially those which came from Kuczynski's pen, depict the genesis and development of industrial capitalism as little more than Lenin's concept of the "eve of the proletarian revolution," and the parliamentary system as simply an instrument of dominance for the bourgeoisie—here obviously connected to the KPD's underestimation of the Weimar democracy but without reference to those Communist dissidents of the KPD Opposition, who had defended the constitution of the first German republic.[11]

From another perspective, however, the accomplishments of the Communist exile's historical writings are indeed evident in contrast with those of the so-called Third Reich-driven historiography. Here it suffices to be reminded of: Jürgen Kuczynski's work on the situation of the proletariat, especially the foreign workers in Nazi Germany; Alfred Meusel's social historical consideration of German foreign policy and also his studies of the family under the Nazi rule; and not to forget Albert Schreiner's towering volumes on military science dealing with German armament.[12]

The re-immigrated historians in the GDR and the survivors of the prisons and concentration camps represented a unique tradition of German intellectual history. They were the communist opponents of those scholars who had begun as Hitler's historians and who, after 1945—although naturally no longer along the lines of Nazism—formed the historical disciplines in West Germany.

In contrast to some of their comparable West-German polar opposites, the GDR historians at no point in their lives supported, justified, or trivialized a racial-biological war of extermination. Often, they themselves barely escaped from Nazi Germany. Their academic accomplishments as well as deficits cannot be considered in isolation from their tragic fate—above all their decision to seek, in East Germany, an alternative to the course of German history as it had been played out up to that time.

The SED in the years immediately following the war still included Communists and Social Democrats. It became, however, a Stalinist party, leaving no room for a democratic, and therefore pluralistic, understanding of antifascism.

According to the official party line, antifascism was simply equated with the GDR and the SED. Only through the rule of the SED, including the command over knowledge-production and research, could social progress be guaranteed. This, grounded in methods of historical research, was to become the core policy on historical studies for SED top leaders and their subordinate party members.

The party leadership regarded the purpose of SED policy on history as being the adaptation of the results of historical research for the legitimization of the given party line. The historians could only accept the requirement of the convergence of scholarly research and politics when they presented the historical process as being in compliance with a Marxist-Leninist understanding of a programmatic policy directed towards the solution of social problems.

It was hardly possible for historians in the GDR to renounce this program, and this was not merely due to the practical consequences. A fundamentally affirmed unity of politics and academic knowledge indicated that there was an intellectual attraction and a politically binding force behind this deformed version of Marxism. Indeed, Marxism was, in all of its various expressions, and is unthinkable without taking its utopian dimension as an article of faith.

The most insightful among East German Marxist historians saw in historical materialism—which they faithfully applied—a stimulating method for research. They, however, did not automatically classify their findings according to the needs of the party leadership.

"No one wants to see," as Walter Markov warned urgently in 1947, "historical materialism, because of its suppression in other parts of Germany, to be compensated for by a monopoly in the Eastern Zone, unless he intentionally wants to see it ruined through inbreeding. What is called for is that all German universities allow for the free competition of both theories and the duty to make them known."[13]

A discussion started, along with the practical partisanship for the socialist project, immediately following 1945, involving the theoretical understanding of history. The vast majority of the GDR historians viewed themselves as Marxist, even when they followed the development of the socialist world with some concern. Some of them maintained the belief that even Stalin could not destroy the basic progressive currency of Marxism.

Ernst Engelberg emphasized that his understanding of partiality (it should be noted how he eventually developed this concept further in the 1970s) had little to do with party institutions and even less to do with the molding of facts according to a mandatory party view of history. To him partiality meant researching the forces that contribute to the progress of history.[14]

By the concept of partiality those researchers who were engaged with, but not uncritically, of the GDR and the SED understood something completely different than automatically cooperating with the system. Moreover, it meant there was no commonality to be found between Walter Markov's non-dogmatic understanding of history and that of Hanna Wolf's—the Rector of the SED Party School—for whom historiography and party propaganda were one and the same. Even so, Walter Markov and his adherents were able to remain in the GDR—in the face of threats of repression—searching for a socialist alternative to the particular historical trend that had been carried out up to that time.

Through 1952 Alfred Meusel could still calmly ward off the accusation of Hanna Wolf, that he propagated the Rankean Objectivity Ideal. "I do not know if Frau Director Wolf is honestly of the opinion that I wish to represent a program of the Rankean school here," he stated at the Historians' Meeting in June of 1952, "rather, I have merely stated that Ranke's work contains some things from which we may learn. And I am definitely committed to this line of thought. . . ."[15]

As the Soviet campaign against the so-called Zionists, Titoists, returnees from the West, and the members of the early communist opposition groups was carried over—albeit to a lesser extent—into the GDR, the historians who had returned also became ensnared in the network of the Party

Control Commission. This especially affected Jürgen Kuczynski as a former associated employee of the American Office of Strategic Services, and also Ernst Engelberg, due to his friendly association with Antonin Hašek, the brother-in-law of Rudolf Slánský, during his exile in Switzerland.[16]

On the one hand, these Communist historians soon found out that the Party apparatus was dependent on the skills that the refugee historians had acquired during their exile, such as foreign-language ability and familiarity with international scholarship. On the other hand, previous contact with Jewish or other relief organizations, to bourgeois politicians, and even to Communists who were considered enemies of the party, could be incriminating or mean, at the very least, a black mark on one's important *Kader* files. Engelberg and the musicologist Georg Knepler attempted in vain to clear the names of some of those who had been indicted in the Prague Slánský trial.[17]

Even Stalin's death on March 5, 1953, did not automatically lift the threat or the de facto practice of repression. However, in the end, none of the historians had to suffer the fate of Paul Merker, who as late as March 1955, was sentenced, through a secret trial, to serve a prison term.[18]

Thus it was not until the 1970s that that such works, which had as their subject the personal experience of exile or persecution, appeared from the historians here in question, e.g., Jürgen Kuczynski's first volume of memoirs, which covered the time up until 1945 (1973), and Karl Obermann's memories of his exile in France (1984).[19] In the literary estate of Albert Schreiner and Alfred Meusel, biographic descriptions can be found that substantiate the texts that were published in the GDR.[20] It was not until 1988 that Walter Markov discussed openly the circumstances under which he had been expelled from the SED in 1951.[21]

Aside from Markov's autobiography and Kuczynski's possibly cryptic or insider-privileged remarks, none of these texts address internal party conflicts. For the survivors of Stalin's camps, a public exposé of one's personal biography was completely out of the question. This was not only, or at least not primarily, the fault of the official reading of the past—which did not systematically stipulate a particular version of Stalin's atrocities—but was rather due to the playing-down of these crimes as merely the "negative effects of the cult of personality."

More often the survivors of Stalin's camps decided simply to return to the GDR, whose official silence through mass-repression seemed convenient for easing into the single possible opportunity to deal with the worst chapter of their biography: that is, to build, through silence, a protective shield against one's own tormenting questions. Going to the Federal Republic of

Germany was not merely a political decision made by some of the other camp survivors, but rather it was often due to the debt they felt they owed to their innermost need, to process the terrible events through crying out or through writing.[22]

Despite all the coercion and suffering inflicted by their own rank and file, for those historians the "General Line" of the party remained in principle outside any critique. They swore, without giving any critical analysis to the idea, that the working class and "its party" were the prominent forces in socialist society. Faith in the ultimate superiority of socialism united these historians—despite all their underlying differences—with the SED leaders and their party apparatus.

In general, this must have led these historians, despite diverse individual differences, to an impoverished and dualistic world view—a mindset of good and evil, which pigeon-holed the subtle Marxist class analysis into a friend-or-foe schema. Whoever rejected this way of thinking would inevitably come to be considered "a counter-revolutionary," and a "bourgeois relic." Within this conception of history there was no place for the idea of a council democracy or a multiparty democracy as the prerequisite for the self-government of the working people.

From the very beginning a relationship vis-à-vis the institutions of the SED arose that contributed decidedly to the subordination of the historical disciplines under paternalistic party guardianship: Even professionally experienced, and to some extent critical historians like Ernst Engelberg or Leo Stern, during their controversies, appealed more than once to the Central Committee apparatus as the highest authority, and thereby assisted it in acquiring the decision-making power that they themselves would eventually come to experience. This general loss of political voice was not simply taken by the Central Committee's apparatus through force, but it was also the historians who brought this loss upon them.

Did these historians simply collude to acquiesce to the SED? Joining the party, and returning to East Germany may look like part of a pact among like-minded individuals, although the ultimate implication of this was submission—even if it did not always turn out to be the case. At any rate, with the rigid classification system within the party structure, a democratic conception of socialism had to weather some damage. This, which to some was a sensitive dilemma, was intensified by the SED exercise of power and its subsequent resistance to critical ideas. Nevertheless, none of them ended their connection to the Party, without which socialism seemed unthinkable.

What is the significance of all this for scholarly work and its effects? Through their critique of capitalism, the founders of GDR historiography wanted to expose the underlying roots of social disaster and thereby perform the service of making a contribution to the prevention of fatally flawed social developments, in both the present and the future. On one hand, Marxist theory offers a point of departure for investigating the historical continuity of various historical developments ranging from imperialism, militarism, and political anti-Semitism to fascism. On the other hand, dogmatic axioms often preclude the realistic assessment of bourgeois society.

West Germany: Traditional and Modern Historiography

As already stated, West German historiography after 1945 showed notable lines of personal continuity with the historical profession in Hitler's Germany. The continuities in methodological approaches were also remarkable in the first decade after the fall of the Nazi state. In this period, scholarly debates took place within a relatively small and confined circle of conservative university professors. West German historians adopted the political notion of totalitarianism in order to interpret the Nazi state. Totalitarianism in its rude, specifically German form equated communism with Nazism: the term fascism was carefully avoided. Consequently, Gerhard Ritter, an outspoken proponent of this paradigm, denigrated communist resistance to Nazi Germany as being allegedly in service of a similar totalitarian power, i.e., the Soviet Union.[23] He also emphasized that the existence of modern mass democracy would provide a fertile ground for demagogic leaders, able to forge mass parties and to erect totalitarian people's states; nothing of that phenomenon should be classified as specifically German.[24]

Hans Rothfels, another important strategist of Westernization policy in historical scholarship, sought to build an intellectual bridge between conservative circles in Bonn and Washington. Like Ritter, Rothfels evaluated Hitler's conservative enemies as the true representatives of German resistance and denied Prussian militarism as responsible for the rise of Nazism.[25] Ritter, Rothfels and Friedrich Meinecke saw Nazism as part of a movement that had its roots in mass democracy arising in the wake of French Revolution.[26] The "Third Reich" was seen as a modern form of one-party and one-ideology dictatorship based on a combination of repression, propaganda, and the manipulation of the masses. This view both served, as Mary Fulbrook wrote, "to condemn Nazism and Hitler as evil, while at the same time asserting that Nazism neither arose from long-term trends in German history, nor had any intrinsic relationship with the German people, who appear simply to have bumped into it and been blown off their proper course."[27]

In April 1957 it was Werner Conze, recently appointed at Heidelberg University, who initiated a conference entitled "The Social History of the Modern World" in Bad Ems. Thus the West German spa became the birthplace of the *Arbeitskreis für moderne Sozialgeschichte*, the Workshop for Modern Social History. The participants, among them Theodor Schieder, openly demanded a new conceptual form of structural history.[28] Nine years later Hans-Ulrich Wehler published the essay collection, *Modern Social History*, and argued that nineteenth-century Germany had undergone only a partial modernization. The economic sphere was modernized, but the social sphere remained conservative in its structure.[29]

Wehler, like Fritz Fischer, who otherwise cannot be counted as a member of this group, explained that it was the aim of the reactionary German elites to retain power that led to the outbreak of the First World War, the failure of the Weimar Republic, and the coming of Nazi Germany.[30] Wehler, as well as Jürgen Kocka, attempted to analyze social processes of German society from the perspective of modernization, industrialization, and the creation of modern Europe.[31]

This use of methods of the social sciences to analyze history challenged East Germany's historians who had, until then, almost solely focused on a coherent social theory as an instrument for analysis, i.e., Marxism. This group of West German historians, soon to be labeled as Bielefeld School, took Marx's analysis of society as a starting point to combine it with other major influences, such as Max Weber or the French *Annales* School.

On the other hand, most of their East German counterparts, particularly of the second generation that followed the founder-fathers, remained confined to a rather narrow conception of Marxist-Leninist thought that did not allow them to ask critical questions to the Party leadership's preconceived outlines for scholarly research. In a self-critical reevaluation, the East German historian Helga Schultz pointed out that social history in the GDR had reached high standards in the 1960s, but came to a halt with Karl Marx, thus it could no longer keep up with the accelerated process of innovation of social history in the Western world.[32]

The fact remains that Marxist historians in the early GDR were devoting their attention to areas of research that up until then had only rarely been addressed in the German universities, such as the research of revolutions or the history of Marxism and the workers' movement. They were working out, if not at times tending to overestimate, the roll of the mass population and the factors of material life as the primary and deciding forces in the process of history. Their works were, in this regard, a challenge to historical studies in the Federal Republic of Germany, which consequently were also gradually taking up these problems and doing so in a way that was actually, at least in part, more open and productive than what was generally possible in the GDR.[33]

Who could seriously contend that the following are not important contributions to German historical scholarship of that generation and beyond: Walter Markov's research on the French Revolution or on nationality problems in the Balkans; Jürgen Kuczynski's multivolume *History of Worker's Conditions under Capitalism* or his historical studies of everyday life; Ernst Engelberg's Bismarck biography and also his investigation of Social Democracy under Bismarck; Leo Stern's large-scale editions on the history of the German workers' movement; the work of Hans Mottek covering economic history and environmental research; or Karl Obermann's historical presentation of the Revolution of 1848 and the process of class formation in pre-revolutionary years? The question of whether Mottek or Obermann, who during their exile took their first steps into what would become lifelong careers in history, would have been able to write such works under different conditions than in the GDR is just as well left open. The same can be said in regard to any concluding judgments, regarding Alfred Meusel or Albert Schreiner, whose creative apex as researchers had already been secured in the period of their lives prior to their return. Any verdict over Arnold Reisberg's and Wolfgang Ruge's works should be prefaced with the question of how their innermost reserves were able to motivate them at all, after decades of suffering in Soviet camps, so that they were still able to apply themselves to historical writing.

It should also not be neglected that East German historians of the second generation succeeded in presenting a set of remarkable publications on a variety of topics. These included monographs on the reformation, the social history of the working class and the peasantry, on non-proletarian parties and organizations in Imperial Germany and the Weimar Republic, comprehensive accounts on Germany in both world wars, and biographical and sociohistorical research on anti-Nazi resistance. Not the same positive judgment, however, can be given with regard to East German historical works on the history of the GDR, West Germany or the history of twentieth-century communism.

After the Collapse of the GDR: What Remains?

The fall of the Berlin Wall and the opting of many East Germans for a quick unification with West Germany ended not only communist rule in the GDR; the East German state itself and its political culture, including its historiography, ceased to exist. Within a few months, the world that East German communists had created all but vanished. Their values were now marginalized in the Federal Republic; the antifascist biographies of the founder-generation of the GDR commanded little respect in the political mainstream.[34]

The end of the GDR abruptly compelled the surviving founder-figures of East Germany's historiography to reflect on their shared responsibility for the breakdown of this state. Jürgen Kuczynski recognized his personal responsibility for a blatantly repressive system, to which the people had increasingly turned their backs.

Shortly before his death he wrote that one must

> discriminate between human failure and historical failure. When Kant said that "good intentions" are what matters, perhaps (?) he was right in terms of judging human character. But man also has, I think, a historical character. And it is here that I, as well as so many of my friends, have failed. Neither Harich nor Havemann, and quite possibly not even I in 1956–57 [when Kuczynski openly placed some of the dogmas of GDR ideology in question], but also I, when one traces the entire history of the GDR and my activities. In history what counts is not good intentions, not the honest endeavor, but only success. And in that I have simply been a complete failure. Indeed the point is to change the world, not merely to make it a bit more bearable by being a good example.[35]

Historical analysis and historical faith came together, wrote Wolfgang Ruge, in a critical account. Out of this arose what he described as the "cardinal mistake" of the GDR historians: this mistake was to conceive reality "under the fascinating influence" of Marxist-Leninist theory, "distortedly misconceived and accordingly represented." He pointed out that:

> seduced by our preconceived convictions, we dismissed, or at least trivialized, the multifaceted economic, political, ideological, and moral signs of decay that were all around us. Only now did we really acknowledge them for the first time as the historical career of socialism and its outcome, from its beginnings, through Stalinism and stagnation up until its disintegration can and must be assessed. There is no excuse for this serious neglect that many bad details about the practice of "really existing socialism" are only now becoming known. What we knew—and personally I

> have to say: what I knew—should have been enough to realize the absurdity of a conception of society in which the appeal to grandiose goals is used to sanctify the deployment of criminal means.[36]

The collapse of the GDR raised the subsequent question of what standard should be used to judge the historical scholarship that had been produced there. Nothing seemed more natural to the historians and publicists of the Federal Republic than to impose the pluralistic West German model of historical studies as the measure with which to judge the success or shortcomings of the eastern German historians. This was the ideal by which the commissions in charge of handling the final accounts, and the rebuilding of eastern German historical institutions (which, by the way, did not only consist of West Germans) oriented itself.

The severity of the critique and self-critique of the eastern German historians upon the first encounter with them and the historical inheritance of the GDR—which all too often was stigmatized as a burden from the past—was fed, not insignificantly, by the findings of the "fathers" of West-German historical studies that later historians would present at the end of the 1990s.[37] These findings about historians, who after 1945 were granted a second chance—unlike most of the post-1990 GDR researchers—were for West Germans often sobering, but nothing new to the East Germans who had studied this history.

Indeed, in the GDR there was research initiated by re-immigrants and carried on by their students that provided lucid information about perpetrators, accomplices, and also the compliance of German historians with Nazism. Justifiably the propagandistic style of these works has been subjected to critique; it has also made problematic their reception in the Federal Republic. However, if one keeps in mind that the initiators of these works were anti-Nazis or victims of Nazism—including Ernst Engelberg, Leo Stern, as well as many of their students such as Werner Berthold (b. 1923) and Walter Schmidt (b. 1930)—the sometimes-acerbic formulations certainly take on a new light.

The Cold War adversely affected both of the German states. As the French historian of the Communist International, Pierre Frank, pointed out, "the result was the *mutual* intensification of reactionary tendencies, originating from two clearly different societal foundations."[38] Certainly the distortion of historical observations made by historians in both of the German states led to a self-induced blockade in the processing of the past—and not only in the West. Georg Iggers's assessment remains worthy of discussion, according to which

> it was not until the end of the 1960s that a pluralistic historical scholarship in the Federal Republic was possible for the first time, although a fundamental difference remained between the two states in regard to the mechanisms for disciplining nonconforming historians: the FRG, with its rule of law, and the GDR with a dictatorship.[39]

This contribution has dealt with one of the problems within the dynamic fields of academic knowledge and politics and at the same time poses some implicit questions on the subject of political ethics. The debate over German historians during the Nazi period, as well as over the handling of history in the individual departments in both German states, raise also questions about the quality control of present academic standards.

Indeed, the historical academics of the two German states did have an influence on each other—albeit an indirect one—even during the Cold War, as has been discussed above. At the beginning of the 1950s, Marxist and non-Marxist history educators, in both instruction and research, coexisted with one another in the GDR. At the beginning of the next decade the non-Marxist historians, to the extent that there were any remaining in the GDR at all, had been condemned to a marginal existence. The interference of the Party impeded or strangled any serious research, as far as it was not in agreement with the wishes of the SED apparatus.

The rigid and paternalistic control of the Party over academic knowledge had exclusively negative results. Historians, especially Marxists, who supported this policy ultimately worked against their own interests as researchers. Every critique of the founding-figures among East German historians who shared in this counterproductive relationship of scholarship and political interests is stuck with a counter-question: what chance did they have in the Federal Republic of Germany? For example, unlike England, the West German historians' guild never offered Marxists full citizenship. Had it been otherwise, some decisions about the liquidation and the continued existence of GDR institutions after 1990 could have very well turned out differently.

What remains of East German historiography? For the overall majority of works by East German historians it is the case (as it is for historical works in general) that they are products of their own particular time and that they are written so that a new generation may improve and surpass them. It is part of the historian's trade—in contrast to that of the architect or even the philosopher—that the names of some fortunate historians remain engraved in collective memory with regard to their moral value longer than their works. Their shelf life is usually already determined by the immediately following generation. Yet it still remains an open question: who will be remembered longer by posterity, these historians who seamlessly switched over from the 'Third Reich' to the Federal Republic; or those historians who resisted Hitler, who only in the GDR were given a chance at a career, and who were ready to pay the price for all this? The question of what remains of the legacy of East-German historical scholarship and of the body of historical knowledge that came out of the GDR is one for which this author, unlike some of his colleagues, does not presume to provide a definitive answer.

Notes

1. Arthur Rosenberg, "Die Aufgabe des Historikers in der Emigration," Emil Julius Gumbel (ed.), *Freie Wissenschaft: Ein Sammelbuch aus der deutschen Emigration* (Strasbourg, 1938), reprinted in: Mario Kessler (ed.), *Deutsche Historiker im Exil: Ausgewählte Studien* (Berlin, 2005), here p. 27.

2. Parts of this essay had been published under the title: *Exile Experience in Scholarship and Politics: Re-emigration of Historians to East Germany*, translated by David Schrag, in Mario Kessler, *On Anti-Semitism and Socialism: Selected Essays* (Berlin, 2005), 167–82.

3. See Mario Kessler, *Exilerfahrung in Wissenschaft und Politik: Remigrierte Historiker in der frühen DDR* (Cologne etc., 2001).

4. For some of these historians see Heinz Heitzer et al. (eds.), *Wegbereiter der DDR-Geschichtswissenschaft: Biographien* ([East] Berlin, 1989). See also Lothar Mertens, *Lexikon der DDR-Historiker: Biographien und Bibliographien zu den Geschichtswissenschaftlern aus der Deutschen Demokratischen Republik* (Munich, 2006), and my critical review in the Internet journal *H-Soz-u-Kult*, August 14, 2007.

5. See Martin Kröger and Roland Thimme (eds.), *Die Geschichtsbilder des Historikers Karl Dietrich Erdmann: Vom Dritten Reich zur Bundesrepublik* (Munich, 1996), 59–78.

6. On Anrich's career under Hitler and his role in post-war West Germany, see Lothar Kettenacker, "Ernst Anrich und die Reichsuniversität Straßburg," Christian Baechler et al. (eds.), *Les Reichsuniversitäten de Strasbourg et de Poznan et les résistances universitaires 1941–1944* (Strasbourg, 2005), 83–96.

7. Michael Burleigh, *Germany Turns Eastwards: A Study of Ostforschung in the Third Reich* (Cambridge, UK, 1988), 237–38, and Gerd Voigt, *Russland in der deutschen Geschichtsschreibung 1843–1945* (Berlin, 1994), 313–14, made references to Schaeder. See the biography by Gerlind Schwöbel, *Leben gegen den Tod: Hildegard Schaeder* (Frankfurt-Main, 1995).

8. Statement, quoted from: Karola Fings and Cordula Lissner (eds.), *Unter Vorbehalt: Rückkehr aus der Emigration nach 1945* (Cologne, 1945), 164.

9. See the author's viewpoint: Mario Kessler, "The Soviet Style of Power: Some Notes on the SED," *Russian History/Istoire Russe, XXIX (2002),* Nos. 2–4, 317–27. Reprinted in: *idem, On Anti-Semitism and Socialism,* 135–48.

10. Karl Obermann, Joseph Weydemeyer: *Pioneer of American Socialism* (New York, 1947); Alfred Meusel, *Die deutsche Revolution von 1848* (Berlin, 1948); *idem, Das europäische Sturmjahr* (Berlin, 1948).

11. For this dissident communist current, see Theodor Bergmann, "Gegen den Strom": *Die Geschichte der Kommunistischen Partei-Opposition,* 2nd ed. (Hamburg, 2001).

12. Jürgen Kuczynski, *The Economics of Barbarism: Hitler's New Economic Order in Europe* (London, 1942); *idem, Germany Under Fascism: 1933 to the Present Day* (London, 1944); Alfred Meusel, *Germany's Foreign Policy (London, 1938); idem,* "National Socialism and the Family," *The Sociological Review, XXVI (1936*), 166–86; Dorothy Woodman [i.e. Albert Schreiner], *Hitler treibt zum Krieg* (Paris, 1934); *idem, Hitlers Luftflotte startbereit* (Paris, 1935); A. Müller [Schreiner], *Hitlers motorisierte Stoßarmee* (Paris, 1936); Albert Schreiner, *Vom totalen Krieg zur totalen Niederlage Hitlers* (Paris, 1939).

13. Walter Markov, "Historia docet?," *Forum: Zeitschrift für das geistige Leben an den deutschen Hochschulen, 1947,* No. 1, 8–9, quoted from: *Idem, Kognak und Königsmörder:' Historische Miniaturen* ([East] Berlin and Weimar, 1979), 19–20.

14. Engelberg, who, in the 1950s and 1960s followed a more dogmatic position, developed a rather open-minded approach after his retirement. See, e.g., his posthumously published writings *Wie bewegt sich, was uns bewegt? Evolution und Revolution in der Weltgeschichte,* ed. by Achim Engelberg (Stuttgart, 2012).

15. "Historiker-Tagung, 7. und 8. Juni [1952]," Archiv der Berlin-Brandenburgischen Akademie der Wissenschaften, Alfred Meusel Papers (ABBAW, NL Meusel), No. 618.

16. For details see Kessler, *Exilerfahrung in Wissenschaft und Politik,* 113–41and 236–39.

17. See Ernst Engelberg's letter of 1January 14, 1951, to the Central Party Control Commission (ZPKK) in: Stiftung Archiv der Parteien und Massenorganisationen der DDR im Bundesarchiv, Berlin (SAPMO-BArch), DY 30/IV 2/4/124, 285–86, and Knepler's letter of November 30, 1952, ibid., 159–62.

18. See Jeffrey Herf, "East German Communists and the Jewish Question: The Case of Paul Merker," *Journal of Contemporary History,* XXIX (1994), 627–61; Wolfgang Kießling, *Partner im "Narrenparadies": Der Freundeskreis um Noel Field und Paul Merker* (Berlin, 1994); Mario Kessler, *Die SED und die Juden—zwischen Repression und Toleranz: Politische Entwicklungen bis 1967* (Berlin, 1995), 52–105.

19. Jürgen Kuczynski, *Memoiren: Die Erziehung des J. K. zum Kommunisten und Wissenschaftler* ([East] Berlin and Weimar, 1973); Karl Obermann, *Exil Paris: Gegen Kultur- und Bildungsabbau im faschistischen Deutschland* ([East] Berlin, 1984), 8–42 (autobiographical notes).

20. Schreiner's autobiographical notes can be found in a Stasi file (collected material about Schreiner). See *Der Bundesbeauftragte für die Unterlagen des Staatssicherheitsdienstes der ehemaligen DDR (BStU), MfS-Zentralarchiv, HA IX/11,* Vol. 286. Meusel's notes are collected in: ABBAW, NL Meusel, No. 1.

21. See Walter Markov, *Zwiesprache mit dem Jahrhundert: Dokumentiert von Thomas Grimm* ([East] Berlin and Weimar, 1989).

22. See Wolfgang Ruge, *Berlin-Moskau-Sosswa: Stationen einer Emigration* (Cologne, 2003), 439. See the expanded version of the memoirs: *Gelobtes Land: Meine Jahre in Stalins Sowjetunion,* ed. by Eugen Ruge (Berlin, 2012).

23. See Gerhard Ritter, *Carl Goerdeler und die deutsche Widerstandsbewegung* (Munich, 1964), 108–09.

24. See *idem, Europa und die deutsche Frage* (Munich, 1948), 193–95.

25. See Hans Rothfels, *The German Opposition to Hitler* (Chicago, 1948). There are several German editions of this book.

26. See Friedrich Meinecke, *Die deutsche Katastrophe: Betrachtungen und Erinnerungen* (Wiesbaden, 1946).

27. Mary Fubrook, *German National Identity After the Holocaust* (Cambridge, UK, 1999), 114.

28. See Winfried Schulze, *Deutsche Geschichtswissenschaft nach 1945* (Munich, 1993), pp. 254–65.

29. Hans-Ulrich Wehler (ed.), *Moderne deutsche Sozialgeschichte* (Cologne, 1966).

30. See Konrad H. Jarausch, "Der nationale Tabubruch: Wissenschaft, Öffentlichkeit und Politik in der Fischer-Kontroverse," Martin Sabrow et al. (eds.), *Zeitgeschichte als Streitgeschichte: Große Kontroversen seit 1945* (Munich, 2003), pp. 20–40; *Imanuel Geiss,* "Zur Fischer-Kontroverse—40 Jahre danach," Ibid., pp. 41–57; Klaus Große Kracht, *Zeitgeschichte als Streitgeschichte: Historische Kontroversen in Deutschland nach 1945* (Göttingen, 2005), pp. 47–67.

31. See Georg G. Iggers, *Deutsche Geschichtswissenschaft: Eine Kritik der traditionellen Geschichtsauffassung von Herder bis zur Gegenwart* (Vienna, 1997), pp. 328–64.

32. Helga Schultz, "Was bleibt von der Geschichtswissenschaft der DDR?," *Österreichische Zeitschrift für Geschichtswissenschaft,* 2 (1991), 2:22–46.

33. See several contributions in: Alexander Fischer and Günter Heydemann (eds.), *Geschichtswissenschaft in der DDR: Historische Entwicklung und kritische Bilanz,* 2 Vols. ([West] Berlin, 1988–1990). After 1990 Fischer and Heydemann wrote, following the Zeitgeist, much more critical about East German historiography than they did in the two-volume work. Of note is the well-balanced evaluation by Andreas Dorpalen, German History in *Marxist Perspective: The East German Approach* (Detroit, 1985).

34. Catherine Epstein, *The Last Revolutionaries: German Communism and Their Century* (Cambridge, MA and London, 2003), 244–57 convincingly shows how the surviving members of the GDR's founder generation tried to come to terms with the upheavals of 1989–90 and its consequences. On the founding fathers after

1989, see also Mario Kessler, "Gründerväter der DDR-Geschichtswissenschaft und der Umbruch 1989: Jürgen Kuczynski, Wolfgang Ruge und Ernst Engelberg," Klaus Kinner and Helmut Meier (eds.), *Politikum Geschichte: Die Rolle der Geschichte in öffentlichen Diskussionen* (Berlin, 2009), 47–62.

35. Jürgen Kuczynski, *Fortgesetzter Dialog mit meinem Urenkel* (Berlin, 1996), p. 81.

36. Wolfgang Ruge, "Nachdenken über die Geschichtswissenschaft der DDR," *Zeitschrift für Geschichtswissenschaft, 41* (1993), 7:584–85. Reprinted in: Idem, *Beharren, kapitulieren oder Umdenken: Gesammelte Schriften 1989–1999*, ed. by Friedrich-Martin Balzer (Berlin, 2007), here p. 336.

37. See, e.g., the discussion on the 42nd Conference of the German Historical Association at Frankfurt-Main 1998, as documented in: Winfried Schulze and Otto Gerhard Oexle (eds.), *Deutsche Historiker im Nationalsozialismus* (Frankfurt-Main, 1999).

38. Pierre Frank, *Geschichte der Kommunistischen Internationale*, Vol. 2 (Frankfurt-Main, 1981), 783. My emphasis.

39. Iggers, *Deutsche Geschichtswissenschaft*, 428. While quite a number of historians see East German historiography as part of German *Wissenschaftstradition* and make comparisons with its West German counterpart, much less research is made so far on GDR historiography as part of a Soviet-styled model of science and scholarship in East and East Central Europe. See Frank Hadler and Georg G. Iggers, "Überlegungen zum Vergleich der DDR-Geschichtswissenschaft mit den ‚gespaltenen' Historiographien Ostmitteleuropas nach 1945," Georg G. Iggers et al. (eds.), *Die DDR-Geschichtswissenschaft als Forschungsproblem, Beiheft 27 der Historischen Zeitschrift* (Munich, 1998), 433–44.

2

Where Did Historical Studies in the German Democratic Republic Stand at the Eve of Unification?

GEORG G. IGGERS

Any study of historiography in the GDR must, of course, take into consideration the very different conditions under which historical studies were conducted there—and in other socialist countries—from those that prevailed in the West.[1] Western historians have contrasted the pluralism of interpretative approaches in the West with the limits that an official interpretation of history placed in the work of the historian in the socialist countries. As it has been crudely put, historians in the West derived their findings from the evidence; those in the socialist countries fitted their evidence into their preconceived conclusions. This, of course, is a vast oversimplification on two counts. No historical study is free of prior assumptions that guide the research. Nor has research has been as free in the West or as directed in the East as this juxtaposition suggests. As Winfried Schulze and Klaus Große Kracht have documented in a study of the West German historical profession from 1945 to 1960[2] and others have shown for the periods before, a conservative nationalistic orientation dominated the universities in Germany since the mid-nineteenth century and fairly effectively barred dissenting historians from university positions.[3]

While historians who had served the Nazi regime were quickly reintegrated into the West German historical profession after 1945, Walter Markov, who had spent ten years in a Nazi prison as a Communist, in

1946 was denied the opportunity of submitting the second dissertation ("Habilitation"), required for university teaching, at the university of Bonn and left for what became a distinguished career at the Karl Marx University in Leipzig.[4] Only in the 1960s did a younger generation introduce a more critical perspective on the German past and more diverse methodological and conceptual approaches into the West German universities.[5]

Nevertheless, even before the emergence of critical voices and alternative methodological approaches in the 1960s the pressures for conformity in West Germany were by no means comparable with those in East Germany, where very soon after 1945 party and state assumed direct political control over research, teaching, publication, and recruitment. After a brief period of transition until about the mid-1950s, when so-called bourgeois, i.e., non-Marxist, historians coexisted with historians who represented the viewpoint of the Socialist Unity Party (SED), the latter, once cadres of professionally trained historians were available, assumed a monopoly in the universities, research institutions, and schools. Very early after 1945 the guidelines were laid for historical research and writing.[6] The resolutions promulgated by the SED at its party congresses in the early 1950s and reiterated by Walter Ulbricht demanded that historical research, writings, and teaching were to be partisan (*parteilich*), i.e., function in the service of the party.[7] A major task of the historian was to be the polemical confrontation with historical interpretations in the capitalist countries. Marxism-Leninism was to serve as the sole comprehensive theoretical framework for the study and writing of history.

The ideological guidelines were closely integrated into a system of political control and discipline of the historical profession. The recruitment process enforced ideological and political conformity. Admission to the university required an *Abitur* from the *Erweiterte Oberschule*, which followed the basic eight, more recently ten, grades. Admission for study rested not only on academic performance but very heavily on nonacademic factors such as involvement in the youth organization of the party, in the earlier years of the GDR also on class background, whereby membership in the working class was interpreted broadly enough to favor the children of local party functionaries.[8] Active church membership or refusal to belong to the party youth organization, the Free German Youth (FDJ), eliminated many. Similar criteria were involved in admission to university. Not always in the natural sciences, but generally in the social sciences, including history, party membership played an important role as did, in the case of male students, the willingness to serve an extra year and a half in the armed forces in addition to the compulsory eighteen months of military service. By the

1960s virtually all full professors of modern history were members of the Socialist Unity Party or, occasionally, one of the parties associated with it in the National Front.[9]

The disciplining of Walter Markov and Jürgen Kuczynski in the 1950s as well as of young historians in 1988 who protested the ban in the GDR of the Soviet magazine *Sputnik* demonstrated how even limited dissent among loyal party members was not brooked.[10] Among church historians at the theological faculties of the universities, there were as expected a number of scholars who were neither Marxists nor members of the Socialist Unity Party, but who were nevertheless committed to interpreting the Christian experience in a socialist society.[11] A non-Marxist social historian of international reputation, Karlheinz Blaschke, was unable to obtain a university post; after losing his position at the Saxon State Archives in Dresden, he was able to find poorly paid employment as a historian only at the church-operated Theological Seminary in Leipzig, not a part of the university, and was appointed professor only after 1990 in Dresden.[12]

Similarly the major publishing houses, among which the Akademie Verlag and the Verlag der Wissenschaften were the most important, published exclusively works written from a Marxist-Leninist viewpoint, as did the state-financed scholarly periodicals. Religiously oriented publishers, such as the Union Verlag, provided limited opportunities for the publication of other viewpoints, but the Union Verlag, as the publishing house of the Christian Democratic Union in the GDR, had only restricted leeway for dissent and divergence. Occasionally publication in the West was approved or tolerated. Thus, little room was left for dissent and nonconformity.

History occupied a very important role second only to Marxism-Leninism in the hierarchy of academic disciplines because of the special function it served in legitimizing the regime—hence the subordination of historical research and writing to the party. The mechanisms of enforcing conformity were thus much more evident and direct than in the Western democracies. The key institution that coordinated research and teaching was the *Rat für Geschichtswissenschaften*, the Council for the Historical Sciences, directly attached to the Central Committee of the Socialist Unity Party.[13] This committee supervised the "Central Plan for the Sciences of Society," in which the overall plan for the entire profession of historians in institutions of higher education and research in the GDR formed an important part. The Institute for Marxism-Leninism, in addition to preparing in cooperation with its parallel institution in the Soviet Union the edition of the works of Marx and Engels, concerned itself with ideological conformity, as did the Academy of Social Sciences, which until the fall of 1989 was attached to the Central Committee of the Party. Since 1990, both institutions were renamed and underwent significant changes and reduction in personnel, but were dissolved soon after.

Research was highly centralized in the mammoth Academy of Sciences of the GDR with its very large number of researchers, patterned closely on the Soviet Academy of sciences. The six universities, the teacher's colleges, and the technical universities were conceived primarily as teaching institutions (although professors and assistants, like their counterparts in the West, were expected to do research). As German unification approached in the course of 1990, the great diversity between the organizational framework of research and higher education in the two parts of Germany became very apparent. West Germany, where research was conducted largely at the universities, had no institution comparable to the Academy of Sciences in the GDR. At the universities in the GDR, moreover, the areas of teaching and study not dealing directly with the political aspects of the modern period were badly underrepresented, as were medieval and ancient history. Marxism-Leninism, as the official and only ideology of studies in the social sciences and thus of history, further limited the possibilities of research and expression. The ideology, moreover, led to the ritualized language in the form of a terminological code that prevented intellectually honest communication.

Within this highly centralized system of control with its prescribed conceptions of history and society, there nevertheless existed at all times a degree of diversity and broad areas in which independent work was possible, although more so in the last two decades of GDR's existence than in the previous twenty years after the consolidation of power by the SED in the 1950s. Several scholars have described the GDR of the post-Stalin era as an authoritarian rather than a totalitarian society.[14] In practice under no modern regime, neither of the Soviet nor the Fascist model, has the state or the party ever succeeded in attaining complete control over historical research or writing.[15] Subtle forms of conformity and of dissent often reinforced or weakened central control. The Communist regime in the GDR, despite its control of mass media and of police power, was never able to generate the degree of consensus among historians, that alas, the Nazi regime was able to solicit; in part this was because the latter succeeded for a long period where the former failed in establishing its claim to national legitimacy among the historians it sought to control. There developed a very large gulf between the published work of the historians and their official pronouncements on the one hand and what they really thought on the other. Again the ritualized language to which we referred imposed a conformity that to the reader who could not read between the lines and note the silences appeared total.

One of the sad aspects of the historical profession in the forty years of the existence of the GDR was the failure of many historians to take advantage of the limited possibilities for free expression that existed. Historians in the GDR with whom I have spoken were not convinced that the reluctance to explore new directions in social history and even in sensitive areas like the study of fascism was fully the result of regimentation. The restrictions that governed the work of the historians do not by themselves explain why new methods and subject matters, for example, in the study of everyday life and culture and of mentalities, which were well-established not only in the West but also in Poland and Hungary and were not entirely absent in the Soviet Union, were pursued in the GDR only to a very limited degree. Moreover, research was not as closely monitored as the existence of the Council for Historical Science and the master plan for the profession seemed to suggest. The historians at the universities and at other research and teaching institutions were consulted but seldom provided input into new imaginative directions. Nor did the plan prevent them from following their research interests and, provided it remained within the general guidelines of Marxist doctrine, to find a publisher.

In part, the (limited) opening in historical scholarship also resulted from the desperate desire of the GDR government to gain international acceptance and respectability. Very early GDR historians began to participate in international conferences.[16] The requirements of scholarship that would be taken seriously by the international community of scholars thus came into conflict with ideology. Notwithstanding the ritual citations of Marx, Lenin, Brezhnev, and Honecker, in earlier years of Stalin and Ulbricht, and the invocation of simplistic class analysis, GDR historians, as Andreas Dorpalen demonstrated, often made very substantial contributions to international scholarship, especially in less sensitive areas of study such as agrarian history and the history of the Middle Ages.[17]

The normalization of international relations through the treaties of the early 1970s, with which not only the Western powers but also West Germany recognized the existence of the German Democratic Republic as a member of the international community of nations, made international scholarly dialog easier, although the GDR continued to maintain barriers to the free exchange of scholars between the two Germanies, and particularly with West Berlin. The 1980s saw an increasing amount of international exchanges involving senior but also in some cases junior scholars and doctoral candidates, which in the second half of the 1980s more frequently included the Federal Republic of Germany. The growing opening and sophistication of scholarship in the GDR made theses exchanges meaningful. Exchanges and cooperative projects dealt with a broad variety of topics, from the meaning and character of the Protestant Reformation to comparative studies of the bourgeoisie in nineteenth-century Europe, from the historical and theoretical significance of Max Weber to the Nazi regime.

The opening in historical studies in the 1970s and 1980s was accompanied by changing assessment of the German past. Beginning with Erich Honecker's succession to Walter Ulbricht as First Secretary of the Socialist Unity Party in 1971, which coincided approximately with the treaties of the early 1970s granting the GDR international recognition, a reorientation took place in the assessment of the German past. One the one hand the SED now rejected the older hope of a unified socialist Germany as well as the West German conception of "two states but one nation" and stressed that not language or ethnicity but class and social system were the basis of nationhood, in other words that the GDR represented a socialist German nation; on the other hand the party claimed the entire German past as the "heritage" (*Erbe*) of the socialist nation. To be certain the "heritage" that constituted the whole of the past, good and bad, was distinguished from the positive "tradition" on which the GDR could build its sense of national identity.[18]

The basis on which the new socialist nation, the GDR, sought to establish its legitimacy was thus much broader than the "progressive" tradition that it formerly had claimed, although it continued to identify itself with these "progressive" traditions. Historians were, however, called upon now to do justice to the past and to avoid the former schematic approach that had distinguished sharply between "progressive" and "reactionary" personalities and forces. The concept of "tradition" in its traditional sense was now understood more broadly to comprehend not only the heroic line from Thomas Müntzer through Karl Marx and August Bebel to Karl Liebknecht and Ernst Thälmann and finally the leaders of the GDR—and perhaps as a second thought the unnamed working poor who in Brecht's words had built Thebes—but also those who in paving the way for German nationhood had created the possibility of a socialist Germany.

The five-hundredth anniversary of Luther's birth in 1983, which overshadowed that of the hundredth recurrence of the date of Karl Marx's death, was an occasion of reassessing the role of Luther as initiator of a broad revolutionary movement including all oppositional classes and strata.[19] Biographies of great men, particularly those of Martin Luther by Gerhard Brendler, of Frederick II by Ingrid Mittenzwei, and of Otto von Bismarck by Ernst Engelberg played a crucial role in the reassessment of the German past.[20] It should not be neglected that the attempts by the official GDR historians to lay claim to the German national tradition as part of the positive heritage of the GDR—i.e., essentially the Prussian tradition—have been disquietingly oblivious of the antidemocratic aspects of this tradition. Luther is thus modernized with little willingness to recognize the premodern aspects of his thought—and identically his anti-Semitism.[21]

Yet this call for a relatively new openness had only limited bearing on those who topics that bore directly on the legitimacy of the GDR regime and its relationship to the Soviet Union, although here too there was gradual movement before 1989 toward greater honesty. The role of the Communist Party in the last months of the Weimar Republic, the fate of German Communists who had fled to the Soviet Union, and, of course, the Hitler-Stalin Pact continued to be taboos.[22]

Nevertheless, even in these areas of study, there was perceptible movement toward greater openness in the 1970s and 1980s. Questions that before had been shunned were now approached cautiously.[23] Thus Joachim Petzold began in the mid-1970s to recognize the limitations of the so-called monopoly capitalism thesis, to which he still adhered, to explain the broad basis of popular support for the Nazis.[24] Kurt Gossweiler who otherwise rejected a critical approach toward Stalin's crimes, called for a comparative study of fascism to understand more clearly the specific context within Nazism arose in Germany.[25] Dietrich Eichholtz published a path-breaking multivolume study of German war economy during WWII that discussed in great detail the general and specific aspects of the interrelationship between German industrial capitalists and Nazi leaders.[26] Finally Kurt Pätzold began a serious investigation of anti-Semitism and Jewish persecution,[27] while Helmut Eschwege's works on the same topic remained underrated during the whole time of the GDR.[28]

By 1989 GDR scholarship on Nazism and the Holocaust had reached the point where it could finally make its contribution to international scholarship. Two events in 1989 reflected how far GDR scholarship had gone and how far it still had to go. In May 1989 American and GDR historians held a conference on terror and resistance under the Nazis in which there was a very open exchange of research findings and interpretations.[29] In time for the fiftieth anniversary of the outbreak of WWII, GDR historians published a volume on the road to war that still began with an article on the central role of finance capital in determining German policy and ended with a discussion of the attitude of German Communists in 1939 toward the Hitler-Stalin Pact, seen by them generally as a defensive move on the part of the Soviet Union, but with no mention of the secret protocols on the division of Eastern Europe.[30]

In practice, although never in theory, there has always been a distinction in the GDR between political and social history. Paradoxically in a historiography that labeled itself as Marxist, social history was given a subordinate role to political history. It was rather marginalized. And yet because it was marginalized, it also enjoyed a degree of relative freedom. Social history may thus have offered its practitioners a partial way out of their dilemma between their own understanding of Marxism, which called for a history from below, and Marxist-Leninist doctrine, which imposed the primacy of party and state.

The new social and cultural history of the late 1970s and 1980s derived a great deal of its inspiration from fields at the margins of the discipline of history proper, folkloristics (*Volkskunde*), economic history, and regional history. This history succeeded in laying the foundations for an extensive study of what it called *Kultur und Lebensweise*, that is, culture conceived in a very broad sense as encompassing the material conditions of life, work, housing, food, clothing, but also sociability and attitudes. The major research projects of social and cultural historians moved in diverse directions: Hartmut Zwahr in his study of the formation of the working class in Leipzig took into account kinship factors crossing class lines; Helga Schultz introduced demographic factors patterned on the *Annales*; Jürgen Kuczynski as well as Wolfgang and Sigrid Jacobeit treated the role of everyday life.[31] The historians of the Magdeburger Börde project investigated the many sides of life in a process of the modernization of the countryside.[32] The same did Jan Peters, Lieselott Enders, and Hartmut Harnisch in their edition of peasants' diaries from the eve of the industrial revolution.[33]

As this volume discusses in detail, German unification was marked by the replacement of the majority of East German historians by West Germans at East German universities, although a very few, such as Hartmut Zwahr (University of Leipzig) were retained in their posts or as Jan Peters (University of Potsdam), Helga Schultz (University of Frankfurt-Oder), and Wolfgang Küttler (Max Planck Institute for the History of Sciences). Much later Peter Hübner, Mario Kessler, Michael Lemke, André Steiner, and a few others were appointed at the newly founded Center for Contemporary History (*Zentrum für Zeithistorische Forschung*) in Potsdam, and Matthias Middell became head of the Center for Advanced Studies (*Zentrum für Höhere Studien*) at the University of Leipzig. The one institute which had transcended political and cultural borders, the Institute for Universal and Cultural History, founded by Karl Lamprecht at the beginning of the century, which had no parallel in West Germany and which with Walter Markov and Manfred Kossok had placed African and Latin American studies on a new basis, was dissolved with unification. A number of younger historians, including Matthias Middell and Gerald Diesener sought to rescue the institute without formal university support and published the most important German journal of comparative, global history, *Comparativ*, relatively ignored in West Germany. In brief the period after 1990 did not see a fruitful integration of East and West German historiography with significant impulses for the rejuvenation of historical studies generally in Germany but largely a continuation of West German patterns of researching and writing history little affected by unification.

Notes

1. Parts of this essay are based on: Georg G. Iggers, "Introduction" to: idem (ed.), *Marxist Historiography in Transformation* (New York and Oxford, 1991), 1–37. See idem, "New Directions in Historical Studies in the German Democratic Republic," *History and Theory*, 28 (1989), 1:59–77; idem, "Geschichtswissenschaft und autoritärer Staat: Ein deutsch-deutscher Vergleich (1933–1990)," *Berliner Debatte Initial*, 2 (1991), 2:125–31.

2. Winfried Schulze, *Geschichtswissenschaft in Deutschland nach 1945* (Munich, 1989, paperback ed. 1993); Klaus Große Kracht, *Die zankende Zunft: Historische Kontroversen in Deutschland nach 1945* (Göttingen, 2005). See also Ernst Schulin (ed.), *Deutsche Geschichtswissenschaft nach dem 2. Weltkrieg 1945–1965* (Munich, 1989).

3. See Wolfgang Weber, *Priester der Klio: Historisch-sozialwissenschaftliche Studien zur Herkunft und Karriere deutscher Historiker und zur Geschichte der Geschichtswissenschaft, 1800–1970* (Frankfurt-Main, 1985); also Georg G. Iggers, *The German Conception of History: The National Tradition of Historical Thought from Herder to the Present*, 2nd ed. (Middletown, CT, 1983); Bernd Faulenbach, *Ideologie des deutschen Weges: Die deutsche Geschichte in der Historiographie zwischen Kaiserreich und Nationalsozialismus* (Munich, 1980); Hans Schleier, *Die bürgerliche deutsche Geschichtsschreibung der Weimarer Republik* (Berlin, 1975); on the social and intellectual context of the German professoriate, see Fritz K. Ringer, *The Decline of the German Mandarins: The German Academic Community, 1890–1933* (Cambridge, MA, 1969).

4. See Sven Heitkamp, *Walter Markov: Ein DDR-Historiker zwischen Parteidoktrin und Profession* (Leipzig, 2003), 110–18, and Manfred Neuhaus et al. (eds.), *"Wenn jemand seinen Kopf bewusst hinhielt . . .": Beiträge zu Werk und Wirken von Walter Markov* (Leipzig, 1995). See now Markov's posthumously published autobiography: *Wie viele Leben lebt der Mensch: Eine Autobiographie aus dem Nachlass* (Leipzig, 2009).

5. See Georg G. Iggers, *The Social History of Politics: Critical Perspectives in West German Historical Writing since 1945* (Leamington Spa, 1985), especially the introduction. See also Hans-Ulrich Wehler, "Geschichtswissenschaft heute," Jürgen

Habermas (ed.), *Stichworte zur 'geistigen Situation' der Zeit*, vol. 2 (Frankfurt-Main, 1979), 709–53. See also Mario Kessler's essay in this volume.

6. See, e.g., Günter Heydemann, *Geschichtswissenschaft im geteilten Deutschland* (Frankfurt-Main, 1980); idem and Alexander Fischer (eds.), *Geschichtswissenschaft in der DDR*, 2 vols. (Munich, 1988–1990); Konrad H. Jarausch (ed.), *Zwischen Parteilichkeit und Professionalität: Bilanz der Geschichtswissenschaft der DDR* (Berlin, 1991); idem and Matthias Middell (eds.), *Nach dem Erdbeben: (Re-) Konstruktion ostdeutscher Geschichte und Geschichtswissenschaft* (Leipzig, 1994); Ilko-Sascha Kowalczuk, *Legitimation eines neuen Staates: Parteiarbeiter an der historischen Front—Geschichtswissenschaft in der SBZ/DDR 1945 bis 1961* (Berlin, 1997); Georg G. Iggers et al. (eds.), *Die DDR-Geschichtswissenschaft als Forschungsproblem*, Beihefte der Historischen Zeitschrift, N.F., No. 27 (Munich, 1998); Martin Sabrow, *Das Diktat des Konsenses: Geschichtswissenschaft in der DDR 1949–1969* (Munich, 2001); Mario Kessler, *Exilerfahrung in Wissenschaft und Politik: Remigrierte Historiker in der frühen DDR* (Cologne etc., 2001); Lothar Mertens, *Priester der Klio oder Hofchronisten der Partei? Kollektivbiographische Analysen zur DDR-Historikerschaft* (Göttingen, 2006).

7. See Siegfried Lokatis, *Der rote Faden: Kommunistische Parteigeschichte und Zensur unter Walter Ulbricht* (Cologne, etc., 2003).

8. See, e.g., Mary Fulbrook, *The People's State: East German Society from Hitler to Honecker* (New Haven, CT, and London, 2005), 120–23.

9. In the early years after 1945, "bourgeois" historians, like Otto Hoetzsch, Heinrich Sproemberg, Fritz Rörig, Fritz Hartung, Eduard Winter, Hellmut Kretzschmar, Karl Griewank, Friedrich Schneider, Hans Haussherr, and Martin Lintzel occupied professorships in the Soviet Zone of Occupation and the GDR. See Harm Klueting, "Parteilichkeit war wichtiger als Objektivität," *Frankfurter Allgemeine Zeitung*, 8 May 1990, and the literature mentioned in footnote 6. For biographical notes of almost all East German professors of history see Lothar Mertens, *Lexikon der DDR-Historiker: Biographien und Bibliographien zu den Geschichtswissenschaftlern aus der Deutschen Demokratischen Republik* (Munich, 2006). From East German perspective see Heinz Heitzer et al. (eds.), *Wegbereiter der DDR-Geschichtswissenschaft: Biographien* (Berlin, 1989). On Hoetzsch see Gerd Voigt, *Otto Hoetzsch 1876–1946: Wissenschaft und Politik im Leben eines deutschen Historikers* (Berlin, 1978); Uwe Liszkowski, *Osteuropaforschung und Politik: Ein Beitrag zum historisch-politischen Denken und Wirken von Otto Hoetzsch*, 2 vols. (Berlin, 1988); on Griewank see Tobias Kaiser, *Karl Griewank (1900–1953): Ein deutscher Historiker im "Zeitalter der Extreme"* (Stuttgart, 2007). Walter Markov was excluded from the SED in 1951 because of political deviation but ultimately retained his chair. After polling colleagues in the GDR, I was able to find to find only Wolfgang Jacobeit and Bernd Töpfer, historians and full professors at the Humboldt University who were not members of the SED or one of the parties associated with it.

10. On Markov's case see Heitkamp, *Walter Markov*, 148–58; on Kuczynski see Kessler, *Exilerfahrung*, 131–41, and Horst Haun, *Kommunist und "Revisionist": Die SED-Kampagne gegen Jürgen Kuczynski (1956–1959)* (Dresden, 1999); on the

disciplined historians in 1988 see Rüdiger Horn's interview with *Der Stern*, no. 22 (23 May 1990), 25–27.

11. See Friedemann Stengel, *Die Theologischen Fakultäten in der DDR als Problem der Kirchen- und Hochschulpolitik des SED-Staates bis zu ihrer Umwandlung in Sektionen 1970/71* (Leipzig, 1998).

12. See Karlheinz Blaschke, "Als bürgerlicher Historiker am Rande der DDR: Erlebnisse, Beobachtungen und Überlegungen eines Nonkonformisten," Karl Heinrich Pohl (ed.), *Historiker in der DDR* (Göttingen, 1997), 45–93.

13. See Heydemann, *Geschichtswissenschaft im geteilten Deutschland*, 177–78, and also Walter Schmidt, "Geschichte zwischen Professionalität und Politik: Zu zentralen Leitungsstrukturen und -mechanismen in der DDR," *Zeitschrift für* Geschichtswissenschaft (cited hereafter as ZfG), 40 (1992): 11, 1030.

14. To name but a few with special reference to the interrelationship of East German historical scholarship, ideology, and institutions: Georgi Verbeek, "Kontinuität und Wandel im DDR-Geschichtsbild," *Aus Politik und Zeitgeschichte* (9 March 1990), 30–42; Martin Sabrow, "Das Wahrheitsproblem in der DDR-Geschichtswissenschaft," *Tel Aviver Jahrbuch für Deutsche Geschichte*, XXV (1996), 233–57; idem (ed.), *Geschichte als Herrschaftsdiskurs: Der Umgang mit der Vergangenheit in der DDR* (Cologne, etc., 2000).

15. On Nazi attempts to control the German historical profession, see the pioneering works of Max Weinreich, *Hitler's Professors: The Part of Scholarship in Germany's Crimes Against the Jewish People* [1946] (New Haven, CT, and London, 1999), of Helmut Heiber, *Walter Frank und sein Reichsinstitut für die Geschichte des neuen Deutschlands* (Munich, 1966), and of Karl Ferdinand Werner, *Das NS-Geschichtsbild und die deutsche Geschichtswissenschaft* (Stuttgart, 1967). Among more recent studies, see Michael Burleigh, *Germany Turns Eastwards: A Study of Ostforschung in the Third Reich* (Cambridge, MA, 1988); Karen Schönwäler, *Historiker und Politik: Geschichtswissenschaft im Nationalsozialismus* (Frankfurt-Main and New York, 1992); Willi Oberkrome, *Volksgeschichte: Methodische Innovation und völkische Ideologisierung in der deutschen Geschichtswissenschaft 1918–1945* (Göttingen, 1993); Martin Kröger and Roland Thimme, *Die Geschichtsbilder des Historikers Karl Dietrich Erdmann: Vom Dritten Reich zur Bundesrepublik* (Munich, 1996); Iggers, *Deutsche Geschichtswissenschaft*, 319–28; Margareta Kinner, *Karl Alexander von Müller (1882–1964). Historiker und Publizist*, Dissertation (University of Munich, 1998); Peter Schöttler (ed.), *Geschichtsschreibung als Legitimationswissenschaft 1918–1945* (Frankfurt-Main, 1997); Götz Aly, *Macht-Geist-Wahn: Kontinuitäten deutschen Denkens* (Frankfurt-Main and Vienna, 1997); Winfried Schulze and Otto Gerhard Oexle (eds.), *Deutsche Historiker im Nationalsozialismus* (Frankfurt-Main, 1999); Thomas Etzemüller, *Sozialgeschichte als politische Geschichte: Werner Conze und die Neuorientierung der westdeutschen Geschichtswissenschaft nach 1945* (Munich, 2001); Joachim Lerchenmüller, *Die Geschichtswissenschaft in den Planungen des Sicherheitsdienstes der SS* (Bonn, 2001); Ingo Haar, *Historiker im Nationalsozialismus: Deutsche Geschichtswissenschaft und der "Volkstumskampf" im Östen*, 2nd ed. (Göttingen, 2002); Mathias Beer and Gerhard Sewann (eds.); *Südostforschung im*

Schatten des Dritten Reiches: Institutionen-Inhalte-Personen (Munich, 2004); Eduard Mühle, *Für Volk und deutschen Osten. Der Historiker Hermann Aubin und die deutsche Ostforschung* (Düsseldorf, 2005).

16. See Karl Dietrich Erdmann, *Die Ökumene der Historiker: Die Internationalen Historiker-Kongresse und das Comité des Sciences Historiques* (Göttingen, 1987).

17. See Dorpalen, *German History in Marxist Perspective.*

18. There is an extensive literature on "Erbe und Tradition." For a collection of main statements see Helmut Meier and Walter Schmidt (eds.), *Erbe und Tradition in der DDR: Die Diskussion der Historiker* (Berlin, 1988). For a self-critical reevaluation of this conception as well as of the two-nation theory see Walter Schmidt, *Das Zwei-Nationen-Konzept der SED und sein Scheitern: Nationendiskussionen in der DDR in den 70er und 80er Jahren* (Berlin, 1996). See also Jürgen Hoffmann, *Wie weiter mit der deutschen Nation?* (Berlin, 1990); Gerhard Naumann and Eckard Trümpler, *Der Flop mit der DDR-Nation: Zwischen Abschied von der Idee der Konföderation und Illusion von der Herausbildung einer sozialistischen Nation* (Berlin, 1991); Jürgen Reuter, *Die Abgrenzungspolitik der DDR von der Bundesrepublik Deutschland in den siebziger und frühen achtziger Jahren*, Phil. Diss. (University of Bonn, 1991).

20. See "Thesen über Martin Luther: Zum 500. Geburtstag," *ZfG*, 29 (1981), 10:879–93; Hartmut Lehmann, "Die 15 Thesen der SED über Martin Luther," in: Fischer and Heydemann (eds.), *Geschichtswissenschaft in der DDR*, vol. 2, 215–34; Horst Barthel et a. (eds.), *Martin Luther: Leistung und Erbe* (Berlin, 1986); Martin Roy, *Luther in der DDR: Zum Wandel des Lutherbildes in der DDR-Geschichtsschreibung* (Bochum, 2000); Laurenz Müller, *Diktatur und Revolution: Reformation und Bauernkrieg in der Geschichtsschreibung des "Dritten Reiches" und der DDR* (Stuttgart, 2004), pp. 260–276. See also Horst Dähn and Joachim Heise (eds.), *Luther und die DDR: Der Reformator und das DDR-Fernsehen 1983* (Berlin, 1996).

20. Gerhard Brendler, *Martin Luther: Theologie und Revolution* (Berlin, 1983); Eng. ed.: *Martin Luther: Theology and Revolution* (Oxford and New York, 1991); Ingrid Mittenzwei, *Friedrich II. von Preußen: Eine Biographie* (Berlin, 1979); Ernst Engelberg, *Bismarck*, vol. 1: *Urpreuße und Reichsgründer* (East and West Berlin, 1985); vol. 2: *Das Reich in der Mitte Europas* (Berlin, 1990).

21. This is even partly true of Brendler, *Martin Luther*, although he does frankly discuss Luther's anti-Semitism (on pp. 435–38 of the German edition). See also Joachim Petzold, "Missachtung und Ausbeutung Luthers zur Zeit der faschistischen Diktatur," in Barthel et al. (eds.), *Martin Luther*, 435–40.

22. See Hermann Weber, "'Weiße Flecken' in der DDR-Geschichtsschreibung," *Aus Politik und Zeitgeschichte* (March 1990), 3–15; Idem, "Weiße Flecken," in *der Geschichte: Die KPD-Opfer der Stalinschen Säuberungen und ihre Rehabilitierung* (Frankfurt-Main, 1989).

23. See Dietrich Eichholtz and Kurt Gossweiler (eds.), *Faschismus-Forschung: Positionen, Probleme, Polemik* (Berlin, 1980).

24. As late as 1977 the volume *Unmastered Past* reiterated the position adopted at the 7th Comintern Congress in 1935 that fascism, under which German Nazism was subsumed, is "the open terrorist dictatorship of the most reactionary, most

chauvinistic, and most imperialistic elements of finance capital." Gerhard Lozek et al. (eds.), *Unbewältigte Vergangenheit: Kritik der bürgerlichen Geschichtsschreibung der BRD*, 3rd ed. (Berlin, 1977), 334. See also Joachim Petzold's books: *Konservative Theoretiker des deutschen Faschismus* (Berlin, 1978); *Die Demagogie des Hitlerfaschismus* (Berlin, 1982); *Faschismus: Regime des Verbrechens* (Berlin, 1984). See also his posthumously published autobiographical text: *Parteinahme wofür? DDR-Historiker im Spannungsfeld von Politik und Wissenschaft*, ed. by Martin Sabrow (Potsdam, 2000).

25. See Kurt Gossweiler, *Aufsätze zum Faschismus.* 2 Vols. (Berlin, 1988).

26. See Dietrich Eichholtz, *Geschichte der deutschen Kriegswirtschaft.* 3 Vols. (Berlin, 1969–1996); reprint in 5 vols.: Munich, 1999.

27. See Kurt Pätzold's books: *Faschismus-Rassenwahn-Judenverfolgung: Eine Studie zur politischen Strategie und Taktik des faschistischen deutschen Imperialismus* (Berlin, 1975); *Verfolgung, Vertreibung, Vernichtung: Dokumente des faschistischen Antisemitismus 1933 bis 1942* (Leipzig, 1983); *Pogromnacht 1938*, with Irene Runge (Berlin, 1988): See also Pätzold's partly self-critical autobiographical account: *Die Geschichte kennt kein Pardon: Erinnerungen eines deutschen Historikers* (Berlin, 2008).

28. See Helmut Eschwege's books: *Kennzeichen J. Bilder, Dokumente, Berichte* (Berlin, 1966); *Selbstbehauptung und Widerstand: Deutsche Juden im Kampf um Existenz und Menschenwürde 1933–1945*, with Konrad Kwiet (Hamburg, 1984). Eschwege, who was excluded from the SED during the anti-Semitic campaign of 1952–53, worked as librarian in Dresden, but was never admitted to a research position. See his autobiography *Fremd unter meinesgleichen: Erinnerungen eines Dresdener Juden* (Berlin, 1991).

29. For GDR contributions, see Akademie für Gesellschaftswissenschaften beim ZK der SED (ed.), *Deutscher Faschismus: Terror und Widerstand* (Berlin, 1989).

30. Dietrich Eichholtz and Kurt Pätzold (eds.), *Der Weg in den Krieg: Studien zur Geschichte der Vorkrkriegsjahre 1935/36 bis 1939* (Berlin, 1989). See the opening article by Eichholtz, "Das Expansionsprogramm des deutschen Finanzkapitals am Vorabend des 2. Weltkrieges," 1–39, and the concluding article by Heinz Kühnrich, "Der deutsch-sowjetische Nichtangriffsvertrag vom 23. 8. 1939 aus der zeitgenössischen Sicht der KPD," 517–51.

31. See Hartmut Zwahr, *Zur Konstituierung des Proletariats als Klasse: Strukturuntersuchung über das Leipziger Proletariat während der industriellen Revolution* (Berlin, 1978); Helga Schultz, *Berlin 1650–1800: Sozialgeschichte einer Residenz* (Berlin, 1987); Jürgen Kuczynski, *Geschichte des Alltags des deutschen Volkes.* 6 Vols. (Berlin, 1981–86); Wolfgang and Sigrid Jacobeit, *Illustrierte Alltags- und Sozialgeschichte des deutschen Volkes*, vols. 1 and 2 (Leipzig and Cologne, 1986–87), vol. 3 (Münster, 1995).

32. See Hans-Jürgen Rach and Bernhard Weissel, *Landwirtschaft und Kapitalismus: Zur Entwicklung der ökonomischen und sozialen Verhältnisse in der Magdeburger Börde vom Ausgang des 18. Jahrhunderts bis zum Ende des ersten Weltkriegs.* 2 Vols. (Berlin, 1978); Heiner Plaul, *Landarbeiterleben im 19. Jahrhundert: Eine volkskundliche Untersuchung über Veränderungen in der Lebensweise der einheimischen*

Landarbeiterschaft in den Dörfern der Magdeburger Börde [. . .] (Berlin, 1979); Hans-Jürgen Rach and Bernhard Weissel (eds.), *Bauer und Landarbeiter im Kapitalismus in der Magdeburger Börde: Zur Geschichte des dörflichen Alltags vom Ausgang des 18. bis zum Beginn des 20. Jahrhunderts* (Berlin, 1982); Hans-Jürgen Rach et al. (eds.), *Die werktätige Dorfbevölkerung in der Magdeburger Börde: Studien zum dörflichen Alltag vom Beginn des 20. Jahrhunderts bis zum Anfang der 60er Jahre* (Berlin, 1986).

33. See Jan Peters et al. (eds.), *Märkische Bauerntagebücher des 18. und 19. Jahrhunderts: Selbstzeugnisse von Milchviehbauern aus Neuholland* (Weimar, 1989).

3

The Revenge of the Krupps?

Reflections on the End of GDR Historiography

WILLIAM A. PELZ

> There are some men of letters who do not model themselves on the present,
> but study the past in order to criticize the present age.
> They confuse and excite the people.
> It is expedient that these be prohibited.
>
> —First Emperor of China[1]

During the Cold War, Walter Ulbricht is reported to have remarked that Germany was now two countries: one for the Krupps [big business][2] and one for the Krauses [common people]. This was naturally a gross propagandistic oversimplification but there was a grain of truth in this statement all the same. If the German Democratic Republic (GDR) was neither democratic nor much of a republic due to its Stalinist repressive apparatus, it is none the less true that big business (the Krupps) and even former Nazis[3] played a significant role in creating the Federal Republic of Germany (FRG). Adenauer, leader of the West Germans, was eager to put the horrors of fascism behind him, and as early as 1946, before he could have known who had or had not been responsible for war crimes, "urged that ordinary members of the Nazi party 'finally' be left in peace."[4]

Particularly during the hotter moments of the Cold War, the two conflicting social systems existing on German soil produced highly politicized histories. This is far from surprising given the truth of George Orwell's observation that whoever controls the past controls the future and whoever controls the present controls the past.[5] In the West, anyone in the past who had opposed exploitation or oppression ran the risk of being smeared as anti-democratic, totalitarian or, maybe worse, written out of the history books entirely. Of course, in the GDR things were no better with even leftists as noble as Rosa Luxemburg being slandered for being "anti-Leninist."

Still, despite their significant flaws and shortcomings—most notably the grip Stalinist ideology held on so many—the historians of East Germany established an important school of historiography. Among their strengths was a committed antifascism that, in contrast with the West, was willing to explore the dark corners of the Nazi period. Unlike many Western historians, historians of the GDR recognized the existence of class struggle and the roles played by history's less powerful actors.

While the German Peasants' Revolt (1525) was given a place of honor in most histories in the GDR[6] and in East Berlin's *Museum for German History*, in West Germany the 100,000 peasant victims of the counter-revolutionary repression urged on by Martin Luther often rated, at best, a bare mention. Naturally, all these struggles were expropriated by the Eastern state in an attempt to legitimize it. Yet, despite all attempts at censorship and control, the ruling Socialist Unity Party (SED) was never able to totally silence competing voices such as the history of the international brigades in the Spanish Civil War.[7]

In the end, historians in both German states were, in many ways, prisoners of their social-economic systems.[8] In the East, one had to worry about offending SED party bureaucrats who obsessively defended the "party line." Most pointedly in the early years of the GDR, particularly when Stalin was alive, there was little freedom to explore historical science outside the borders delineated by the Soviet Union. Given the nature of Stalinism, there should be little wonder at this state of affairs.[9]

Yet, in capitalist Germany, in most ways more free of controls, there was typically little future for historians questioning an educational system that placed capitalism as the bedrock value of society. One does well to remember that during the period of the *Berufsverbot*,[10] a young academic was given a six-month sentence (suspended) for calling the Federal Republic a "repainted Coca-Cola can," while "red" hunting became all the rage in some West German educational institutions.

With unification, what some thought would be a joining of equals quickly revealed itself to be more in the nature of a victory of the FRG over the GDR, of West over East. Unlike Cato who thundered "Carthage must be destroyed" at the end of every speech,[11] Western politicians promised to let a thousand flowers bloom in the new Eastern states. They never specified the true cost of this project. One cost that became apparent early on was that leftist intellectuals, whether supporters of the SED state or not, were to be scapegoats. West Germany, and particularly the conservative politicians running it, saw unification as a chance to purge the East of those who held anti-capitalist, or even non-capitalist, worldviews.[12]

GDR professors in what were considered sensitive fields, like history, were "wound down" or discharged. It is true, as an American leftist living in East Berlin commented, some of these were "narrow dogmatists, disciplinarians or worse [but] many were respected scholars."[13] He goes on to argue that even those "in nonpolitical fields had to face West German 'Expert' panels which 'tested their competence and moral record.' Professional jealousy, political views or theoretical disagreements could trigger firings."[14] Textbooks from the old days were replaced with more West-oriented, capitalist-friendly editions. English textbooks, for example, were purged for making various radical comments such as stating blacks in the U.S.A. were disadvantaged."[15]

Soon the discourse shifted from historians being politically subversive (or at least biased) to historians being overabundant and redundant. That is, the "market"[16] was used as an argument to drastically cut back on funding for historical sciences. "The market" was accepted as the final judge by many East German historians who unwittingly played into the hands of those who sought to control the creation of academic positions that might be home to critical East German historians. As John A. Weaver notes: "In short, the "market" assured that Western standards of research and teaching would be used to evaluate former East German historians, and Western models of the university would be adopted to (re)structure the former East German system. [. . .] In this climate of scarcity, the best former East German historians could do is hope the "market" would be kind."[17]

In fact, approximately three-quarters of East German University academics lost their jobs. Nor was this merely a case of replacing SED supporters with younger untainted East Germans. One study found that between 1994 and 1998, of the 1878 professors employed in the Eastern states, only slightly over a hundred came from the East.[18] Many have wondered why. Certainly a victorious capitalist West would want to remove the old Eastern functionaries from key positions of power. Yet, what was the harm in letting recognized scholars of Ancient India continue their work in Sanskrit at Humboldt University?[19]

The GDR Historical Association appealed to their West German counterparts for help adjusting to the *Wende*, the transformation of the years 1989–1990. There had been hope for a renewal and even rebirth of the historical sciences in East Germany, and some had believed that a stronger and better social history would emerge. Some had argued that a renewed socialism would require a revitalized leftist historiography. Very soon, however, the Western historians demanded "the all but wholesale dismissal of their Eastern colleagues . . . [by 1994] it looks though the Marxist-Leninist tradition has indeed almost vanished."[20]

First, I contend that these purges were part of the process of Western colonization of the former GDR.[21] The idea of applying the language and analysis of colonial and post-colonial discourse to the relations between two industrialized countries within the same (cultural, linguistic, and historical) nation may seem absurd. Still, if one can get beyond the obvious racial element in traditional European colonialism, the history of the former GDR since 1989 fits broadly into a familiar colonial tradition. As a controversial argument made in *Kolonialiserung der DDR* stated:

> If one equates colonialization not with the invasion of colonial troops [. . .] with massacre of 'natives' etc., but rather focuses on the fundamental issues: the destruction of an 'indigenous' economic structure, the exploitation of available economic resources, *the social liquidation of not only the political elite but also the intellectuals of a country*, along with the destruction of [. . .] a population's identity, then one can indeed say that a colonization process in the very precise sense of the word, has taken place in the former GDR.[22]

If one takes any classic study of, say, the British in South Asia and substitutes "East German" for "Indian," the text would be remarkably similar. If all the gods of India were held to be monstrous and false, so, too, were all the ideas and beliefs in the former East Germany. As Edward Said commented, "Orientalism is fundamentally a political doctrine willed over the Orient because the Orient was weaker than the West, which elided the Orient's difference with its weakness."[23] In this colonialization project, historians were of particular importance, since one of the prime goals of the West was to present a version of the past that would characterize the GDR as the West's evil 'other' (much like Edward Said discussed the "orient") while simultaneously the FRG sought validation for its own existence "as a superior, enlightened German state."[24] The old GDR had to become integrated into the West, albeit in a subordinate position.

My second argument is that the elimination, or, at the very least marginalization of Marxism, socialism and any type of critical anti-capitalist historical research was a priority. This aim was pushed by right-wing ideologies who attempted to reduce the entire complex experience of the German Democratic Republic[25] to a story of villains and heroes. In this narrative, East German historians become nothing more than jaded pens put to paper to serve the totalitarian state.

It was also a direct result of the imposition of a market-based relation to the historical sciences. That is, historians were implicitly asked: how would they pay their own way and contribute to the new united Germany and her (capitalist) economy? In other words, history itself was devalued and the value of the left's history fell towards zero. This was not limited to Stalinist propaganda that sometimes passed as history in the old GDR days. Despite its at times wrongful misappropriation by the Stalinists, Marxism retains vital tools for the historian.

A renewed Marxist paradigm could "avoid the postmodern abyss that promoted nihilism and relativism . . . [and it would] combine the idea of seeing history as a social and cultural construction with the traditional notion of social history, which focuses on the development of social classes, capitalism, and liberal democracy."[26] Both Georg Iggers and Konrad Jarausch have pointed out that numerous GDR historians employed methods underdeveloped in the FRG, such as everyday history and the French Annales tradition. The prime goal of their work was not to legitimize the SED state, but to create sound scholarship within a Marxist framework.[27]

Sadly, such work has been dismissed as propaganda when it is not simply ignored. The institutions that once employed critical thinkers have been downgraded. As an English language article on education in the former GDR pointed out, none of the nine recognized "elite universities" are located in the five Eastern states. This is partially because the red taint of the GDR combined with Western colonial condescension resulted in most private donations as well as most of almost two billion Euros of state money going to institutions in the West.[28] If the institutions of the former GDR would learn their place, "have the courage not to try to do everything and play to their strengths" and "stay within their limits,"[29] they may yet aspire to prosper as lesser versions of their former illustrious selves.

The tragedy of the destruction of East German historiography is not just about the careers terminated, the lives ruined, or the students left unenlightened. It is part of the larger project of a Western colonization that seeks to bury Marxism along with any other left-wing critics. It is an attempt to teach Germans and others that, in Thatcher's words, there is no alternative to the current capitalist system. What we have witnessed since 1989 is not so much German unification as the revenge of the Krupps. In the final analysis, the revenge of history may well prove more powerful than the wishes of even the strongest capitalists.

Notes

1. Edict quoted in D. Twitchett and M. Loewe (eds.), *Cambridge History of China*, vol. I (Cambridge, MA, 1986), 69.

2. For a popular English language survey of this family, see William Manchester, *The Arms of Krupp* (Boston, 1968).

3. See the classic, if dated, work by T. H. Tetens, *The New Germany and the Old Nazis* (New York, 1961).

4. Jeffrey Herf, *Divided Memory: The Nazi Past in the Two Germanys* (Cambridge, MA, 1997), 378.

5. This remark appears in his famous anti-authoritarian novel *1984.*

6. Some might say overly so.

7. Josie McLellan, *Anti-Fascism and Memory in East Germany: Remembering the International Brigades, 1945–1989* (Oxford, 2004).

8. For a brilliant discussion of historians and German History, see Konrad H. Jarausch and Michael Geyer, *Shattered Past: Reconstructing German Histories* (Princeton, NJ, 2002).

9. For a fuller discussion of Stalin and Stalinism, see Roy Medvedev, *Let History Judge* (New York, 1989).

10. Term for the 1972 Anti-Radical Decree that, applied selectively, banned people with radical views from working in government jobs—most significantly teaching. See Gerard Braunthal, *Political Loyalty and Public Service in West Germany: The 1972 Decree against Radicals and its Consequences* (Amherst, MA, 1990).

11. Marcus Porcius Cato the Elder: "Delenda est Carthago"

12. Peter Marcuse, " 'Wrapping up' East Germany: Purge of Communists and Socialists in Eastern German Universities," *The Nation,* December 1991.

13. Victor Grossman, *Crossing the River: A Memoir of the American Left, the Cold War and Life in East German* (Amherst and Boston, 2003), 256–57.

14. Ibid., 257.

15. Miriam Widman, "In East, English Classes Purge Textbooks of Old Ideology," *International Herald Tribune*, February 11, 1992.

16. The phrase the "market" is put in quotation marks because this concept was used beyond (objective) economic realities to justify what were essentially (subjective) political ends.

17. John A. Weaver, *Rethinking Academic Politics in (Re)unified Germany and the United States* (New York, 2001), 189–90.

18. Noted by Thomas Ahbe, quoted in: Paul Cooke, *Representing East Germany Since Unification: From Colonization to Nostalgia* (Oxford and New York, 2003), 3.

19. Grossman, *Crossing the River*, 257.

20. Stefan Berger, "Historians and Nation-Building in Germany after Reunification," *Past & Present* (August, 1995), 10.

21. One early left-wing critique of this phenomena is Dorothy Rosenberg, "The Colonization of East Germany," *Monthly Review* (September 1991). For an

alternative analysis, see Heather M. Stack, "The 'Colonization' of East Germany? A Comparative Analysis of German Privatization," *Duke Law Review*, 46 (1997), no. 5.

22. Quoted in Cooke, *Representing East Germany*, 2. My emphasis.

23. Edward Said, *Orientalism* (New York, 1978), 204.

24. Cooke, *Representing East Germany*, 41.

25. See a different approach that goes beyond the simplistic "good guys" and "bad guys" model in Mary Fulbrook, *The People's State: East German Society From Hitler to Honecker* (New Haven, CT, 2005).

26. Weaver, *Rethinking Academic Politics*, 85.

27. Ibid., 72.

28. Daniel Schulz, "Silent Stars," *The Atlantic Times* (July, 2008), 14.

29. Ibid.

4

"Once Upon a Time . . ."

Losses in Scholarly Competence as a Result of German Unification

HELMUT MEIER

Proposal: This essay deals with the Institute for the History of the German Working-Class Movement at the Academy of Social Sciences that was attached to the Central Committee of the Socialist Unity Party of Germany.

Embellished records, which unfortunately determine the public reception of how the GDR was integrated into the Federal Republic of Germany and the consequences arising therefrom, consider the transformation of the East German higher education system to have been successful. Though some of the personalities involved in this transformation have expressed regret concerning the excesses that occurred and admit that trivial mistakes were made, they consider these to have been either exceptional or inevitable.[1]

Just as civilian losses in armed conflicts are depreciatingly described as collateral damage, so the fact that tens of thousands of GDR scholars were summarily removed from their academic posts is labeled a successful transformation of East German scholarship. The odd regret changes nothing and helps no one. Almost from one day to the next, the bulk of GDR academics were catapulted into unemployment or early retirement. Within the briefest possible time, GDR higher education was replaced by the West German system; GDR-trained staff were reduced to an insignificant minority of marginal importance. To the extent that they were allowed to stay in their institutions at all, they were kept out of all relevant posts. The incredible statement made in Wildbach-Kreuth, by a Christian Social Union member of parliament on how to deal with East German academics, is evidence that this marginalization was intended. He stated quite unequivocally: "[n]o need to put them into prison camps. We'll just marginalize them."[2] There is ample evidence from supposedly serious authors indicating that this attitude was and is widespread. Take for example Michael Wolffsohn, who considers the replacement of elites a "minimal requirement if one wants to come to terms with the GDR past and an indispensable act of political hygiene,"[3] or Arnulf Baring who considers GDR academics "unusable" due to their lack of expert knowledge.[4] A particularly macabre manner of justifying the way GDR academics were treated was to compare them to Nazi sympathizers within West German academia, who were generally permitted to continue working following the conclusion of World War II, arguing that the same mistake could not be repeated with the East Germans.

The bulk of West German scholars contributed toward this radical exchange of elites, while certain East Germans were more than willing to assist them. While such procedures are not unusual in times of radical social upheaval, it should nevertheless be noted that the events of 1989–90 were supposedly a peaceful and constitutionally agreed upon amalgamation of two states, and not the military occupation of a vanquished enemy.

What precisely occurred in the fields of higher education and scholarship has been extensively investigated and discussed by a number of authors.[5] Given this deliberate destruction of GDR academia, it could not be expected that institutions representing specific features of the GDR system would be treated with greater tolerance: namely, the scholarly and political research institutions of the Socialist Unity Party of Germany and the other member parties of the National Front, the trade union federation, and other mass organizations.

The chances of even a fraction of these institutions' scholarly capacities surviving the transition were minimal. Only a handful of scholars employed by them were able to find permanent or even temporary employment in other academic institutions following the end of the GDR. I will demonstrate the extent of the waste of scholarly capacities in this sector by taking the academic staff of the Academy for Social Sciences attached to the SED Central Committee, in particular the Institute for the History of the German Working-Class Movement, as a case study.

Nobody employed in academic institutes attached to the ruling SED party believed that the entire scholarly potential employed there, which was enormous, would be allowed to carry on. Vague hopes were however entertained that a limited number of staff might be financed by a trust fund attached to the Party of Democratic Socialism. These plans immediately encountered legal difficulties. The Federal German (that is, West German) establishment was not interested in drafting timely legislation to resolve the matter. Decisions were instead delayed or even evaded, leading to a seemingly endless back-and-forth, in the course of which an irreversible process of self-elimination set in.

The Party of Democratic Socialism, which succeeded the SED-PDS,[6] was struggling to establish a stable position for itself within the Federal German political system while also confronting widespread public hostility. This hostility prevented the party from realizing that they would eventually also require a scholarly apparatus of their own. Moreover, a faction of the newly established PDS leadership were themselves hostile to these "party intellectuals;" they felt that the party should dispense with the dogmatic academics "inherited" from the past. Fundamental, thorough analyses were not in demand at the time; instead, brief statements in line with public opinion were fashionable.

The staff employed by the Academy of Social Sciences had no option but to either apply for work at other institutions or to carry on their academic work in associations and project groups on a volunteer basis, so as to retain their scholarly competence. The prior option proved hopeless for this class of scholars. Thus Professor Jürgen Hofmann's application to the project "Files of the Prussian Ministries of State," for which his competence was amply established by his research into the Camphausen-Hansemann ministry, was not even considered worthy of a reply. His previous place of employment immediately disqualified him as an applicant. However, this left only the latter option, which was mostly taken by older staff members of the former party academy, because they were able to provide for themselves through retirement, whether planned or early. The younger staff members had no choice but to take on any sort of job or to resign themselves to unemployment and abandon their academic careers. They were, alternatively, forced to take on work they were not qualified for in order to provide for themselves and their families.

These scholars were subjected to all the negative labels that other GDR citizens were as well. This applied to other groups more discriminatingly, inasmuch as they were, in the period of transition, either eliminated on account of "lack of personal integrity," or of "lack of expert knowledge," or as a result of "transformation of staff structures."[7] The academic staff of party institutions were denounced as "people close to the system," representing the ruling party and in agreement with its basic concepts, thus making them "culprits." Their academic qualifications and expertise as well as their positions were considered to be the result of their political adaptability. The staff of these institutions could moreover not count on the solidarity of their colleagues in state universities and other academic institutions.

Guided by an unacknowledged prejudice, the scholars in question were considered to have lost their right to exist, following the disappearance of the GDR. The fact that these academic institutions had been raised to the status of controling authorities and became seats of academic councils by the last university reform in the GDR had triggered a great deal of envy, as the scholars employed there were thus authorized to guide the work of other national institutes of higher education and research. It was their responsibility to represent and carry out the policy of the SED vis-à-vis other academic institutions. This was often rightly felt by university and academy staff to be an imposition. The Institute for the History of the German Working-Class Movement at the Academy of Social Sciences, in fact, refused, for objective and functional reasons, to be made the seat of the council for historical research. The honor was then awarded to the Institute of Marxism-Leninism.

It is therefore not surprising that the self-dissolution of the Academy of Social Sciences, the Institute of Marxism-Leninism, the "Karl Marx" party school and the Institute for Economic Management were hardly noticed by the public, nor was their disappearance regretted. These institutions were all totally ignored in the report on "East Berlin's academic contributions to united Berlin," conducted by the SPD-PDS Senate of Berlin, to explore how the academic inheritance of the GDR had been integrated into Berlin's academic ventures, despite the fact that they were all located in East Berlin.[8] It is well known that the temporary admittance of scholars employed by these institutions into newly established academic associations was immediately publicly denounced. The new institutions were accused of "harboring camp-followers of the SED" and threatened with the loss of funding or of legal status. The campaign against the *Luisenstädtische Bildungsverein* in Berlin illustrates this. Denouncing every effort to allow academics from these party institutions to carry on in any capacity was a frequently used weapon in anticommunist campaigns.

The old Cold War concepts of "the enemy" were thus happily revived.

Consequently, only the most persistent and expert representatives of this academic faction continued on with their research, albeit in a more modest scope. It was conducted on a largely voluntary basis, often entailing an abandonment of employment at the scholar's own expense. The toxic atmosphere of constant hostility and discrimination (to which established academia happily contributed) proved to be particularly humiliating for those concerned.

The most committed scholars among this group of academics were aware from the very beginning that a profound and self-critical investigation of the perspectives they had hitherto held was indispensable for the credibility of all future research. Scholars attempted to deal with this challenge in various ways. They renounced outdated viewpoints, openly conceded errors, misjudgments, and deficits in their own work, and bravely turned to new ways of addressing problems. A great deal of evidence backs up this assertion. A wealth of publications by former members of the Institute for the History of the German Working-Class Movement attached to the Academy of Social Sciences were submitted, such as those by Rolf Richter,[9] Helmut Meier,[10] Jürgen Hofmann, Annette Neumann,[11] Gerhard Lozek,[12] Alfred Loesdau[13] Wladislaw Hedeler, Horst Helas, Klaus Kinner, and Elke Reuter.[14]

Gerhard Lozek, for example, criticized (a) the simplified and dogmatic historical concept of progressive and linear socioeconomic formations; (b) the incorrect evaluation of the post-1917 era; (c) the mechanical approach to the conformity of the historical process to historical laws and to the concurrence of historical findings with the party line; (d) the claim to philosophical and scientific truth; and, (e) the historical role played by the proletarian vanguard "party of a new type" and all conclusions arising there from. He described these points as

> very grave deficits, errors, and handicaps harming GDR historiography. Added to this was a simplified concept of progress, which made problems of historical alternatives and the idea of open-ended history, plurality, open-mindedness, and the individual as a historical subject taboo.[15]

These efforts were, as a rule, officially ignored. Those that were not were exceptions proving the rule.[16]

A thorough examination of the working methods and findings of scholars attached to the Academy of Social Sciences and other institutions—established by the SED to influence scholars in the GDR and acquire knowledge necessary for governance—reveals that serious research was nevertheless also conducted, even during GDR times. Of course, scholars working for these institutions were exposed to certain constraints they felt unable to resist. After all, the scholars in these institutions had largely joined the party on grounds of honest conviction and were therefore wholeheartedly committed to the successful construction of socialism in the GDR. This was a balancing act that necessitated compromises, which led to self-censorship and scholarly inconsistencies.

Still, even in such instances, scholarly research brought consequences of its own. One had to face facts, even if they were incompatible with previously held beliefs and expectations. Analyzing the numerous papers and expert opinions produced by the institutes of the Academy of Social Sciences, one finds that they reveal numerous problems and conflicts which lay at the root of socialism's defeat. Proposals were made as to how these problems and conflicts could be overcome. Unfortunately, as a rule these did not meet with the approval of the party leadership or the GDR government directing said research. Admittedly, criticism of the dominant party line and demands for reform were not made with sufficient determination. This experience is certainly one of the outstanding reasons why during the crisis of autumn 1989 the bulk of those employed by the party academy were no longer willing to support the ossified policy pursued by the party leadership. Their political resignation arose from the profound disappointment concerning their many attempts toward reforms, all of which had failed. They had realized that the slogan calling for the unity of scholarship and politics, which they had long supported, had been a mistake. This so-called "unity" had merely led to scholarship subordinating itself to the whims of ruling politicians, ultimately harming both scholarship as well as politics.

The expertise of scholars employed in these institutions was, after all, well known outside of the GDR as well. Scholars of the Academy were frequently invited to conferences and symposia where they were subjected to drastically less anticommunist slander than during the transition period. Instead they were regarded as strategic partners and respected experts in their fields. One illustration of this is the joint elaboration of the statement "The Dispute between Ideologies" by representatives of the SPD-*Grundwerte* (basic values) Commission and scholars attached to the Academy of Social Sciences in 1987.[17] Another case in point is that in 1986 Alfred Loesdau was asked to attend a conference on research into the GDR in Conway, New Hampshire, USA. His paper was later published in *Studies in GDR-Culture and Society*, New York. Lothar Bisky was another member of the Academy invited to the same conference. In May 1989, Helmut Meier from the Historical Institute and Gudrun Langendorf from the Institute for Economics were invited to Britain to attend a conference in Nottingham, convened on the occasion of the 40th anniversary of the GDR. The University of Oldenburg, on the occasion of their Ossietzky Festival in 1987, asked Professor Otto Reinhold, the chancellor of the Academy of Social Sciences, to send scholars competent to make contributions on the subjects of "the future of labour" and "future trends in national traditions." Sociologist Frank Adler and historian Helmut Meier accepted the invitation.[18]

More examples can easily be provided to demonstrate that the participation of scholars from the Academy of Social Sciences at conferences in the Federal Republic of Germany and other western countries, to discuss certain academic problems was much appreciated and that interesting contributions from these scholars were expected. Lothar Mertens's publication on the institutions of the Academy cannot, therefore, be considered an accurate presentation of the activities, achievements, and function of this institution.[19] It is a misleading overview, one of many attempts, to present the GDR as an academic desert whose scholarly institutions produced no achievements at all and were thus rightly doomed.[20]

An instance of the total losses or, at least, serious inroads into the scholarly potential took place at the Institute for the History of the German Working-Class Movement attached to the Academy of Social Sciences since its dissolution on January 31, 1991.

At that time the permanent staff of the institute comprised eight full professors, three assistant professors, six senior assistants with a doctorate, four staff members with a doctorate and two without this qualification, three assistants, among them one with a doctorate. Adding to this highly qualified staff were a number of temporary academic staff, comprising six research students in training for a professorship and nineteen German and two Soviet post-graduate students. These staff members worked in five research departments, forming work teams engaged in special areas of research.

The department for the history of the German working-class movement from 1917 to 1945 focused, on the one hand, on the history of the social and economic activities of the Communist Party of Germany during the period of the Weimar Republic, thereby investigating problems that were not dealt with elsewhere by GDR historians. Both the visions of the Communists, with respect to how to solve the housing question and their attempts to implement them, were explored. On the other hand, research also centered on antifascist resistance and the problems of antifascism in the GDR.

A research venture, which was unique to the GDR, was undertaken on the subject of "The Socialist Nation and Historical Consciousness." Thus, the development of the historical consciousness of GDR citizens was investigated beginning in 1967. A number of extensive sociological opinion polls were undertaken, yielding interesting results. GDR historical propaganda was then analyzed in light of the poll results.[21]

The other research focus in the department was the national status of the GDR. It attempted to overcome simplified political concepts concerning the establishment of a socialist nation. This work only began in 1987–88 and could therefore not produce any practical results. Investigations into the development of contractual relations between the GDR and the Federal Republic of Germany, however, did yield initial findings.

Research into the history of the SED's economic policy pursued was one of the institute's earliest undertakings. Their particular focus was to investigate the concept and its implementation by the party in the 1940s and 1950s as well as since the 1970s. Later, scholars of the institute also investigated GDR-USSR economic relations.

For many years, scholars probed the relations between the SED and different social groups in the GDR, particularly the relations of the party to cooperative farmers, to craftsmen and to the intelligentsia. An important object of research was the relation between the state and the churches and between the state and practicing Christians.

The use of unpublished sources compiled by enterprises, as well as district and regional administrations, in the course of these investigations into SED policy made them particularly valuable. These investigations made use of a considerable amount of insider experience and internal material, which could easily be complemented by archive material and publications.

In the course of the 1960s, investigations were undertaken into "the bourgeois historiography and the ideological debate on history" which, for the first time, dealt with Federal German historiography and eventually also covered the history of historiography in the United States, in Britain, and in Italy. Its central subjects were the political and theoretical concepts of non-Marxist historiography (such as the doctrine of totalitarianism). Increasingly, as the publication "Historiography in the 20th Century, Historiography in Modern Times and Historical Philosophy in Western Europe and the United States" published in 1998 proves, analyses of the findings were focused on specific theoretical problems of historiography and were subjects dealt with by the institute's research teams.

Following the dissolution of the Academy of Social Sciences the academic staffs of the Institute for History lost their jobs and were confronted with the need to provide for themselves. The older staff members were able to retire or take an early retirement package, which provided them with at least basic means of existence. This allowed them to carry on with their academic research without worrying about how to eke out an existence. This was the case for five of the eight professors employed by the Institute for the History of the Working-Class Movement. Two more professors and two senior assistants as well as one female academic staff member managed to find temporary employment, albeit under difficult and fluctuating conditions. The jobs they found would nowadays be called precarious and were poorly remunerated. One of the lecturers was able to find more or less secure employment in an institute he had co-founded. Most of the junior staff were obliged to manage by seeking additional employment outside their profession, i.e., they went into self-employment, into nursing or elderly care, became traveling salespersons for insurance companies or other services. This compelled the majority of them to give up their scholarly ambitions. In view of their proven competence this was the regrettable normality.

Given these circumstances, it is somewhat remarkable how much academic work former institute members have managed to produce since 1990. They could, of course, have been far more productive had their potential not been so irresponsibly wasted and pushed into the "secondary academic culture." Had they been allowed to cooperate with institutionalized academia or establish new research institutes, they would doubtlessly have made valuable contributions to the scholarly work performed there. This potential was wasted because the necessary political will was lacking.

There are a number of facts to be dealt with to appreciate the scope of this wastage. Since 1990, former staff from the Institute for the History of the German Working-Class Movement at the Academy of Social Sciences have participated in many academic activities, including political informational and educational work, public debates, and academic conferences. Their number of published contributions is considerable, and they continue to relate contemporary research into the history of the working-class movement from 1918 to 1945; see Elke Reuter's publications and co-publications for examples.[22] Antifascism in the Communist Party, the SED and in the GDR—a subject initially taken up in the 1980s—is being expanded to the present period, particularly in terms of its relevance to the struggle against modern right-wing extremism and neo-Nazism; the work of Rolf Richter and Horst Helas must be mentioned in this regard. Their ongoing relevance can be seen in the bibliographies of these scholars compiled and published on their birthdays.[23] In the 1990s, Rolf Richter was involved in several projects training young people to enable them to resist and overcome right-wing extremist views and activities. Horst Helas wrote about Berlin's *Scheunenviertel*, which provided important information regarding the daily lives of Jews in Berlin and the racist misdeeds organized by the Nazi regime against them.

Utilizing the methodical and theoretical experience gained in the course of empirical investigations into historical consciousness in the GDR, a group of scholars belonging to the *Gesellschaftswissenschaftliche Forum* (Forum for Social Sciences), supervised by Jürgen Hofmann and assisted by Helmut Meier, undertook research, for a number of years, into identity in East Germany. This research sent questionnaires to addresses provided by the Brandenburg Ministry for Internal Affairs. Though this opinion poll was statistically not representative, the findings were still very informative—as is evident if one compares them with investigations conducted by relevant mainstream institutions. These findings were presented at public symposia and published.[24] The project group submitted a short contribution to the Commission to Investigate the Social and Political Changes in the new Federal States (KSPW).[25]

Staff of the former department of historiography under Gerhard Lozek produced a monograph on non-Marxist western historiography, which had already been an integral part of research and publishing planning in the GDR. It was printed at the time of the *Wende* (the term denoting the political transition of 1989–90), and thus it was feared that it would suffer the fate of so many other GDR-era projects which failed to see the light of day. The publication of the book is indebted to Gerhard Lozek's staying power and the willingness of the publisher, Fides, to take considerable risks,[26] and it was very much appreciated by experts.[27] Alfred Loesdau who was also involved in the project continued his research on U.S. historiography and political science.[28]

Research into the policies pursued by the SED were discontinued due to the loss of scholars: Rolf Leonhard und Helga Kanzig died, while others were obliged to take up employment outside their profession to support their families, as they could find no work in their own fields. One exception to this unfortunate development was the research on relations between the state and the churches and SED policy toward the churches undertaken by Joachim Heise from the Institute for Comparative State-Church Research established and run by Horst Dähn.[29]

Some staff members from the former Institute of History at the Academy took up investigations in other, sometimes new, fields. In recent years, Alfred Loesdau took up intensive investigations into the history of Berlin's allotment plot gardens. Under his direction, a team of experts produced an interesting publication dealing with historical and current problems of the allotment plot garden movement and its role in the urban development of Berlin.[30] Helmut Meier reviewed, from a topical point of view, debates on inheritance and tradition in the GDR and its practical relevance.[31] He also published a history of the GDR *Kulturbund* (Cultural Workers Association).[32] In addition, he researched the life and relevance of Constantin Frantz.[33] During his limited period of research at the Institute for Comparative Studies on Church and State, Rolf Richter investigated into the Russian Orthodox Church in Berlin.[34] Jürgen Hofmann, one of the spokesmen for the historical commission attached to the PDS (now Die Linke) executive committee, presented statements on various historical events and problems. He also wrote on topical problems of the history of the labor movement and of the GDR.[35]

This contribution only deals with permanent staff of the Institute for the History of the German Working-Class Movement at the Academy of Social Sciences at the time of its dissolution. It does not refer to the activities and achievements of temporary staff. The facts presented here do not, by any means, represent a complete survey of all publications produced by the scholars referred to. Thus, the works mentioned in this paper are merely exemplary, demonstrating how productive the scholars were, who lost their jobs when the institute was dissolved from one day to the next, forcing them to fend for themselves under completely different conditions. It would have served the national German interest better had they been allowed to continue working in their fields, but the political will to do so was lacking. We can only record the irreparable losses incurred and underscore the activities and findings achieved despite these extremely difficult circumstances.

It leaves me to state that the intended total elimination of scholars of the GDR was not fully achieved in as much as the scholars from the Institute for the History of the German Working-Class at the Academy of Social Sciences courageously continued to work in their fields and produce respectable results. To show this was the intention of this contribution. In conclusion let me demonstrate the following paradox: the undesirable and non-esteemed voices of East German scholars have become, for scholars abroad, an integral part of academia in present-day Germany and even evidence of the pluralism of opinions. Their contributions exist and must be acknowledged. In Germany, however, they are still taboo. And, as much as possible, ignored. As a rule, no discourse deals with them objectively. From this angle, one could consider this an illustration for the cunning of history, as pointed out by Hegel.

Translated by Hanna Behrend

Notes

1. See Stifterverband der deutschen Wissenschaft (ed.), *10 Jahre danach. Zur Entwicklung der Hochschulen und Forschungseinrichtungen in den neuen Ländern und Berlin* (Essen, 2002). These were the proceedings of the joint symposium convened by Wissenschaftsrat, Stifterverband, and Volkswagen Foundation on February 8–9, 2002, at Berlin town-hall.

2. Gesellschaft zum Schutz von Bürgerrecht und Menschenwürde e. V. (ed.), *Unfrieden in Deutschland: Weissbuch 2: Wissenschaft und Kultur im Beitrittsgebiet* (Berlin, 1993), 7.

3. Michael Wolffsohn, "Doppelte Vergangenheitsbewältigung," Klaus Sühl (ed.), *Vergangenheitsbewältigung 1945–1989: Ein unmöglicher Vergleich?* (Berlin, 1994), 40, 42.

4. Arnulf Baring, *Deutschland, was nun? Ein Gespräch mit Dirk Rumberg und Wolf Jobst Siedler* (Berlin, 1991), 59.

5. See Stefan Bollinger and Ulrich van der Heyden (eds.), *Deutsche Einheit und Elitenwechsel in Ostdeutschland* (Berlin, 2002).

6. This was the abbreviation of Socialist Unity Party of Germany-Party of Democratic Socialism.

7. Roland Bloch and Peer Pasternack, "Die Ost-Berliner Wissenschaft im vereinigten Berlin: Eine Transformationsfolgenanalyse," *Institut für Hochschulforschung an der Martin-Luther-Universität Halle-Wittenberg, Work Report, No. 2/04* (Halle, 2004), 34.

8. See ibid.

9. Rolf Richter, "Aus der Rede von Prof. Dr. Rolf Richter, Akademie für Gesellschaftswissenschaften, auf der Kundgebung Berliner SED-Mitglieder am 9. November 1989," Manfred Behrend and Helmut Meier (eds.), *Der Schwere Weg der Erneuerung: Von der SED zur PDS, a Documentation* (Berlin, 1991); idem, "Antifaschismus vor neuen Anfängen," *Beiträge zur Geschichte der Arbeiterbewegung*, vol. 32 (1990), no. 6; idem, "Über Uneingelöstes im Antifaschismus der deutschen kommunistischen Bewegung," *Gibt es erledigte Frage an die Geschichte? Beiträge auf dem Wissesnchatlichen Kolloquium zu Ehren des 65. Geburtstages von Prof. Dr. habil. Dr.h.c. Walter Schmidt* (Berlin, 1995).

10. Helmut Meier, "Anliegen und Ergebnisse der Erbe- und Traditionsdebatte in der Geschichtswissenschaft der DDR," Eberhard Fromm and Hans-Jürgen Mende (eds.), *Vom Beitritt zur Vereinigung: Schwierigkeiten beim Umgang mit deutsch-deutscher Geschichte* (Berlin, 1993); idem, *Geschichtsbewusstsein und historische Identität in der DDR: Versuch einer kritischen Bilanz* (Hefte zur ddr-geschichte no. 31) (Berlin, 1996).

11. Jürgen Hofmann and Annette Neumann (eds.), *Die Klasse in Aufruhr: Der 17.Juni 1953 in Berliner Betrieben* (Berlin, 2003).

12. Gerhard Lozek, *Totalitarismus—(k)ein Thema für Linke?* (Pankower Vorträge, no. 1), (Berlin, 1997); idem (ed.), Geschichtsschreibung im 20. Jahrhundert: Neuzeithistoriographie und Geschichtsdenken im westlichen Europa und in den USA (Berlin, 1998), idem, "Zu Erfahrungen der DDR-Geschichtswissenschaft bei der Analyse und Kritik der nichtmarxistischen Historiographie," Alfred Loesdau and Helmut Meier (eds.), *Zur Geschichte der Historiographie nach 1945: Beiträge eines Kolloquiums zum 75. Geburtstag von Gerhard Lozek* (Berlin, 2001).

13. Alfred Loesdau, "Zur Erforschung der USA-Historiographie nach dem II. Weltkrieg in der DDR," Rainer Schnoor (ed.), *Amerikanistik in der DDR: Geschichte-Analysen-Zeitzeugenberichte* (Berlin, 1999).

14. Elke Reuter, Wladislaw Hedeler, Horst Helas, and Klaus Kinner (eds.), *Luxemburg oder Stalin: Schaltjahr 1928. Die KPD am Scheideweg* (Berlin, 2003).

15. Gerhard Lozek, "Zu Erfahrungen der DDR-Geschichtswissenschaft bei der Analyse und Kritik der nichtmarxistischen Historiographie," Loesdau and Meier (eds.), *Zur Geschichte der Historiographie nach 1945*, 21.

16. See Stefan Berger, "Was bleibt von der Geschichtswissenschaft der DDR? Blick auf eine alternative historische Kultur im Osten Deutschlands," *Zeitschrift für Geschichtswissenschaft*, 50 (1992), no. 11, 1023–1024.

17. See Harald Neubert, *Zum gemeinsamen Ideologie-Papier von SED und SPD* (hefte zur ddr-geschichte, no. 18), (Berlin, 1994); Erich Hahn, *Positionen zum SED/SPD-Dialogpapier von 1987: Nach-Lese in veröffentlichten und bisher unveröffentlichten Quellen* (hefte zur ddr-geschichte, no. 84), (Berlin, 2003).

18. See Friedrich W. Busch (ed.), *Perspektiven gesellschaftlicher Entwicklung in beiden deutschen Staaten—Materialien eines Symposions aus Anlaß der Ossietzky-Tage 1987 an der Universität Oldenburg* Oldenburg, 1988), esp. 159–60.

19. See Lothar Mertens, *Rote Denkfabrik? Die Akademie für Gesellschaftswissenschaften beim ZK der SED* (Münster, 2004).

20. See Eberhard Fromm, "Review" of Lothar Mertens, Rote Denkfabrik? Die Akademie für Gesellschaftswissenschaften beim ZK der SED. http//www.der-deutsche-intellektuelle.de/html/mertens.html.

21. See Marco Demantowski, "Der Beginn demoskopischer Geschichtsbewußtseins-Forschung in Deutschland: Die Forschungsgruppe 'Sozialistisches Geschichtsbewusstsein' am Institut für Gesellschaftswissenschaften beim ZK der SED," *Zeitschrift für Geschichtsdidaktik*, 4 (2005), no. 4.

22. See Elke Reuter et al., *Luxemburg oder Stalin*; Günther Fuchs, Erwin Lewin, Elke Reuter, and Stefan Weber (eds.), *"Brüsseler Konferenz" der KPD von 1935*, CD-ROM (Berlin, 2000); Klaus Kinner and Elke Reuter, *Der deutsche Kommunismus. Selbstverständnis und Realität*, vol. 2: *Gegen Faschismus und Krieg (1933–1939)* (Berlin, 2005).

23. See Horst Helas, Reiner Zilkenat et al. (eds.), *Antifaschismus als humanistisches Erbe in Europa. Festschrift zum 60. Geburtstag von Prof Dr. Rolf Richter* (Berlin, 2005); Reiner Zilkenat et al. (eds.), *Antisemitismus und Demokratiefeindschaft in Deutschland im 20. Jahrhundert: Festschrift zum 60. Geburtstag von Dr. Horst Helas* (Berlin, 2007).

24. See Detlef Eckert, Jürgen Hofmann, and Helmut Meier (eds.), *Zwischen Anschluß und Ankunft—Identitätskonflikte und Identitätssuche der Ostdeutschen auf dem Weg zum Bundesbürger* (Potsdam, 1992); Jürgen Hofmann, Erhard Weckesser, and Rüdiger Beetz (ed.), *Zwischen Anschluss und Ankunft, Vol II: Beiträge zur einer ostdeutschen Zwischenbilanz. Materialien eines wissenschaftlichen Kolloquiums* (Potsdam, 1994); Helmut Meier and Erhard Weckesser (eds.), *Ost-Identität: Konjunkturelle Erscheinung oder längerfristige Bewusstseinslage? Beiträge des dritten wissenschaftlichen Kolloquiums zum Thema "Zwischen Anschluss und Ankunft" am 16.März 1996 in Potsdam* (Berlin, 1996).

25. Projektgruppe "Identitätswandel," *Kurzstudie: Identitätskonflikte, Reaktionen und Neuorientierungen in der ostdeutschen Bevölkerung beim Übergang in die Gesellschaft der Bundesrepublik Deutschland (Report),* Project Nr. AG 5/38 (Berlin, October 1992).

26. See Lozek (ed.), *Geschichtsschreibung im 20. Jahrhundert.*

27. See Gerhard Lozek, "Zu Erfahrungen der DDR-Geschichtswissenschaft [. . .]," 26–27.

28. See Loesdau, "Zur Erforschung der USA-Historiographie nach dem II. Weltkrieg in der DDR;" idem, "Zur Historiographie der USA nach 1945," Loesdau and Meier (eds.), *Zur Geschichte der Historiographie nach 1945*, 135–41; Alfred Loesdau, "Die Sozialwissenschaften in den USA zwischen Nonkonformismus und regierungspolitischem Engagement: Zum Verhalten US-amerikanischer Gesellschaftswissenschaftler unter den Bedingungen globaler Konflikte an der Wende zum 21. Jahrhundert," Gesellschaftswissenschaftliches Forum. Interdisziplinäre Online-Zeitschrift, no. II (May 2008), www.gewiforum.de.

29. See Joachim Heise, "Das Institut für vergleichende Staat-Kirche-Forschung," Heiner Timmermann (ed.), *Die DDR: Politik und Ideologie als Instrument* (Dokumente und Schriften der Europäischen Akademie Otzenhausen, vol. 26 (Berlin, 1999). See also Horst Dähn and Joachim Heise (eds.), *Luther und die DDR: Der Reformator und das DDR-Fernsehen 1983* (Berlin, 1996).

30. Alfred Loesdau et al., *Kleine Gärten einer großen Stadt: Die Kleingartenbewegung Berlins in nationaler und internationaler Sicht* (Berlin, 2007).

31. See Helmut Meier, *Geschichtsbewusstsein und historische Identität in der DDR. Versuch einer kritischen Bilanz* (hefte zur ddr-geschichte, no. 31) (Berlin, 1996); idem, "Zu Formen des praktischen Umgangs mit Erbe und Traditionen in der DDR," Heiner Timmermann (ed.), *Die DDR: Politik und Ideologie als Instrument* (Dokumente und Schriften der Europäischen Akademie Otzenhausen, vol. 86) (Berlin, 1999).

32. See Helmut Meier, *Der Kulturbund im politischen System der DDR in den siebziger Jahren* (hefte zur ddr-geschichte, no. 62) (Berlin, 2000).

33. See Helmut Meier, "Constantin Frantz (1817 bis 1891): Verfechter von Antisemitismus in der deutschen Ideologiegeschichte," *Rundbrief 1-2007* (AG Rechtsextremismus und Antifaschismus beim Parteivorstand der Linkspartei/PDS) (Berlin, 2007), 52–58; idem, "Constantin Frantz' Schrift 'Louis Napoleon' im Vergleich mit dem Marxsschen '18. Brumaire,' " *Jahrbuch für Forschungen zur Geschichte der Arbeiterbewegung*, vol. 6 (2007), no. III, 48–57.

34. See Rolf Richter, *Aus dem Leben der russischen orthodoxen Kirche in Berlin* (Berlin, 1999).

35. See Jürgen Hofmann "Anton Ackermann über den „besonderen deutschen Weg," Klaus Kinner (ed.), *Wege aus der Katastrophe: Debatten über ein Nachkriegsdeutschland und nationale Wege zum Sozialismus im europäischen Vergleich* (Leipzig, 2006); idem, "Arbeitermilieu und Rechtsextremismus: Zur Genesis und Dimensionen eines historischen und aktuellen Problems," *Jahrbuch für Forschungen zur Geschichte der Arbeiterbewegung*, vol. 6, no. 1 (2007); idem and Michael Schneider (eds.), *Arbeiterbewegung und Rechtsextremismus* (ITH-Berichte, No. 41), (Leipzig, 2007).

5

German Unification and the Debate of the West German Social Sciences

STEFAN BOLLINGER

In the summer of 2008, one of the leading research institutes in Germany declared that the disparity in living conditions between East and West Germany, regarding the per capita income, would continue for another 320 years.[1] Thus German unity remains, more than twenty years after the fall of the Wall, largely incomplete. Tensions, contradictions, and conflicts are perhaps the inevitable consequence of a process that, in the final analysis, did not amount to a true unification of equals, but rather the absorption of the East by West Germany. One still has to agree with Rolf Reißig's insight, that in terms of contemporary Germany we are dealing with one state but two separate societies.[2] A brief glance across the U.S. border to Canada might drive home how lasting such real and perceived inequalities are, as the long-standing grievances of the Franco-Canadians illustrate.

One Country: Two Societies, One Scholarly Tradition?

The legacy of the Cold War (experiencing 45 years of postwar history very differently on opposite sides of the Iron Curtain in two separate social and political systems of two mutually exclusive ideologies of Western capitalism and Soviet-style socialism) reinforces the current line of division in as-of-yet un-united Germany. Persisting economic inequalities between the East and the West of Germany also underscore this. One feature of this still unresolved conflict is the role and the experiences of the GDR elites, mainly its intelligentsia.[3] Within the East German intelligentsia, the historians and political scientists are merely one case among many—albeit a unique one. The GDR elites and the GDR intelligentsia have radically lost influence and power. The fact that Germany today is governed by Chancellor Angela Merkel, who is not only a former East German citizen but also a former activist of the Communist Party youth organization (FDJ—Free German Youth) and part of the GDR intelligentsia, cannot obscure this watershed demotion of East Germany's scholars and intellectuals in contemporary Germany. The old GDR intelligentsia, the core supporters of the state, have been almost summarily dismissed from their professorships and other positions. Today they have to survive on odd jobs, if they were not old—and lucky—enough to opt for regular or early retirement. While younger former members of the GDR intelligentsia have found new jobs, those new jobs are usually far below what they are really qualified for. They usually have to work under the supervision of West German bosses, being subject to West German interests, as well as cultural and social structures. Those East German scholars and intellectuals who did not qualify for early retirement had to learn the oft-grim reality of being evaluated by Western superiors, the insecurities of only temporary employment, and being *abgewickelt* (dismissed from their posts).

Of course, the old GDR intelligentsia is partly responsible for their radical loss of status and influence. The intellectuals, including the historians, have for too long uncritically supported policies that paid lip-service to the humanistic values of socialism while simultaneously allowing its deformation, abuse, and truly undemocratic incarnation. Large parts of the old GDR intelligentsia argued only very late, too late, for an anti-Stalinist, democratic and, *at the same time*, pro-socialist independent East Germany. The collapse of the GDR happened very quickly and the willingness of most rank-and-file East Germans to try out a presumably better version of socialism evaporated rapidly after the fall of the Wall and the massive intrusions of West German influences on the disintegrating East. The East German intelligentsia were, due to its support of the old regime, defanged, demoralized, and soon pushed aside, not only by East German dissidents but also by opportunists, at the first the pull and gravity of West German academic structures.

Can there really be a truly unified country when, without war and out of a peaceful revolution, the intelligentsia of a whole country is condemned to unconditional surrender? Apparently "East Germany was to experience again what all of Germany already experienced in 1945, namely unconditional surrender," noted the leading West German political scientist Klaus von Beyme.[4] In the unconditional capitulation of an undeclared war—the losers of this conflict are at the mercy of the victors!

It seems that there is ample reason to look back at this process (its missed opportunities and the intentional destruction of people's professional lives) with anger. This is not as much a problem that pertains to my own biography, inasmuch as I have established myself on the periphery of mainstream scholarship, within the so-called second scholarly culture, which by the way justifies its existence only if it challenges the pieties and certainties of the reigning mainstream.

A conference that probes into the fate of what is left of the GDR's scholarly culture is a good idea. It should be food for thought that this conference takes place here in North America and not in Germany! After all, for certain self-appointed West German victors of history there is only a history of success, where those who were excluded do not count except as triumphs and new conquests.[5] Others have warned early on that this wholesale exclusion was deeply problematic and will come back to haunt us all. Jürgen Mittelstrass stated, years ago, that the process should be reconsidered, addressing as well as ameliorating those injustices.[6] Yet improvements never really happened, and now it is all history.

It is no longer about correcting those mistakes—for that, it is already too late—but about remembering what could have been and what has been irrevocably lost. It is now time to assess the price paid for those exclusions. We must come to understand how a society that excludes ultimately loses out on opportunities that integration would have provided. After all, it is not merely that part of contemporary Germany feels itself at a disadvantage, but also that social alternatives to the status quo are suppressed.

Who Controls One's Own Identity?

GDR intellectuals, including historians, were heavily involved in the attempt to build a socially just socialist society, even though the party leadership had always looked at them with a mixture of distrust and contempt. They were considered unreliable from the onset and especially in moments of crisis. Yet, the vast majority of the GDR's historians were committed to their state's version of socialism and tried to look at its myriad shortcomings as inevitable birthing pains and merely temporary problems.[7] Those intellectuals and historians were at certain moments (like during the de-Stalinization that started in 1956, the very relative liberalizations of the early 1960's, as well as during the 1970s and 80s) increasingly willing to critique the bureaucratic and anti-intellectual policies of the party apparatus—demanding a more democratic socialism. Nevertheless, the GDR's social scientists, and especially its historians, were most certainly not among the avant-garde of such efforts. It is mainly the GDR's artists and writers who come to mind, as fighters for a better socialism rather than its social scientists. There were, however, courageous individuals among the latter group, like Leo Kofler, Ernst Bloch, Wolfgang Harich, Hermann Klenner, Gunther Kohlmey, Fritz Behrens, and others, who worked toward more humane socialist alternatives. When it comes to historians and scientists in the neighborhood of history, only a handful of names stand out, such as those of Walter Markov, Manfred Kossok, Uwe-Jens Heuer, and Jürgen Kuczynski, who initiated critical discussions, and thus, from time to time, ended up in conflicts with the party, while always defending not only a Marxist approach but also the ideals of the GDR and its socialist system.

Especially in the field of historical scholarship, the SED always understood that the intellectual foundations of its hold on East German society very much depended on a coherent vision of history, which was closely tied to the party line and entailed massive propaganda efforts. One has to agree with what the then-young historian Bernd Florath and others, who stated openly, right after the collapse of the GDR:

> [a]s historians they have failed at a key point of their own intellectual self-definition, namely to keep a critical distance to those in power and to criticize the abuses of power. They did not only not behave like mature citizens of the scholarly community but indeed failed to apply to themselves their own critical standards and methodological considerations when it came not to the past but to their own situation.[8]

The fact that these historians have too often participated in an uncritical fashion has very much proved burdensome for the GDR historians of the 1989–1990 watershed and thereafter. It robbed them of the opportunities to influence public opinion, in favor of their ideal of a democratic socialism. Distortions, one-sidedness, outright falsifications, as well as ideologically justified ignorance, robbed many of them of their voices, at least at first. Many found themselves in a defensive position, especially vis-à-vis the handful of oppositionists who now voiced their complaints and dissatisfaction very aggressively in organizations such as the *Independent Historians Association* (that was explicitly founded to challenge and oppose the GDR's historians' establishment). All of this robbed them—like the other state-supporting and state-employed producers of ideology in the GDR—of leverage, while interacting and competing with their West German Colleagues. The West Germans often ceased to be mere colleagues and turned into judges, who now had the right and the power to evaluate and pass judgment on their

East German counterparts. The West German historians were now in a position to decree that their eastern counterparts lacked scholarly credentials and were ideologically compromised.

The consequences of this encounter are well known: by the mid-1990s, the West German-dominated restructuring of East German academia resulted in over 70 percent of East German academics being victimized one way or another and losing their employment. Hansgünter Meyer calculated that out of the 7,516 East German full and associate professors in 1995, about 5,000 were dismissed (66.5%). From the 31,400 assistant professors and adjuncts, 19,400 (61.8%) had their positions eradicated.[9] Historians, political scientists, philosophers, and people employed in the legal profession were especially affected by this "weeding-out" process, given that they, contrary to East Germany's economists, could not find adequate second careers in the private sector.

More important than the loss of institutional support and full-time employment is the removal of East German intellectuals, including the voices of East German historians, from public debate, which, by and large, rendered East Germans silent. The post-Communist political elites of East Germany were very much under-represented on the federal level and in the purely Eastern-German governmental, administrative, and higher-education apparatus, and also in the media. They were statistically, and in term of their sensibilities, dominated by the West's cultural priorities. These people paid the price of having been disenfranchised from their own history and biographies, sometimes willingly and other times not. Thus the West German perspective and interpretations of history very much shaped the public, publicized, and scholarly mainstream. To this Western mainstream, the East largely represented totalitarianism and the continuity of dictatorships—emphasizing any similarities between the Nazis and the Communists.[10] Coming to terms with the past, exclusively under the auspices of being victors in the Cold War, allows little room for self-reflection and self-correction. East Germans have at times responded to these pressures by withdrawing into their private spheres and/or by stubbornly challenging the Western-dominated mainstream, without honing their critical and dialectic self-criticism. This is not just the problem of "normal" East Germans but also of many of its intellectuals and former GDR historians.

What is lost in all of this is a systematic and common search for unity: a reflection on similar problems, similar detours, and the forces of divisive Cold War loyalties on both sides. Apart from a few rare exceptions, in the contemporary discussion on the GDR, the theory of totalitarianism reigns supreme, and the *Eigensinn* (or dynamics and complexities) of East German society is rendered invisible or insignificant. The key problem here is the continuation of the Cold War "by other means": the intentional discrediting of the socialist idea. As Werner Mittenzwei in his collective portrait of the GDR intelligentsia stated:

> [a] continued dialogue between anti-Communist thought in the West and Marxist thought in the East was not in their [West Germany's ruling elite] interests, instead the point was to completely eliminate the Eastern perspective or at least to render it impotent through marginalization.[11]

What took center stage for West German anticommunists was the entire Socialist concept, not just its Stalinist deformation. Thus, what was to be discredited was the idea of a Democratic Socialism, as propounded by the Party for Democratic Socialism (now Die Linke).

The Absence of a Discussion

At first there certainly were discussions between East and West German historians, sociologists, and political scientists.[12] They focused on the identification and acceptance of the ideological boundaries of GDR scholars, as well as the attempt to grasp and overcome the deficits of Marxist-Leninist understanding—without ceasing to be Marxist.

Yet this discussion was largely replaced by a discourse that focused on the dictatorial character of the GDR. One of its crucial consequences was the wholesale dismissal of the East German academia from institutions of higher education and their replacement by West Germans. This immensely complicated any real dialog between East and West German scholars.

In times of a supposed "end of history" (in Francis Fukuyama's words), the legitimacy of any socialist project seemed to be hopelessly outdated. Even many West German liberal and social-democratic historians could not fully escape this *Zeitgeist*. As a consequence, Marxist and other leftist approaches were marginalized and even social history itself was put on the defensive. What followed instead was the renaissance of various theories of totalitarianism. The "end of the Cold War" and Western triumphalism demoted East Germany's historians virtually overnight from once-respected partners to vanquished outcasts.

Despite of these developments, some leading West German publicists, foremost Christoph Klessmann and Peter Bender, emphasized the necessity to write post-1945 German history from a comparative perspective.[13] One of the few examples for an East-West cooperation was the project Deutsche

Zeitgeschichte (German Contemporary History) that was sponsored by the Rosa Luxemburg Foundation and resulted in a massive scholarly handbook.[14]

Discussions Without a Partner

Yet despite such promising examples, much of post-1945 history is increasingly being written from the perspective of the winners of the Cold War. There are some notable exceptions, as some publications from the Zentrum für Zeithistorische Forschung at Potsdam and from the Institut für Zeitgeschichte at Munich and Berlin illustrate.

It must also be said that historians and other social scientists who were educated in the GDR are frequently discriminated against in the job market. Senior positions such as C4 professorships (distinguished professorships) and C3 professorships (full professorships) at East German institutions of higher learning exclusively are offered to West German candidates.[15] The also neglects the specific background of East Germans, who otherwise would have offered life experiences and work in two different scholarly and intellectually environments. Even the fact that *Die Linke* has been part of governing coalitions in several East German states, including Berlin, has not changed this overall situation.

Several industrious East German scholars have been instrumental in establishing a *zweite Wissenschaftskultur* ("Secondary Scholarly Culture" or alternative scholarly network), which exists largely outside the official academic institutions. This network organizes conferences and workshops, as well as producing a series of books that are on par with mainstream Western publications.[16] Among these initiatives, Rolf Reißig's Berlin-Brandenburg Institute for Social Scientific Studies (BISS) needs to be mentioned. This focuses on the transformation process of East Germany since 1990 and reflects primarily the experiences of their East German contemporaries. In the beginning the BISS was largely ignored by the "mainstream," but increasingly gained respect and recognition. It is now succeeded by an *Innovationsverbund Ostdeutschlandforschung*, a sociologists' project that focuses on innovative research on East German society, which is attached to the Technical University of Berlin.

Despite its modest beginnings, over the years the output of the "Second Scholarly Culture" has been increasingly well-received by "mainstream" scholars. To name but a few are the sociological journal *Berliner Debatte Initial*, and *Berliner Gesellschaft für Weltkriegs- und Faschismusforschung*, a network of scholars from East and West on European fascism, and *Gesellschaftswissenschaftliches Forum*, a platform of social scientists from the former

GDR. The *Rosa Luxemburg Foundation*, a think tank largely connected with the party Die Linke also needs to be mentioned. It established regional branches all over Germany, such as "Helle Panke" in Berlin, as well as offices in a number of foreign countries.[17] During the last years, a growing number of established scholars, some of them non-Marxists, participated in discussions that were mainly organized by the Rosa Luxemburg Foundation.[18]

Losses for All of Germany?

Such otherwise abstract processes must also be understood on the more concrete level of personal experience. In addition, we should consider these developments not only in terms of individual career trajectories, but also on the level of how this impacts the entire scholarly discourse all over Germany. For example, East German universities indeed suffered from many flaws and political and ideological limitations. Yet there were also some specific strengths, such as a far more favorable student-professor ratio than was customary at West German universities and a more permanent position below the level of senior professors. In addition, students and young instructors with children were especially supported with scholarships.

Despite the dogmatic nature of the regime, East Germany's universities also fostered in the 1980s a critical scholarship in some select disciplines, such as in sociology of labor and families and in some fields of historical research. This included the history of the European Reformation Age, research on the Enlightenment Period, and early bourgeois revolutions, particularly in England and France, as well as the social history of workers, peasants, and artisans. The historiography of both World Wars, as well as state and society in Imperial Germany until 1945, deserves special mentioning.

Most of these critical East German scholars advocated a renewed and improved socialist GDR, not its incorporation into the West. Of course, those socialist sensibilities were rejected and dismissed as hopelessly naïve by West German elites.

Ironically, the almost wholesale marginalization and dismissal of East German scholars deprived united Germany of a much-needed specific expertise that would have been a potential asset in the transformation and democratization of East German society. This includes scholars with specific knowledge of areas outside Germany; especially those East Germans who had studied in the Soviet Union and other Eastern European countries possessed significant familiarity, with languages, customs, and networks that were now considered superfluous unless in specific trades and business.

Often highly specialized and competent experts in areas such as African, Near Eastern, and Latin American studies lost their academic positions, largely because they were East Germans. Many of them were pushed into completely unrelated lines of employment, such as insurance, banking, and advertisement. Such a process, of forced de-professionalization, largely destroyed their linguistic, social, and cultural competence. The successful integration of ever-larger numbers of refugees into Germany, refugees from around the world, would benefit immensely from the now-lost skills and abilities of these East German experts.

Another related problem is the retirement of progressive West German university professors who were appointed in the decade of reform after 1968. Their academic successors are almost exclusively devoted to the ideas and the political agenda of neo-liberalism. This created imbalances and overall impoverished the range and diversity of German academic culture. Thus, the exclusion of East German scholars and the generational shift in the West contributes to a neoliberal hegemony that is ultimately harmful for a pluralistic academic culture.

Translated by Axel Fair-Schulz and Mario Kessler

Notes

1. See Hubert Beyerle, "Osten in 20 Jahren auf Westniveau," *Financial Times Deutschland* (June 19, 2008). http://www.ftd.de/politik/deutschland/:Wirtschaftswachstum%20Osten%20Jahren%20Westniveau/374843.html [accessed: June 20, 2008]; see also Institut für Wirtschaftsforschung Halle—IWH, "Konjunktur aktuell: Ostdeutsche Wirtschaft: Kein aufholendes Produktionswachstum 2008 und 2009," *IWH-Pressemitteilung*, No. 22/2008 (June18, 2008). http://www.iwh-halle.de/d/publik/Presse/22-08.pdf [20 June 08, 21:57].

2. See Rolf Reissig, *Die gespaltene Vereinigungsgesellschaft: Bilanz und Perspektiven der Transformation Ostdeutschlands und der deutschen Vereinigung* (Berlin, 2000).

3. See for facts and historical process: Stefan Bollinger, and Ulrich van der Heyden (eds.), *Deutsche Einheit und Elitenwechsel in Ostdeutschland* (Berlin, 2002); Stefan Bollinger, Ulrich van der Heyden, and Mario Kessler (eds.), *Ausgrenzung oder Integration? Ostdeutsche Sozialwissenschaftler zwischen Isolierung und Selbstbehauptung* (Berlin, 2004); Arno Hecht, *Die Wissenschaftselite Ostdeutschlands. Feindliche Übernahme oder Integration?* (Leipzig 2002).

4. Klaus von Beyme, "Der kurze Sonderweg Ostdeutschlands zur Vermeidung eines erneuten Sonderweges: Die Transformation Ostdeutschlands im Vergleich

der postkommunistischen Systeme," *Berliner Journal für Soziologie*, no. 3 (1996), 309.

5. See Jürgen Kocka and Mayntz, Renate (eds.), *Wissenschaft und Wiedervereinigung: Disziplinen im Umbruch* (Berlin, 1998).

6. See Jürgen Mittelstrass, "Lasst uns noch einmal über die Bücher gehen . . . (Interview)," *Leibniz intern*, no. 12 (2002), 12.

7. See a collective biography: Werner Mittenzwei, *Die Intellektuellen: Literatur und Politik in Ostdeutschland von 1945 bis 2000* (Leipzig, 2002); see also Jürgen Kuczynski, *"Nicht ohne Einfluss:" Macht und Ohnmacht der Intellektuellen* (Cologne, 1995).

8. Bernd Florath, "Verpasste Möglichkeiten? DDR-Historiker in den sechziger Jahren," *Utopie kreativ*, nos. 73–74 (1996), 64.

9. See Hansgünter Meyer, "Integration statt biologische Lösung. Eine Untersuchung mit einer Aussicht," Bollinger et al. (eds.), *Ausgrenzung oder Integration?*, 264–68.

10. See Peer Pasternack, *Gelehrte DDR: Die DDR als Gegenstand der Lehre an deutschen Universitäten 1990–2000* (Wittenberg, 2001).

11. Mittenzwei, *Die Intellektuellen*, 526.

12. See Rainer Eckert, Wolfgang Küttler, and Gustav Seeber, Gustav (eds.), *Krise-Umbruch-Neubeginn: Eine kritische und selbstkritische Dokumentation der DDR-Geschichtswissenschaft 1989/1990* (Stuttgart, 1992); Hartmut Kaelble, Jürgen Kocka, and Hartmut Zwahr (eds.), *Sozialgeschichte der DDR* (Stuttgart, 1994).

13. Christoph Klessmann, *Die doppelte Staatsgründung: Deutsche Geschichte 1945–1955*, 5th ed. (Bonn 1991); Idem, *Zwei Staaten, eine Nation: Deutsche Geschichte 1955–1970* (Göttingen, 1988); Peter Bender, *Episode oder Epoche? Zur Geschichte des geteilten Deutschland* (Munich, 1996); Idem, *Deutschlands Wiederkehr: Eine ungeteilte Nachkriegsgeschichte 1945–1990* (Stuttgart, 2007).

14. See Clemens Burrichter, Detlef Nakath, and Gerd-Rüdiger Stephan (eds.), *Deutsche Zeitgeschichte von 1945 bis 2000: Gesellschaft -Staat-Politik. Ein Handbuch* (Berlin, 2006).

15. See Peer Pasternack, "Desintegration und Integration. Die Ost-Berliner Wissenschaft im vereinigten Berlin," Roland Bloch and Peer Pasternack, *Die Ost-Berliner Wissenschaft im vereinigten Berlin: Eine Transformationsfolgenanalyse. HoF Wittenberg-Institut für Hochschulforschung an der Martin-Luther-Universität Halle-Wittenberg e.V. Arbeitsberichte. no.* 2/04, 100.

16. See Stefan Berger, "Was bleibt von der Geschichtswissenschaft in der DDR? Blick auf eine alternative historische Kultur im Osten Deutschlands," *Zeitschrift für Geschichtswissenschaft*, no. 11 (2002), 1016–1034.

17. Key publications connected with these initiatives include: *Rosa-Luxemburg-Stiftung: Texte, Manuskripte, Standpunkte, Schriften*; *Jahrbücher für Forschungen zur Geschichte der Arbeiterbewegung*; *Hefte zur DDR-Geschichte*; *Pankower Vorträge*; *Texte & Argumente*; *Diskurs*, *Osteuropa in Tradition und Wandel*, and others. Karl Dietz Verlag (publishing house) and the daily newspaper *Neues Deutschland* deserve special attention.

18. See Andreas Herbst, Gerd-Rüdiger Stephan, and Jürgen Winkler (eds.), *Die SED: Geschichte-Organisation—Politik: Ein Handbuch* (Berlin, 1997); Gerd-Rüdiger Stephan et al. (eds.), *Die Parteien und Organisationen der DDR: Ein Handbuch* (Berlin, 2002); Stefan Bollinger (ed.), *Das letzte Jahr der DDR: Zwischen Revolution und Selbstaufgabe* (Berlin, 2004).

6

Anticommunist Purge or Democratic Renewal?

The Transformation of the Humboldt University, 1985–2000[1]

KONRAD H. JARAUSCH

During the heady fall of 1989 observers from abroad watched the overthrow of Communism in Germany with mixed emotions. On the one hand the dramatic television news photos of the mass exodus, peaceful demonstrations, and the fall of the Wall generated much sympathy for the recovery of freedom in the GDR. On the other hand the growing groundswell for unification with the FRG aroused considerable concern about the return of a German nation-state and the accompanying extension of Western institutions to the East.[2] Anglo-American historians noted with surprise that well-known Marxist colleagues of the Humboldt University like Kurt Pätzold or Günter Vogler were losing their positions and leading Western scholars like Heinrich August Winkler or Hartmut Kaelble were taking their place. Members of the German Studies Association (GSA) and Conference Group for Central European History (CGCEH) therefore debated resolutions which cautioned against a wholesale purge of Eastern institutions, while acknowledging the need for improving academic standards.[3] But in the heat of the transition, such warnings were generally ignored.

Two decades later individual memories as well as historical evaluations of the transformation of the East German universities have become rather polarized. One view, propagated mostly by dismissed scholars alleges an "anti-Communist purge" of personnel well as a restoration of "capitalist conditions." This victimization narrative emphasizes the drastic reduction of the professoriate which threw a large number of GDR academics out of work. Moreover, the critical version claims that internal reform efforts were shunted aside and Western structures imported instead, which amounted to a kind of academic *Anschluss* or takeover, invoking the notorious term for Hitler's conquest of Austria. In a bitter collection of documents on the conflicts over the reshaping of the history department, Kurt Pätzold complains about the "ignorance or devaluation of the internal initiatives" at democratization and the "imposition of the West-German (West-Berlin) educational system."[4] This polemic against the takeover by a triumphant West ignores his own repressive behavior toward his students in order to assume the role of a hapless victim.

In contrast, the leading proponents of the transformation tell a success story of a fundamental renewal of Eastern universities, though, as the historian Jürgen Kocka admits, the process may have overshot its mark somewhat. Since GDR universities were "anything but a palladium of opposition," the internal reformers had to be supported "from above and outside" in order to achieve an actual new beginning. The sociologist Renate Mayntz argues that the plurality of actors such as the state governments, the Conference of Ministers for Cultural Affairs (KMK), the science council (WR) and the foundations offered various versions of the Western model to choose from. No matter whether the form was a complete liquidation or a more moderate restructuring, both approaches replaced people and changed content. The reduction of personnel was less due to political cleansing than to financial constraints, while many fields in the natural sciences achieved a considerable mixing of East and West.[5] Even if the transformation failed to renew all German institutions, the positive view maintains that it was a necessary precondition for current reforms.

These contradictory assessments can only be reconciled by clarifying the criteria of evaluation. If one uses the attempts at self-reform as a standard like the former student activist Sven Vollrath, then the "drastic exchange of personnel" will look shockingly high. But if one employs the intellectual reconstitution of departments as a measuring stick, like the legal sociologist Thomas Raiser does, then the restructuring will seem "definitively or at least preponderantly successful."[6] Scrutinizing the "democratic quality" of the process, like the educational researcher Peer Pasternack, will produce a negative evaluation, because the possibilities for participation were reduced by outside intervention. But analyzing the problematic quality of research and teaching under the SED-rule as in the dissertation by Tobias Schulz is bound to yield a more positive judgment.[7] The interpretative challenge is therefore to develop an analytical vantage point that transcends the personal memories of the participants by looking at the transformation of the GDR institutions from a wider perspective of university history.

The following remarks will present a case study of the restructuring of the Humboldt University (HU) with special attention to its controversial historians. This summary of a longer work is based on the files of the university archive, the Ministry of Higher Education of the GDR, and the Science Section of the Central Committee of the SED. It also draws on the official pronouncements in the university newspaper and on the press commentary in the clippings assembled by the public relations office of the HU. This discussion will proceed in four steps. It begins by describing the condition of the university in the mid-1980s, as that provides a baseline for assessing subsequent developments. It will continue with a sketch of the internal efforts at change as their review is indispensable for determining whether self-reform had a chance. It will then address the restructuring from above and outside since its results are at the heart of current controversy. Finally, the conclusion will take a brief look at the difficult arrival in Western normalcy.[8] This approach intends to de-emotionalize evaluations of the process and results of the renewal.

Socialist Scholarship

On October 25, 1985, the Humboldt University celebrated its 175th anniversary before a selected public in the splendidly restored concert hall at the Gendarmenmarkt. Rector Helmut Klein, a professor of education, gave the official address which reflected the growing self-confidence of socialist scholarship. By dynamically linking research with teaching he argued that Wilhelm von Humboldt had founded the academic fame of the institution which the Nobel Prize-winning work of "renowned scholars" had spread around the globe. After Hitler had disgraced German science, the "revolutionary impetus" of liberation by the Red Army had made the establishment of a "socialist *universitas litterarum*" possible. Under the leadership of the working class, "the social basis and function of scholarship had changed fundamentally" toward service for human progress. This ideological inspiration had rendered "research achievements of international rank" possible, reflected in the growing acclaim from abroad.[9] This speech and the *Festschrift* breathed a spirit of success, confidently expecting the victory of socialism.

Due to its ideological partisanship, the conception of "communist education and training" diverged fundamentally from the Western understanding of scholarship. All research was based on "the assertion of Marxism-Leninism as scholarly world view," which provided a method of analysis and determined its results. Another priority, inherited from the labor movement, was the opening of access for children of workers and peasants, which was supposed to generate a new socialist intelligentsia. More important for a country without raw materials was, in Erich Honecker's words, "the *organic connection* of science and production, their close *mutual penetration*." Finally, the university also saw itself as vanguard in the struggle against restorative tendencies in the Federal Republic, "committed to the preservation of peace." This self-image of "a university ideal appropriate for a socialist society" was ideologically determined, socially open and oriented toward applied subjects.[10] For historians the ideological commitment was especially important, since the Marxist classics prescribed many of their topics and guided interpretations.

To the freshmen class of 1985, Rector Klein introduced the HU as "certainly the largest enterprise of Berlin." It had about 19,000 students of whom 3,100 pursued distance learning, 820 were post-graduates, and 600 came from abroad. The institution boasted of "more than 10,000 employees, among them 850 professors and lecturers [as well as] 3,800 [post-doctoral] assistants;" in the field of medicine worked 989 doctors and 3,179 nurses. In terms of disciplines, the HU saw itself as "a 'classical' university, i.e. characterized by quite a broad academic profile," comprising all natural sciences, social sciences, agronomy, the entire spectrum of medicine as well as theology and even some technical subjects. This array was subdivided into thirty-two sections, each of which represented one area of specialization. The HU was led by a rector, supported by five deputies, a scientific council, a social council, and an annual assembly to legitimize central decisions.[11] But on all levels the party exercised its "leading role" through its many secretaries and specific subject-groups so as to maintain control over all decisions.

In spite of paying lip-service to some academic traditions, studying at the HU differed markedly from its Western counterpart, since it was organized in a factory-like manner. For example, all students were required to enroll in Marxist-Leninist courses to strengthen their class-consciousness by introducing them to the ideological classics and discussing contemporary issues. They were also supposed to belong to the Free German Youth (FDJ) which further indoctrinated them, demanded harvest duty, and organized their free time. Moreover, each year a socialist competition was held in which students showed off their accomplishments in order to garner prizes and premiums. Even the leadership of the university had to keep exact count of the graduation numbers and the post-graduate degrees, since the annual plan treated them as products of academic training. Due to the high number of required courses, the ubiquity of ideological indoctrination as well as the additional social commitments, studying was highly structured, leaving all too little time for creative thought and leisure activities.[12]

Within this framework of Marxist teaching, the task of the historians was to offer research support for a narrative that justified the existence of the GDR as "the better Germany." Initially they concentrated on exploring understudied areas like the heritage of the working class, but eventually they expanded their scope to include also the problematic traditions of Prussia. At the same time the curriculum included lectures on the Socialist world system so as to generate solidarity with the Soviet Union and the national liberation movements. Much effort also went into refuting the bourgeois interpretations of West German historians who were derided as NATO-stooges or as neo-Fascists for treating postwar Germany as one nation. Due to Soviet sensibilities and ideological blinders, this involved ignoring the Hitler-Stalin pact of 1939 and slighting the racial dimension of the Holocaust. Many were competent researchers, but when ideology and sources collided, most chose, like Siegfried Prokop, to support the party line.[13] History at the HU was therefore an uneasy amalgam of professionalism and partisanship.

The leadership of the university was nonetheless conscious of the rapid development of international scholarship and tried to keep up with its progress through its own development plans. In this effort it focused on technological innovations in microelectronics, robotics, material science, and food production, i.e., on applied areas which were supposed to improve the standard of living. To achieve this end, the SED demanded closer coordination of research with industrial production, insisting on the conclusion of agreements with leading firms which would also open up new funding resources. Even the social scientists were supposed to contribute to the implementation of technical progress in the "developed socialist society," while scholars in the humanities were intended to enrich the culture of the capital. Part of this initiative also involved increased support for the talented and more independence in studying. The key goals were reaching "top-flight international results" and meeting the "world standard"—concepts which revealed the high expectation as well as an awareness of not quite measuring up to them.[14]

Attempts to make the HU more dynamic by founding interdisciplinary centers on microelectronics or peace research failed due to a number of external problems and internal constraints. A first hurdle was the ideological orientation of the university, since the required Marxist-Leninist courses proved perennially unpopular. "The lack of attractiveness was also due to the conflicts at the ideological front. The students have become more critical." A second complaint concerned the "insufficiency of the material basis" which inhibited scientific research: "Due to the lack of modern equipment it will become more and more difficult to reach top international achievements." A third problem was the focus on practical application which stemmed from the party's incomprehension of basic research. "An increasing proportion of economically useful results [was] achieved at the cost of real scientific advances—a dangerous tendency for a university."[15] This grumbling among well-known scholars shows the growing frustration of even loyal academics with the limitations on their work imposed by the SED system.

During the second half of the 1980s isolated voices of criticism swelled into a regular chorus of complaints about state and university. Initially the district secretary could still report the "broad positive resonance" of the last Honecker speech, since there were "only a few illusory views on the role of bourgeois parliamentarianism and the rightist leaders of social democracy." But a growing number of students with "pacifist or class indifferent positions" asked more insistent questions during propaganda sessions or refused military service. At the same time more and more scholars who were disappointed by the lack of appreciation for research and the antiquated technology or got tired of the socialist system, abused "a trip abroad to leave the GDR unlawfully." Loyal SED members were especially angered by the prohibition of the Soviet news magazine *Sputnik*, since they wanted to be able to form their own judgment about Gorbachev's *perestroika* and *glasnost*. In a similar vein, a student group demanded a reform of the FDJ statutes in order to reflect "the ideological diversity of youth" more clearly.[16]

The SED reacted to the erosion of support at the HU by redoubling its ideological propaganda efforts and tightening up disciplinary measures. On the one hand, concerned functionaries appealed to university instructors to "increase the quality and effectiveness of political agitation with the masses" through more personal participation. On the other hand, the party punished perceived transgressions more sharply. When at a symposium in Rome, the literature instructor Peter Böthig lectured on the "artistic cooperation of young poets and painters" and described the cultural scene at the Prenzlauer Berg quarter of Berlin as a "counter-public" sphere, he was accused of spreading "anti-Marxist, antisocialist positions regarding the cultural policy of the party." His characterization had violated a central taboo by suggesting that the SED might not always be right. The ensuing disciplinary hearing expelled him from the university and forced his adviser, Professor Ursula Heukenkamp, to submit to the ritual of self-criticism in order to retain her post. Such overreactions were motivated by fear of losing ideological control.[17]

During the summer of 1989 the Humboldt University therefore made a somewhat contradictory impression. On the one hand, it was the largest and therefore leading institution of the GDR, enjoying international acclaim and fulfilling representative functions in the capital. Through its proximity to the science section of the Central Committee and the Ministry for Higher Education, it had direct access to the political leadership, which both increased its financial resources and made for tighter control. With its scientific "rationalization plan" promoted by the new rector Dieter Hass, it seemed well positioned to meet "the growing demands of the future." On the other hand, many of its laboratories were outdated, much infrastructure was in disrepair, the library was cut off from most new Western publications, and entire disciplines like law, economics, and history were warped by ideological prescriptions.[18] Under the placid surface, discontent was rising among a growing minority of students and professors who were no longer willing to accept the material and intellectual restrictions.

Internal Renewal Attempts

The democratic awakening of East German society in October 1989 finally broke the ban of decreed silence and inspired an astounding outpouring of criticism after decades of conformity. At the fortieth anniversary of the founding of the GDR, the FDJ still marched as usual, but the brutal police repression of a subsequent unauthorized demonstration caused "second thoughts and perplexity" among students who thereupon began to organize a council, independent of the FDJ.[19] Prompted by critical statements of some faculty, the academic Senate formulated an open letter after Honecker's overthrow, welcoming Krenz's "new course of a fundamental renewal of socialist society in the GDR" and supporting his call for "a constructive, open and public dialogue." Democratization, economic reforms, and solutions to ecological problems ought to aim at "the further development of a conception of socialism, which will give it a new lease on life." This was the hour of SED reformers like Michael Brie, Dieter Segert, and Dieter Klein who propagated a democratization of socialism, combining "individual freedom with solidarity."[20]

The peaceful revolution did not start at the HU, yet the civic movement soon drew the university into its vortex. While students and professors demanded the liberation of scholarship, SED functionaries tried to channel the public debate by leading the charge. Suddenly the conformist dean of social sciences Waltraut Falk made unprecedented reform proposals, which demanded a reorganization of "the relationship between science and society, especially science and politics" by ending censorship and control. At the same time she proposed allowing students to govern themselves and making socialism less dogmatic in order to break with the practice of administrative orders. Finally she called for numerous institutional changes such as "the electability of academic leadership positions," the restoration of institutional autonomy, the strengthening of professorial rights—in short a return to that self-government and academic freedom previously denigrated as bourgeois.[21] The SED's authorization of an open dialogue therefore unleashed a flood of criticism that threatened the foundations of socialist scholarship.

Seeking to retain control, the university leadership initiated its own reforms in order to begin the process of democratization. Rector Hass, a chemist, therefore met with the newly elected student council, demonstrating its "recognition as an equal partner" as well as his support for renewal. At the same time the Marxism-Leninism Section proposed a complete transformation of its obligatory courses into an independent "social science curriculum," a kind of general education with a social twist.[22] Pushing for a separation of party and state, the academic Senate also resolved to democratize the leadership structure of the university by making the Scientific Council the legislative and the rector the executive as well as electing new, more credible personalities into both offices as soon as possible. A rehabilitation commission was supposed to correct political injustices such as the removal of academic degrees, and a committee on structure and statute was charged with preparing a new constitution for the university.[23] These initiatives aimed at a liberation of the institution within a reformed but still independent GDR.

Another motor of change from below was the roundtable, founded in late January 1990 to discuss "the current issues of university development." In the beginning it was moderated by the theologian Heinrich Fink and dominated by the PDS with its auxiliaries, but later on representatives of the civic movement and the new political parties joined it as well. Hence, its substantive recommendations vacillated between pressure for further reform and defense of socialist achievements. The round table demanded "the right to be heard on administrative decisions" through the presence of the rector during its deliberations. When it dared question the university leaders on their cooperation with the Ministry for State Security, they did not deny helping the Stasi, but downplayed the importance of their contacts. In structural questions the roundtable tended toward grassroots democracy, demanding more rights for the instructors, students and staff in the various representative organs.[24] Since all important questions were discussed there, the round table, later called *Hochschulpolitischer Rat*, functioned as a kind of rival government.

During the winter of 1990 the faculty reform committee discussed contrasting proposals for a new university statute. Since pre-1968 West German structures appeared too authoritarian and the West Berlin group-representation seemed too strange, the favorite was "a democratized variant of the existing statute of the HU," since its renewal would require the least effort and cost. This version made the council, representing all university members, into the legislature, and maintained the social council as tie to society; the executive, in contrast, was supposed to consist of the rector, his deputies, and the various department heads. The status groups would be represented according to a complicated formula decreasing from professors to instructors to students and staff at 35 to 30 to 25 to 10 percent.[25] The English literature specialist Hans-Joachim Meyer argued for a more drastic alternative which emphasized "freedom of teaching and research" as well as a strengthened "responsibility" of professors and students instead. This statute debate absorbed much energy and proved ultimately fruitless, since its results conflicted with West Berlin law.[26]

Yet in the summer months the effort at self-reform began to stall due to its half-heartedness and defensiveness toward the West. During the rector's election in early April, the irenic Heinrich Fink won out over the unorthodox Marxist Gerd Irrlitz, since the faculty was determined to "maintain an independent HU within the Berlin academic landscape."[27] In his inauguration he clung to the socialist "vision of practicable justice" in contrast to science minister Meyer who warned against making the HU "a left alternative to the Free University."[28] When the latter's president, Dieter Heckelmann, publicly protested against the quick appointment of four dozen Marxists, the HU Senate was "outraged about the manner and tone of the letter." Similarly, many HU members were incensed over the accusation of the journalist Heike Schmoll in the *Frankfurter Allgemeine Zeitung* that Fink had been an "unofficial informant of the Stasi."[29] In contrast to the open self-criticism of Harald Mau, dean of the medical faculty at the Charité, Rector Fink wanted to preserve as much as possible of the GDR in a united Germany.

The limits of self-reform also became apparent through the reluctance of the history section to deal with public accusations that it had taken repressive measures under the SED. Only consistent pressure by victims compelled its new director Adolf Rüger to regret the "humiliations, injustices, discriminations and violations of law" that had been committed between 1956 and 1972. On the basis of the already purged files, he reported on two dozen cases of individuals who were punished by expulsion or jail sentences for critical remarks, for instance on the suppression of the Prague Spring. Some responsible professors like the Reformation historian Günter Vogler excused themselves by pointing to "the fatal principle of combining politics with scholarship," but their victims continued to complain: "Here scholarship was run into the ground and sources were systematically falsified." Especially the well-known National Socialist specialist Kurt Pätzold aroused ill will, since he admitted to having acted from conviction and did not show any sympathy for his former students. "As [a] human being, you just remain speechless."[30]

The HU was ill prepared for unification on October 3, 1990, which also merged the two parts of Berlin into one city-state. It was not really represented in the negotiations in the science council, the conference of cultural ministers and other groups which made proposals for the inclusion of East German higher education into the FRG. In contrast to the other new states, it had to contend with an existing West Berlin science administration which had little knowledge of the transformation problems of the Eastern part of the city and insisted on applying a set of rules that were unknown to GDR academics. Even if some departments like the social sciences had good relations to the FU, the two institutions had grown into Cold War rivals and now had to compete for scarce resources in the same state budget. Due to her impression that the HU was reluctant to change, science senator Barbara Riedmüller-Seel (SPD) demanded the immediate application of the West German higher education law which necessitated the new election of all HU-organs and the completion of a questionnaire, recalling negative memories of de-Nazification.[31]

It took another entire month for the HU leadership to decide on more drastic action in order to forestall the rumored dissolution of half a dozen departments. On November 5 the Senate created an honor committee to investigate Stasi collaboration, abuse of power and corruption so as to "reduce distrust among colleagues." However it could only act on application and did not have direct access to the Stasi files.[32] As a sign of commitment to internal renewal, on December 13 the university council also appointed a "Central Commission on Personnel and Structure" (ZPSK), which was supposed to make suggestions "on the further development of departments" and to undertake "the evaluation of all teaching personnel and scholarly assistants." The individual subject committees were supposed to include West German colleagues, but were dominated by HU members, ensuring that their proposals and evaluation would remain gentle enough.[33] With the additional decision to create a committee to screen election candidates, the HU demonstrated a stronger will to change, even if its implementation continued to lag.

Due to this mixed record, the results of the internal renewal remained rather controversial. On the one hand, some indicators suggested that a genuine effort at democratizing socialism through "a self-cleansing was underway." The student council and roundtable demanded liberating the university from the SED dictatorship and the control of the Stasi. Reform-oriented professors, especially in the natural sciences and medicine, pleaded for setting research and teaching free. And the rector and Senate appointed some panels like the honor committee and the personnel-structure commissions to promote renewal. But at the same time it became evident that Rector Fink only reacted to pressure and that numerous obstacles hindered a comprehensive self-reform. Internal critics grumbled: "Until now, there has only been an ideological change of course, but no [new] scientific development, not to mention a real renewal of personnel." Quoting Gorbachev, media reports therefore created the impression "that the HU is in the same situation as the GDR was a year ago: It comes too late and therefore it is being punished by life."[34]

Intervention from the Outside

With the appointment of the CDU politician Manfred Erhardt, the West Berlin administration took firm control of the renewal process. The new senator had much experience in science management in Baden-Württemberg, and was known to be decisive. His initial impression of the Humboldt University was rather critical—he considered its academic quality "mediocre" and he had "no confidence in self-renewal," since he did not believe that it could pull itself out of the swamp by its own hair, like the legendary Baron von Münchhausen. For this reason he was ready to endorse the compromise decision made by his predecessor Riedmüller-Seel, which secured the further existence of the HU, but insisted on dissolving those disciplines that were especially ideologically tarnished. In the interim as long as a new governing board had not yet been elected, he constituted a "committee of the six," composed in equal parts of HU and Berlin Senate representatives, in order to make all restructuring decisions.[35] With this new instrument the senator and the administration could impose their policy against the wishes of the university.

The decision of December 18, 1989, to "dissolve" half a dozen sections aroused a storm of protest in the HU because hundreds of professors, instructors, and staff people were involved. Though the termination of Marxism-Leninism, police training and science policy hardly caused a ripple, protests against the liquidation of other sections like education, economics, and law as well as philosophy and history were all the more intense, as they were supposed to be reconstituted immediately with new personnel and new curricula.[36] The uproar in the university was great, since the principle that "'termination' supersedes job protection" seemed like a violation of social rights. The academic Senate passed passionate resolutions, students went on strike, and the administration organized media support in defense of the

HU's autonomy. Moreover the HU sued to stop the dissolution, arguing that the provisions of the unification treaty were not supposed to be used for the purpose of *Abwicklung* and that "a careful consideration of each case" was supposed to take place. Hence the administrative courts ruled in favor of the university.[37]

Ironically the legal victory over the administration resulted in an even more drastic intervention, because the supplement to the Berlin higher education law of July 18, 1991, extended the dissolution model to the entire university. Now every section had to be evaluated by a "Committee on Structure and Personnel" or SBK, while every professor had to be newly hired. Composed of West and East German scholars, these SBK panels were supposed to determine the research and teaching profile of each unit, evaluate existing personnel according to its ability and integrity, and select new professors to be appointed.[38] In endless sessions and often drawing on the material of the previous internal reviews, these field committees charted novel intellectual directions and hired fresh personnel in order to make the HU once again competitive. Western members usually dominated the decisions on structure and people since they had broader international experience, wider national contacts and more scholarly publications. The result of their new appointments tended to be a mixture of improved quality and Western patronage.

The history department's conflicts over personnel and content show how difficult it was to confront an unsavory past while organizing a new start. Since its members were reluctant to evaluate themselves, it took pressure from a newly founded *Unabhängiger Historiker-Verband* or Independent Historians' Association (UHV) composed of former victims and critics to force a public reckoning.[39] The renewal committee, chaired by the social historian Gerhard A. Ritter, proposed a structure of fifteen professorships, based on the tripartite tradition of Ancient, Medieval, and Modern History, but also added some innovations in the social, science, and contemporary fields. This SBK kept a few Eastern scholars like Hartmut Harnisch, but offered most professorships to well-known Westerners like Heinrich-August Winkler or Hartmut Kaelble. When the labor courts reinstated some dismissed colleagues such as Kurt Pätzold or Siegfried Prokop in their jobs, the chaos was complete, because two competing faculties existed in the same field of study. Only after the Eastern contracts ran out could the HU boast of "one of the leading institutes in our field."[40]

The resentment against outside intervention came to a head when Rector Heinrich Fink was removed in response to an accusation of Stasi-collaboration by the Gauck Office. His concern for people and advocacy of "democratization, reform and change" from within had created a wide following for him. But to the Western press, his defense of Eastern traditions made him appear as symbol of a widespread lack of willingness to renew. The HU Senate unanimously condemned the "illegal practice of dismissal without notice by the Senator for Science and Research," while the university council asked him to stay in office. During a protest demonstration angry students shouted "nobody is going take away our Heiner," while renowned intellectuals like the writer Christa Wolf declared their solidarity with him. Initially the labor court stopped the firing, but the appellate court dismissed the stay, since it considered the proof of Fink's cooperation with the Stasi convincing.[41] Although an injunction kept the rector from continuing in office, the public controversy over his removal inhibited the process of renewal.

After this emotional conflict, several structural measures sought to improve the functioning of the Humboldt University. A first milestone was the appointment of chancellor Rainer Neumann, an experienced Western administrator, who sought to professionalize the HU administration. A second step was the election of a new Senate which had to decide on the future academic profile and distribution of positions, but at the same time to save 50 million DM.[42] A third stage was the decision to switch to a presidential constitution in order to dampen internal hostilities through the election of a leader from the outside. The best known candidate was the arrogant SPD intellectual Peter Glotz, but the more caring Marlis Dürkop, a Green-politician and rector of the Academy for Social Work, won in a surprise twist, because she was supported by the students and assistants, while the East-Berlin mathematician Bernd Bank became vice president. Encountering a mountain of problems, the new president aimed at "a development towards normalcy, but not mediocrity" in order to restore an atmosphere conducive to academic work.[43]

The most important task was implementing the SBK recommendations for new appointments. Some previous professors who opposed unification went into pre-retirement. Others were excluded due to their Stasi-collaboration, which a student investigation discovered in 180 of 780 cases. But in the natural sciences and medicine many capable Eastern scholars were reappointed, when SBK evaluations could prove their competence. For Western colleagues the HU was attractive due to its prior reputation and location in the capital, while unpaid instructors (*Privatdozenten*) leapt at the chance for a professorship of their own. In relatively neutral fields like agronomy, mathematics, and chemistry, over half of the faculty hailed from the East, and even in some humanities subjects like German, cultural studies, or foreign languages many survived. Only in ideologically compromised areas like history, law, and education were virtually all newcomers from the

West. Somewhat in anticipation in January 1993 Erhardt could proudly maintain that "the merger of two hitherto different academic systems in reunified Berlin has succeeded."[44]

The restructuring of mid-level ranks proved even more contentious as instructors and assistants were more numerous than in the West and most had tenure. For financial reasons alone their number had to be reduced drastically and the ratio of permanent to temporary positions of 80:20 needed to be reversed to give younger scholars a chance. Through a "personnel transition law" all staff members were forced to reapply for the remaining jobs. Due to intensive lobbying, the Berlin administration created 150 supernumerary positions for "academic personnel which were evaluated positively, but for which there were no positions." Supported by trade union advice, many employees contested their dismissal and due to the sympathy of West Berlin labor courts they often reached settlements which allowed them to continue working for several years so that they might find alternative employment. Administrative mistakes of the HU such as missing the deadline for 350 dismissals and downgrading two-fifths of the jobs which had initially been classified too high made this topic a perennial source of "unrest and bitterness."[45]

The overall result of these decisions was a drastic exchange of academic personnel, the magnitude of which resembles the changes after 1945. Only 453 scholars of the 2,755 persons in permanent positions during 1989 remained at the end of 1997; merely 16.5 percent succeeded in surviving. This transition took place in several waves, because during the internal renewal of the PSKs already 119 faculty members and 765 employees left the HU; during the external restructuring by the SBKs another 470 professors and 763 assistants disappeared; and with the phasing out of temporary contracts in 1996 another 55 faculty members and 655 lecturers lost their jobs. In contrast 388 professors were newly hired in searches according to Western law till the end of 1994, 44 percent of which were from the new states. Two-thirds of the full (or distinguished) professors (C4) came from the West, while 55 percent of the C3 professors (roughly translated as associate professors) hailed from the East. Among the employees the number of positions was cut in half, many formerly permanent staff members had to accept temporary jobs and only a limited number were newly appointed from East and West.[46]

The process of renewal from the outside produced mixed results because the struggle over content and personnel was especially intense at the HU. Since the self-reform was stalling during 1990, as the mere change of labels from Marxism-Leninism to Political Science shows, an external intervention was necessary in order to compel more fundamental changes. Unfortunately this Western attempt was sometimes ill-informed, burdened by Cold War animosities and complicated by institutional rivalry between the FU and HU. Although the university now claimed a degree of autonomy, which it had never possessed in the GDR, the Western science administration, enlarged by some Eastern recruits, was nevertheless responsible to the citizens of Berlin for the scholarly profile and financial health of the HU. No doubt, the imposition of the structure-and-appointment commissions (SBKs) was a form of tutelage since it took decisions on content and personnel out of the university's hands. The rude manner and great extent of dismissals also created much unnecessary suffering. Yet this radical approach offered those scholars from the East and West who were capable of mutual cooperation the rare chance of a completely new start.[47]

Arrival in the West

During the mid-1990s the pioneering enthusiasm of new faculty members and students collided not just with the consequences of the transformation, but also with the unresolved problems of the Western system. On the one hand, newly appointed professors like the art historian Horst Bredekamp, were pleased that "the HU has become a fulcrum of the unification process." On the other hand, the "growing pride" was frustrated by the necessity to repair existing buildings, a badly functioning administration, and the antiquated research infrastructure. Even more problematic in the long run was the academic legacy of the old FRG, since the Western system had been in need of reform already before 1989.[48] Especially the appalling under-financing of the universities endangered the rebuilding of the HU, since the Berlin Senate had to maintain three universities with the financial resources that only sufficed for two. The growing funding gap due to the cancellation of federal Berlin subsidies added a sharper edge to many conflicts over profile and personnel which made finding pragmatic solutions difficult.

Fitting the Humboldt University into the established higher education landscape of Berlin created many headaches, since it required painful decisions about the relocation of fields. To relieve duplication, the HU's electronics section was moved to the Technical University, while teacher training in art and music was shifted to the *Hochschule der Künste* (College of Fine Arts). Veterinary medicine was also transferred to the FU, cutting traditional subjects, even if their scholars were supposed to receive special consideration for new appointments.[49]

Yet important additions like the incorporation of the Protestant Academy Berlin-Brandenburg, the consolidation of agronomy and food technology at the HU, the move of natural science departments to a new research campus in Adlershof, and the integration of the Rudolf-Virchow clinics into the Charité met with skepticism, because they diluted already limited financial means. In contrast, new post-unification initiatives like the centers for Great Britain, peace- and extremism-research as well as the interdisciplinary clusters for gender research and ecology hardly got off the ground.[50]

The relocation problems were aggravated by the disastrous efforts of the Berlin Senate to slash the higher education budget. The initial cuts largely spared the HU, but eventually the shrinking budget stopped the rebuilding and rendered all planning obsolete. The first wave rolled in during the summer of 1993 and demanded a 5 percent reduction of positions. Since this created a deficit of 27.8 million DM for 1994, the HU protested against it, opposing the introduction of tuition fees through a budget-structure bill.[51]

More onerous was the Berlin Senate's demand to present a zero growth budget plan for the next two years. In February 1994 the science administration even proclaimed a hiring and investment freeze, which stopped all new appointments and building renovations.[52] Another general reduction of 158 million DM during 1995 for all three universities demanded the elimination of twenty professorships and thirty-four assistant positions at the HU. While the FU and TU, bloated by generous Berlin subsidies, could absorb some reductions, these cuts hit the HU during its rebuilding process and threatened entire curricula.[53]

Frustrated by the continual cuts, Marlis Dürkop resigned in the spring of 1996, opening the way for the election of Hans Meyer as the new president. This well-known constitutional law scholar from Frankfurt University had successfully accomplished the renewal of the law faculty as chair of the SBK and had much prior experience in dealing with bureaucrats and politicians. In contrast to his predecessor, Meyer ran meetings tightly and was adept at pushing his proposals through the academic Senate. He preferred negotiated compromises, joint steps with the other universities, and legally binding agreements.

This change of leadership not only made the internal workings of the university more efficient, but also improved its external image. Since Meyer was closer to the political center, he was better able to communicate the aspirations and needs of the HU to middle class circles in West Berlin, and he placated their anticommunist fears through his reliable personality. Nonetheless, he confronted an almost impossible task, because the across the board reduction created a HU deficit of 24.8 million DM for 1996.[54]

In order to protect the academic core against further cuts, President Meyer pleaded for accepting the university contract, offered by the Berlin Senate. The HU had sued against the "household-structure-law," which sought to close pharmacy and sport at the HU, reduce the Berlin natural sciences by 14 million DM, and introduce tuition fees. Although the alternative of an assured annual lump-sum would shift the distribution-conflicts into the university, it finally offered the "desired security of planning," since it provided reliable figures for decisions on future priorities. Meyer argued that "the precondition for accepting such a contract would be its binding nature and therefore its legal force," while a second prerequisite would be making enough funds available to finance all present personnel. Though the planned reduction of student numbers in Berlin from 100,000 to 85,000 was deplorable, "the universities are well advised to conclude the contract under these conditions, since otherwise additional cuts are imminent." After a controversial discussion the academic Senate accepted the university contract on March 25, 1997: "The agreement merely makes the survival of the Humboldt University possible."[55]

The imposition of an additional reduction of 52 million DM forced a structural discussion on the university, since some "closing of well-functioning areas" became unavoidable. Instead of cutting everywhere like a "lawnmower," the HU leadership chose "to combine the discontinuation of some subjects with reductions in the other areas." To preserve the traditional core, peripheral fields like pharmacy and elementary education had to be sacrificed in spite of the protests of the scholars concerned. The debate between the natural sciences and the humanities was especially bitter, because the former were willing to give up only twenty-two positions, arguing that the build-up of Adlershof demanded "a critical mass" of researchers, while the latter felt discriminated against by the elimination of sixty professorships. Another emotional issue was the abandonment of small subjects like pre-history or their shift to the FU.[56] Since it saw "no alternative" to the reductions, the HU Senate reluctantly accepted their implementation in a "university structure plan" of March 1998, which sacrificed eighty-two professorships, one fifth of the total![57]

The consequences of such cuts for individual fields were drastic, as their effect on the department of history shows. The SBK plan had projected twenty-three professorships, twenty of which were filled by the end of 1994. The university structure plan of 1998 contained only eighteen positions, a reduction of five from the original level. Though this left a fairly large complement, the cuts fell onto innovative positions in American and African history because these were supposed to have been the last hires which had to be stopped. Moreover, two of the existing professorships had "will disappear" notations attached to them, which meant that they were to be cut as soon as the present occupant retired. Since these targets were chosen according to departmental politics, the *kw-Vermerke* (no replacement positions after retirement of the professor) were attached to precisely those areas like comparative European social history which were quite popular with students. There was only a vague effort to avoid duplication with the Meinecke or Kennedy Institutes of the FU, but history was eventually discontinued altogether at the TU, except for the Anti-Semitism Institute and the metropolitan studies program.[58]

In spite of the scandalous budget cuts by Berlin politicians, there were also some encouraging signs that a slimmer HU was gaining new academic excellence in some fields. The most important indicator was the steep rise in foundation grants which already exceeded 106 million DM in 1996, putting "the HU into the leading group of German universities." Similarly impressive was the acquisition of thirteen new doctoral schools (*Graduiertenkollegs*) by 1997, which secured it second place behind Heidelberg University with fourteen. Applications for interdisciplinary research areas (DFG-*Sonderforschungsbereiche*) were increasingly successful as well, especially in the natural sciences, for instance with a cluster on "complex nonlinear processes." The hiring of the best and brightest minds also resulted in some Leibniz-prizes such as the award for physics professor Dieter Rüst. On the national level of the science citation index the HU already occupied first place by the end of the 1990s. . . .[59] Such outside evaluations showed the positive results of the rebuilding effort, which gradually strengthened the confidence of the HU.

The changes during the turbulent decade were so extensive that the new HU had little in common any more with its predecessor except for the name and the buildings. As a result of the hiring of about 400 faculty members and the attractive metropolitan location, the number of students rose substantially to 33,000. Divided into over two dozen departments plus some service areas, the HU was now composed of eleven self-governing faculties. According to its new constitution, it was led by a president under the supervision of a governing board, and was able to try out some administrative and academic innovations due to a special "experiment clause." The return of the capital from Bonn to Berlin also offered contacts to political leaders and the federal bureaucracy which restored its traditional advantage of proximity to important decisions. Finally the build-up of an impressive science campus at Adlershof, the incorporation of the Virchow clinics into the medical complex of the Charité, and the gradual renovation of the representative buildings in the center of the city laid the basis for a dynamic development in the future.[60]

The identity of this "laboratory of unification" nonetheless remained conflicted since different academic cultures clashed about a problematic legacy and the right path into the future. On the one hand, the reputation of the former Friedrich-Wilhelms-University as one of the leading institutions in the world worked as incentive for further achievements. On the other hand, the deplorable record of collaboration with National Socialism and Communism could only serve as warning against further instrumentalization of scholarship.

Due to the disappointments of the unification process many East German scholars fondly recalled the putative warmth of the SED welfare dictatorship, but some were also inspired by the new research opportunities offered by the West. In contrast, Western newcomers arrived with enthusiasm about the possibilities for institution building according to the best international practices, but they tended to be frustrated by the many obstacles to their practical implementation. The discussion of a new mission statement, initiated by the philosopher Volker Gerhardt, therefore failed to reach a consensus because it was not yet clear if this phoenix would rise from its ashes or once again fall to the ground.[61]

Controversial Results

Two decades after the fall of the Wall, the results of the transformation of the HU remain controversial for outside observers as well as internal commentators because undeniable losses contrast with equally clear gains. On the debit side, the drastic reduction of personnel pushed many competent scholars in the humanities and social sciences into unemployment and forced them to establish a "second academic culture" outside of government supported institutions. The pain of this elite displacement has inspired metaphors of "*Anschluss*" or "colonization"'both of which are polemical exaggerations which equate the FRG with Nazi Germany and belittle the free decision of East German citizens. On the credit side, academic freedom has been restored, the research infrastructure rebuilt, and connection to international scientific debates reestablished; in short, a previously somewhat provincial institution has been reinvigorated. Yet the simple "success story" of academic commemorations is equally misleading, since it ignores the human cost of the process.[62] Perhaps the time has come to draw up a more dispassionate and nuanced balance sheet.

Although the HU hardly played a role in the "peaceful revolution," the pressing need for "a change of course in academic policy" was generally accepted in 1989. Even the science section of the Central Committee was ready to admit a lack of "suitable working and living conditions," a lag in "basic innovations," deploring the negative consequences "of linking scholarship and production," and the "low esteem of research and cultivation in the socialist society."[63] But opinions diverged radically on whether such deficiencies could be remedied by reforms *within* socialism or required *the replacement* of the entire system. Initially the HU's self-renewal efforts concentrated on a lengthy debate about a new statute which became obsolete with unification. Only the threat of dissolution prompted a more concerted attempt at change through the PSKs, but the dismissal of Fink diverted energies in a defensive direction. Senator Erhardt therefore insisted on a restructuring from above and outside through the SBK which rewrote curricula, dismissed much personnel, and made new appointments. In contrast to the vigorous self-reform of Jena, this process was more contested in the Cold War atmosphere of Berlin.[64]

Two different conceptions of democratic renewal clashed in the transformation of the HU. Tired of dictatorial tutelage, the internal reformers met in the roundtable of the *Hochschulpolitischer Rat* (a sort of university advisory council) and advocated reforms from below through gradual discussion. Their ideal was grassroots participation in academic self-government so as to create a democratized socialism within an independent GDR. But when three-quarters of East German citizens voted for unification in March 1990, the political basis for the utopia of a third way vanished, since the economic collapse left no alternative but rapid accession to the FRG. The West Berlin science administration, supported by some students and professors, preferred a more drastic restructuring, legitimated by the electoral mandate of a parliamentary democracy. These radical reformers insisted on a sharper evaluation of personnel according to competence and honesty as well as on a complete rewriting of curricula according to Western standards. What one side deplored as takeover from the outside, the other defended as a cleansing necessary for liberating scholarship.[65]

A comparison with other ruptures in the twentieth century shows that in spite of its large-scale dismissals the transformation of the East German universities took generally place within legal norms. In contrast to the half-hearted democratization of the Weimar Republic, the expulsion of innovative, leftist and Jewish scholars by the Nazis during 1933 was brutal and illegal, involving up to one-third of the faculty in some departments.[66] The antifascist restructuring of institutions after 1945 was even more comprehensive and equally tenuous in a legal sense, even if some of the excluded scholars then found new positions in the FRG.[67] Instead of using social categories of race and class, the transformation during unification sought to apply academic standards of discipline structure, scholarly achievement and personal integrity, since only those who did not fit the new profiles, were unproductive or had collaborated with the Stasi were to be excluded. In cases of mistaken judgments, the displaced could also sue.

Although this rigorous exchange of elites produced a "lost generation," it opened new chances for Eastern youth.[68]

What matters most in the long run is less the form of transformation than its academic result—the degree to which the HU will recover its reputation in an increasingly competitive environment. The attractive vision of the founders and the numerous Nobel prizes of the early twentieth century are a challenge for future achievements. But the collaboration of scholars with the National Socialist and Communist dictatorships prohibits an affirmative invocation of the past, requiring "a critical engagement" instead. The East-West mixture of professors and students will only become an advantage, if both academic cultures respect each other. Instead of promoting a marketable corporate identity, the HU needs to develop a dynamic vision of interdisciplinary approach, internationality, and innovation. Many hurdles such as a lethargic administration and insufficient funding still need to be overcome. But in contrast to other East German institutions, the HU has to measure itself on its implicit aspiration to leadership. It will only regain its former vitality if it finds a way to resolve the tension between democratic access and intellectual excellence.[69]

Notes

1. A slightly altered German version of this essay was published under the title "Säuberung oder Erneuerung? Zur Transformation der Humboldt-Universität 1985–2000" in Michael Grüttner et al. (eds.), *Gebrochene Wissenschaftskulturen? Universität und Politik im 20.* Jahrhundert (Göttingen, 2010), 327–51.

2. Konrad H. Jarausch, *The Rush to German Unity* (New York, 1994). See Ilko-Sascha Kowalczuk, *Endspiel: Die Revolution von 1989 in der DDR* (Munich, 2009).

3. For the texts of the resolutions see the newsletters of the GSA and the CGCEH for the winter of 1989/90 (in author's possession).

4. Ingrid Matschenz et al. (eds.), *Dokumente gegen Legenden: Chronik und Geschichte der Abwicklung der Mitarbeiterinnen und Mitarbeiter des Instituts für Geschichtswissenschaften an der Humboldt-Universität zu Berlin* (Berlin, 1996), 5–9.

5. Renate Mayntz (ed.), *Aufbruch und Reform von oben: Ostdeutsche Universitäten im Transformationsprozeß* (Frankfurt, 1994), 283–312. See also Jürgen Kocka and Renate Mayntz (eds.), *Wissenschaft und Wiedervereinigung: Disziplinen im Umbruch* (Berlin 1998).

6. Sven Vollrath, *Zwischen Selbstbestimmung und Intervention: Der Umbau der HUB von 1989 bis 1996* (Dissertation, Berlin, 2008) versus Thomas Raiser, *Schicksalsjahre einer Universität: Die strukturelle und personelle Neuordnung der Humboldt-Universität zu Berlin 1989–1994* (Berlin, 1998), 113 et seq.

7. Peer Pasternack, *"Demokratische Erneuerung": Eine universitätsgeschichtliche Untersuchung des ostdeutschen Hochschulumbaus 1989–1995. Mit zwei Fallstudien: Universität Leipzig und Humboldt-Universität zu Berlin* (Weinheim, 1999) versus the dissertation of Tobias Schulz, "Zur Praxis sozialistischer Wissenschaft: Das Beispiel der Humboldt Universität seit den sechziger Jahren" (Potsdam, 2010).

8. Konrad H. Jarausch, "La destruction créatrice. Transformer le système universitaire est-allemand: le cas de l'histoire," *Civilisations (Winter 2000/1).*

9. Helmut Klein, "175 Jahre Humboldt-Universität: 275 Jahre Charité. Festrede zum Jubiläum," *Humboldt-Universität* (cited hereafter as: HU) 1985/86, no. 9, 5–8. See idem (ed.), *Humboldt-Universität zu Berlin: Überblick 1810–1985* (Berlin, 1985), 147–66.

10. Kurt Hager, "Die Leistungen der Humboldt-Universität—ein würdiger Beitrag zum 35. Jahrestag der DDR," *HU*, 1984/85, no. 5; Klein, anniversary speech, ibid., 1985/86, no. 8; and Erich Honecker, "Aus dem Bericht des ZKs an den XI. Parteitag der SED," ibid., no. 31.

11. Helmut Klein, "Die Aufgaben der Humboldt-Universität zu Berlin in Lehre und Forschung: Referat im Rahmen des 19. Lehrgangs der Genossen Studenten des neuen Studienjahres 1985/86," Humboldt University Archive (cited herafter as: HUA), Bestand Rektorat, Reden und Referate des Rektors, Juli 1985-Dez. 1984, no. 1040.

12. "Lehrgang für junge Genossen am Beginn des Studiums," *HU*, 1980/81, no. 1; Harry Smettan, "Aus dem Bericht der Kreisleitung der SED an die VII. Kreisdelegiertenkonferenz," Ibid., nos. 19/20; See Christoph Kleßmann, *Arbeiter im "Arbeiterstaat" DDR: Deutsche Traditionen, sowjetisches Modell, westdeutsches Magnetfeld (1945 bis1971)* (Bonn, 2007).

13. See Konrad H. Jarausch (ed.), *Zwischen Parteilichkeit und Professionalität: Bilanz der Geschichtswissenschaft der DDR* (Berlin, 1991); Georg Iggers et al. (eds.), "Die DDR-Geschichtswissenschaft als Forschungsproblem," *Historische Zeitschrift*, Special Issue no. 27 (Munich, 1998); Konrad H. Jarausch and Michael Geyer, *Shattered Past: Reconstructing German Histories* (Princeton, NJ, 2003), 61–84.

14. Wissenschaftlicher Rat, "Nationalpreisträger und Akademiemitglieder berieten über die Aufgaben unserer Universität in Auswertung des 3. Plenums und der Beratung des ZK der SED mit den 1. Sekretären der Kreisleitungen," *HU*, 1981/82, Nr. 26; interview with Helmut Klein, "Zur präzisierten Entwicklungskonzeption der Humboldt-Universität," ibid., Nr. 27/28; Harry Smettan, "Es geht um die Erhöhung des Beitrages der Universität für den volkswirtschaftlichen Leistungsanstieg," ibid., no. 35.

15. Critical statements in the protocols of the Senate meetings on February 23, May 31, and June 28, 1988, HUA, Wissenschaftlicher Rat, no. 017.

16. "Information über die Auswertung der Beratung des Sekretärs des ZK der SED mit den 1. Sekretären der Kreisleitung," January 21, 1983; „Bericht über die Erfüllung des Kampfprogramms in den GO," April 16, 1983, in: Foundation for the Archives of the Parties and Mass Organizations of the German Democratic Republic Under the Federal Archives of Germany, Berlin (quoted hereafter as: SAP-

MO-BArch), DY 30/ 8162; Ministerium für Hoch- und Fachschulwesen, "Information über den Mißbrauch von Dienstreisen," November 3, 1987; SED-Kreisleitung der Akademie der Wissenschaften, "Bericht über Ergebnisse und Erfahrungen zur Unterbindung und Zurückdrängung von Übersiedlungsgesuchen," February 2, 1988, all in: SAPMO-BArch, DY 30/7618; petition to the Zentralrat of the FDJ, October 5, 1988, ibid., DY 30/7761.

17. "Information über das innerparteiliche Leben in der Grundorganisation," January 19, 1981, and "Bericht über die Realisierung der Kampfprogramme der GO," August 30, 1982, ibid., DY 30/8163; as well as Hörnig to Hager, June 18, 1985; and Horn, "Bemerkungen zur Rohfassung des Artikels ‚Kooperative Kunstpraxis von jungen Lyrikern und Malern," and further material on the Böthig case, ibid., DY 30/7556.

18. "Die Herausforderung der 90er Jahre. Wie stellen wir uns den wachsenden Ansprüchen an die Zukunft," HU 1988/89, Nr. 28; and "Erste Einschätzung der politisch-ideologischen Diskussion in der ersten Studienwoche," September 22, 1989, ibid., DY 30/7662.

19. "Festakt zum 40. Jahrestag der DDR," HU 1989/90, Nr. 5/6; Richard Schmidt, "Offener Brief an die Mitglieder der FDJ-Kreisorganisation der HU," ibid. See "Urabstimmung zum Studentenrat," ibid., no. 11. and Malte Sieber and Ronald Freytag, *Kinder des Systems: DDR-Studenten vor, im und nach dem Herbst '89* (Berlin, 1993), 84–96.

20. Senate minutes of October 24, 1989, as well as draft of an open letter to all HU-members, HUA, WR 019. Michael Brie, "Was gestern noch richtig war, kann heute falsch sein," *HU*, 1989/90, no. 8; Dieter Klein, "Zwischen Chance und Untergang," ibid., no. 11; Dieter Segert, *Das 41. Jahr: Eine andere Geschichte der DDR* (Vienna, 2008).

21. Hartmut Nieswandt, "Wie verlorenes Vertrauen wiedergewinnen? Wir berichten von der Diskussion während der Kreisparteiaktivtagung am 26. Oktober," *HU*, 1989/90, no. 9; and Waltraut Falk, "Stellungnahme der gesellschaftswissenschaftlichen Fakultät" of November 17, 1989, HUA, WR 019.

22. Leitung der Sektion ML, "Zur Umgestaltung des MLG," *HU*, 1989/90, no. 11; Heike Zappe, "Studentenrat konstituiert," ibid., no. 12.

23. Senate minutes of January 23, 1990, HUA, WR 019; Hartmut Nieswandt, "Neue Alma Mater. Über die Arbeit des 'Ausschusses für Struktur und Statut der neuen Universität,'" *HU*, 1989/90, no. 18, 3.

24. Minutes of the round table sessions, starting on January 24, 1990 in the Vollrath papers. Other documents like membership files and retrospective summaries are in the Pasternack Papers. See also Vollrath, *Zwischen Selbstbestimmung und Intervention*, 49–55.

25. "Arbeitsprogramm zur Bildung demokratisch legitimierter Gremien und arbeitsfähiger Leitungen an der HUB," January 1990; table comparing different statute proposals from A to D of January 5, 1990; "Grundsätze für ein Statut der Humboldt-Universität," February 25, 1990; diverse drafts of January 16 and 30, and March 2 and 5,1990, and draft without date in HUA, WR 026 and WR 48 to 52.

26. Hans-Joachim Meyer, "Gedanken zu einem neuen Bildungswesen in der DDR," and "Vorschlag für eine Universitätsverfassung—Variante (e)," ibid. See "Vorschlag des Ausschusses des Wissenschaftlichen Rates zu Struktur und Statut der HU und Vergleich Variante A und Variante E," *HU*, 1989/90, no. 19/20.

27. Information der Universitätsleitung, "Vorschlag des Ausschusses des Wissenschaftlichen Rates zu Struktur und Statut der HU," of February 2, 1990; Mara Kaemmel, "Konzil," *HU*, 1989/90, no. 28; and Hartmut Nieswandt, "Arbeiten wir miteinander für diese Universität," ibid.

28. Heinrich Fink in the Senate on 15 May 1990, HUA WR 020; idem, "Investitur: Die Rede des neuen Rektors," *HU*, 1989/90, no. 32 versus Hans Joachim Meyer, "Ich weiß, daß viele verzagt und besorgt in die Zukunft sehen," ibid., nos. 33/34.

29. Senate minutes of July 26, and August 1, 1990, HUA WR 020; Heike Schmoll, "Zusammenlegung mit der Universität erreicht: Rektor mit sozialistischer Vergangenheit?" *Frankfurter Allgemeine Zeitung* (cited herafter as: FAZ), September 18, 1990; "Gegen Verleumdungen. Reaktionen auf einen Zeitungsartikel"; "Sich selbst erklären: Rektor stellte sich den Fragen der Medien," *HU*, 1990/91, No. 3.

30. Adolf Rüger, "Kreuz zeigen. Das Institut für Geschichtswissenschaften arbeitet seine Vergangenheit auf," *HU*, 1990/91, nos. 10, 11, 12/3. See Beatrix Herlemann, "Ihre Entschuldigung nehme ich nicht an, Herr Pätzold!," *die tageszeitung* (cited herafter as: *taz*), November 13, 1990; Götz Aly, "Als Mensch bleibst du einfach draußen," *taz*, November 14, 1990; Jan von Flocken, "Die reine Wahrheit oder nichts als lahme Ausreden?" *Der Morgen*, November 17–18, 1990; and letters to the editor by Rainer Eckert and Jörg Judersleben, *taz*, November 26, 1990.

31. Senate minutes of December 4 and 18, 1990, http://dokumente.hu-berlin.de/asprotokolle/, thereafter cited as HU online.

32. Senate minutes of October 23, 1990, and February 21, 1991, HU online; Ehrenausschuss der HU, "Grundsätze für die Arbeit," *HU*, 1990/91, No. 9; Bert Flemming, "Ehre?, . . . es geht neben der Ehre des einzelnen auch um die Ehre unserer Universität,'" ibid., nos. 29/30.

33. Senate minutes of January 17, 1991, HU online; "Zentrale Personalstrukturkommission gewählt," *HU*, 1990/91, no. 14; Heike Zappe, "Eine Anhörung," ibid., nos. 35/36. See Raiser, *Schicksalsjahre*, passim.

34. Anbau, "Selbstreinigung in Angriff genommen," *taz*, December 17, 1990; Gustav Seibt, "Wer zu spät kommt: Aufregung in der Nische, die doch keine war," *FAZ*, December 15, 1990. See Segert, *Das 41. Jahr*, 203, versus Küpper, *Einheitsschmerzen*, 40 et seq.

35. Author's interview with Manfred Erhardt. See "Wissenschaftssenator will 'Abwicklung,'" *Der Morgen*, February 14, 1991; and Anette Schrade, "Klage werde 'Sargnagel' für die HU sein," *HU*, 1990/91. nos. 19/20.

36. Senate minutes of February 5 and 12, 1991, as well as March 19 and 22, 1991, HU online. See Heinrich Fink, "Presseerklärung," and "Zur Lage," *HU*, 1990/91, nos. 15/16; "Eingeschränkt durch das Ergänzungsgesetz sind," ibid., no. 39.

37. "Wird die Uni 'abgewickelt'?," *HU*, 1990/91, nos. 12/13; Heinrich Fink, "Klage," ibid., no. 14; Heinrich Fink, "Zur Lage," ibid., nos. 15/16; "Es kann 'abgewickelt' werden. 'Abwicklung' geht vor Kündigungsschutz," ibid., nos. 19/20; Heinrich Fink, "Presseerklärung des Rektors zur Entscheidung des Oberverwaltungsgerichts," ibid., nos. 35/36; "Abwicklung ist rechtswidrig," ibid., 1991/92, no. 13.

38. Senate minutes of May 7, June 4, and July 10, 1991, HU online; Heidi Damaschke, "Nimbus und Zukunft der Universität," *HU*, 1990/91, nos. 37/38. For an extensive set of records of the deliberations of the SBK-commissions see the Vollrath papers.

39. Some of the key documents of the public debate are collected in Rainer Eckert et al. (eds.), *Hure oder Muse? Klio in der DDR. Dokumente und Materialien des Unabhängigen Historikerverbandes* (Berlin, 1994).

40. Senate minutes of January 14 and May 5, 1992, HU online; Gerhard A. Ritter, "Der Neuaufbau der Geschichtswissenschaft an der Humboldt-Universität zu Berlin—ein Erfahrungsbericht," *Geschichte in Wissenschaft und Unterricht*, 1993, 226–38; Heidi Damaschke, "Große Herausforderung, Neuaufbau des Instituts für Geschichtswissenschaften," *HU*, 1991/92, no. 17.

41. Senate minutes of November 26 and December 3, 1991, HU online. "Der Fall Fink ist ein Fall Humboldt-Universität," *HU*, 1991/92, no. 6; "Wozu Fragen stellen—erstmal Kopf ab"!, and Hans-Dieter Burkhard, "Konzil bittet den Rektor, im Amt zu bleiben," *HU Sonderausgabe*; Heidi Damaschke, "Die Beweise reichen nicht aus," *HU*, 1991/92, no. 8; idem, "Berliner Arbeitsgericht hob fristlose Kündigung von Prof. Fink auf," ibid, Nr. 14; "Unerwarteter Urteilsspruch," *HU*, 1992/93, no. 3.

42. Senate minutes of February 4, 1992, HU online; Heidi Damaschke, "Verwaltung ist nicht Selbstzweck. Kanzler Rainer Neumann," *HU*, 1991/92, no. 6; Anette Schrade, "Erste konstituierende Sitzung des Akademischen Senats, und Kuratorium bestätigte Haushalts- und Stellenplan," ibid., no. 10.

43. Senate minutes of May 27 and August 4, 1992, as well Sitzung des Konzils of July 9, 1992, HU online; Heidi Damaschke, "Das Konzil der Universität stimmte für eine Präsidialverfassung," *HU*, 1991/92, no. 15; "Universitätsleitung nun komplett," *HU Sonderausgabe*; Marlis Dürkop, "Auf dem Weg zur Normalität, nicht zum Durchschnitt," ibid.

44. Senate minutes of January 21, February 25, March 17, April 7, and December 1, 1992, HU online; "Wissenschaftssenator zog Bilanz," *HU*, 1992/93, no. 3; "Was macht man in der Gegenwart mit der Vergangenheit?" and "Zwischen Abwicklung und Neuanfang. SBK am FB Erziehungswissenschaften beendet ihre Arbeit," ibid., no. 4. The figures are from table 4 "SBK-Berufungen bis zum 23. 12. 1994" in Jarausch, "Das Ringen um Erneuerung."

45. Senate minutes of April 14, May 19, and June 2, 1992, HU online; "Chancen für den Mittelbau?" *HU*, 1991/92, no. 13; Marlis Dürkop, "Personalentscheidungen im Zusammenhang mit dem Hochschulpersonal-Übernahmegesetz," *HU*, 1992/93, no. 4; and "Zur Hochschulpersonalübernahme: Aufgaben gingen weit über das 'normale' Maß hinaus," ibid., no. 6.

46. Figures from Raiser, *Schicksalsjahre einer Universität*, 94 et seq., 113 et seq., as well as from Vollrath, *Zwischen Selbstbestimmung und Intervention*, 240 et seq. Comparable numbers for the transformation after 1945 can be found in in the dissertation by Schulz, chapter 1.

47. Arnulf Baring, "Warum ich an die Humboldt-Universität will," *FAZ*, May 11, 1991, versus Gerhard A. Ritter's letter to the editor, ibid., June 10, 1991. See Friedhelm Neidhardt, "Konflikte und Balancen. Die Umwandlung der Humboldt-Universität zu Berlin 1990–1993," *Aufbruch und Reform*, 33–60.

48. "Hochschulen gegen Erklärung der Länderchefs zu Strukturreformen," *HU*, 1993/4, no. 2; "Ein Umbau nach verblichenen Plänen," *Süddeutsche Zeitung* (cited herafter as: SZ), October 14–15, 1995. See Mitchell G. Ash (ed.), *Mythos Humboldt: Vergangenheit und Zukunft der deutschen Universitäten* (Vienna, 1999); and Dietrich Schwanitz, *Der Campus* (Frankfurt-Main, 1995).

49. Senate minutes of June 2, October 6, 1992, and April 2, as well as May 25, 1993, HU online; Marlis Dürkop, "Auf dem Weg zur Normalität, nicht zum Durchschnitt," *HU Extra.*

50. Senate minutes of July 20, August 3, 1993, and March 16, September 20, and December 6, 1994, HU online; "Reizwort Adlershof," *HU*, 1992/93, no. 4; Marlis Dürkop, "Zum Gesetz über die Neuordnung der Hochschulmedizin in Berlin (UniMedG)," *HU*, 1994/5, no. 4; "Adlershof. Eine Chance für die Universität und das Land Berlin," *HU*, 1995/96, no. 7.

51. Senate minutes of July 20 and October 5, 1993; "Keine Generalermächtigung für den Senator," and "Wie billig bekommt man eine Erneuerung?," *HU*, 1993/94, no. 1; "Die Hochschulen stehen im Regen," ibid., no. 3.

52. Senate minutes of November 2, December 7, 1993, February 1 and 25, March 16, June 7, December 6 and 20, 1994, HU online, Marlis Dürkop, "Zur Haushaltssituation der HUB," *HU*, 1993/4, no. 9 and idem, "Wer holt die Kuh vom Eis?" *HU*, 1994/95, no. 1; Horst Bredekamp, "Vorwärtsverteidigung gefragt, und Wissenschaft und Bildung sind Zukunftsinvestitionen," ibid., no. 4

53. Senate minutes of June, 13, July 25, and August 8, 1995, HU online; "SBK-Vorsitzende fordern von Berliner Politikern verantwortliches Handeln," *HU*, 1994/5, no. 8; Marlis Dürkop, "Verlust an politischer Kultur," ibid., 1995/96, no. 4; idem, "Berlin verkennt Bildung als Zukunftsinvestition," ibid., no. 5; and open letter of Marlies Dürkop and Frank Seyffert to the students, ibid., no. 6.

54. Senate minutes of December 17, 1991 and July 2, 1996. See "Ohne Moos, nix los," *HU*, 1995/96, no. 4, "Rechtsstaat beginnt nicht erst, wenn die Kasse stimmt," ibid., no. 6; "Präsidentenwahl," ibid., no. 9.

55. Senate minutes of September 17, October 15, November 5, December 3 and 17, 1995, and January 2, March 25, and May 13, 1997, HU online. "Gefährliches Unicum. Humboldt-Universität wehrt sich gerichtlich gegen Teile des Haushaltsstrukturgesetzes," *HU*, 1995/96, no. 8; "Heftigere Gangart angekündigt," ibid., 1996/97, no. 3; "Ein 'Ja' unter Schmerzen," ibid., no. 6; and text of the contract, ibid., no. 6.

56. Senate minutes of June 10 and 17, September 9, and October 14, 1997, HU online; "Alles andere als Wunschvorstellungen," *HU*, 1996/97, no. 9; "Kürzung von 82 Professoren bis zum Jahr 2000," ibid., 1997/98, no. 1. On top of that the agriculture faculty was to save 11.3 million DM and the administration another 4 million DM.

57. Senate minutes of January 6, 13, and 24, and March 30 and 31, 1998, HU online; "Es geht um die Streichung von 61 Professuren," *HU*, 1997/98, no. 4; Ingo Bach, "Hürdenlauf," ibid., no. 6; "Hochschulstrukturplan beschlossen," ibid.; and "Hochschulverträge paraphiert," ibid., 1998/99, no. 6.

58. Figures from tables 4 and 6 of Jarausch, "Ringen um Erneuerung." See Ritter, "Neuaufbau der Geschichtswissenschaft," 226 et seq. and http://www.geschichte.hu-berlin.de/.

59. "Drittmittelbilanz positiv," *HU*, 1996/97, no. 6; "Humboldt in der Spitzengruppe," ibid., no. 8; "Neuer SFB bewilligt," ibid., 1998/99, no. 9; "Humboldt ist Spitze," ibid., 1999/2000, no. 3, "Leibniz-Preis 2000 für Prof. Dieter Lüst," ibid., no. 2.

60. "Anders als alle Andern. Die HUB entwickelt sich vom Kader-Institut des Sozialismus zur Elite-Hochschule der Zukunft," *UniSpiegel*, December 1, 1999. See Hans-Dieter Burckhard, "Ein Puzzle setzt sich zusammen," *HU*, 1998/99, no. 6.

61. Thomas Möbius und Jörg Nicht, "Phönix im Sturzflug . . . ? Wahrnehmungen des Umbruchs und Strukturwandels an der HUB von 1989–1995," *HU*, 1999/2000, no. 2. See Volker Gerhardt (ed.), *Universität des Mittelpunkts: Beiträge zur Leitbilddiskussion* (Berlin, 2000).

62. BBAW symposium on "Wissenschaft und Wiedervereinigung. Bilanz und offene Fragen," November 24–25, 2009. See Stefan Berger, "Was bleibt von der Geschichtswissenschaft der DDR? Blick auf eine alternative historische Kultur im Osten Deutschlands," *Zeitschrift für Geschichtswissenschaft*, 50 (2002), 1016–1034; Stefan Bollinger et al. (ed.), *Ausgrenzung oder Integration? Ostdeutsche Sozialwissenschaftler zwischen Isolierung und Selbstbehauptung* (Berlin, 2004).

63. This devastating analysis was written by Johannes Hörnig, the long-term higher education department head within the science section of the Central Committee of the SED, for Kurt Hager on October 30, 1989, SAPMO-BArch, DY 30/7720.

64. Michael Ploenus, "Ankunft im vereinten Deutschland. Die Universität Jena zwischen 1989 und 1995," Senatskommission zur Aufarbeitung der Jenaer Universitätsgeschichte im 20. Jahrhundert (ed.), *Traditionen—Brüche—Wandlungen: Die Universität Jena 1850–1995* (Cologne, 2009), 842–77.

65. Pasternack, "'Demokratische Erneuerung,'" 366 et seq., and Raiser, *Schicksalsjahre einer Universität*, 113 et seq. See also the symposium of the Rosa Luxemburg Foundation on "Die Linden-Universität 1945–"990," Berlin, March 19–20, 2009.

66. Herbert Döring, *Der Weimarer Kreis: Studien zum politischen Bewusstsein verfassungstreuer Hochschullehrer* (Meisenheim, 1976); Michael Grüttner, *Studenten*

im Dritten Reich (Paderborn, 1995); Konrad H. Jarausch, "Die Vertreibung der jüdischen Studenten und Professoren von der Berliner Universität unter dem NS-Regime," *Öffentliche Vorlesungen der Humboldt-Universität Berlin*, 37 (1995).

67. Ralph Jessen, *Akademische Elite und kommunistische Diktatur: Die ostdeutsche Hochschullehrerschaft in der Ulbricht-Ära* (Göttingen, 1999); Ilko-Sascha Kowalczuk, *Geist im Dienste der Macht: Hochschulpolitik in der SBZ/DDR 1945–1961* (Berlin, 2003).

68. Roland Bloch and Peer Pasternack, *Die Ostberliner Wissenschaft im vereinigen Berlin: Eine Transformationsfolgenanalyse* (Wittenberg, 2004).

69. Volker Gerhardt, "Ein *Leitbild* für die Humboldt-Universität," *HU*, 1999/2000, no. 1. See Bernd Henningsen (ed.), *Humboldts Zukunft: Das Projekt Reformuniversität* (Berlin, 2008); Konrad H. Jarausch, "Demokratische Exzellenz. Ein transatlantisches Plädoyer für ein neues Leitbild deutscher Hochschulen," *Denkströme*, 1 (2008), 23–52.

7

Research on Fascism and Antifascism in the GDR

A Retrospective

KURT PÄTZOLD

Scholarly discussion of the theoretical foundations, methodology, and findings of the various disciplines is an ongoing process; it is an indispensable precondition for both intellectual and practical progress. In daily academic life no particular fuss is made over this activity. It has come to be expected, and it underlies such time-tested rules and norms as the integrity of the proof underlying every research result.

What happens, however, when a state comes to an end, bringing down with it an entire discipline that played a special role in the collapsing society? This was the process that occurred in the former German Democratic Republic, the GDR. This state, which existed from 1949 to 1989, possessed a diverse and capable historical profession, represented through institutions affiliated with the Academy of Sciences, institutes at universities, and other institutions of higher education, academic societies, seminars and councils, editorial boards of journals, with a plethora of international ties and contacts, some of which had developed a solid contractual basis. Barely a year after unification, all this was destroyed. To discuss the effects of this destruction for East German research and researchers on the topic of fascism and antifascism is the purpose of this essay.[1] Due to space limitations it cannot provide a full-scale examination of the topic.[2]

In 1990, West German commissions evaluated the Academy's historical institutes. The result was that most of their academic employees lost their appointments. Some were sent into early retirement; others were unemployed and had then to seek work in areas more or less related to their qualifications. Only a very few had the prospect of completing critical editions or continuing to document projects. A series of transitional measures prolonged this process and—to use a then applied term—"cushioned" (*abfedern*) the social consequences; but these did not alter the overall effect.

The history departments and institutes in universities and other institutions of higher education had largely been subjected to a procedure, which even the unification treaty designated as "liquidation" (*Abwicklung*).[3] This effectively meant the closing of existing institutes and their divisions, and the termination of all their employees, from professors to custodians and secretaries. This process was followed by the creation of a small number of new research institutions, such as the *Zentrum für Zeithistorische Forschung*, the Center for Contemporary History, in Potsdam. Employees who were fired had the formal right to compete for appointments under the newly created structures, although their prospects for consideration were slim and did, in fact, hardly exist. This was a result partly of downsizing—often justified—of institutes and departments that were too large. More significantly, this "liquidation" was accompanied by the de facto stigmatizing of historians, which naturally decreased or nullified their chances of future employment elsewhere. In fact, to justify this "liquidation," politicians were employing the thesis that GDR historians had been nothing but obedient servants of the SED regime. Thus they had contributed to the "tyranny" (*Unrechtsstaat*), and as such they had forfeited their right to employment as university educators.[4]

In response to this sweeping judgment, some East and West German historians had demanded that a case-by-case review should replace wholesale disposition; criteria for rehire should include a person's academic qualifications for a position, and whether he or she had forfeited the claim to employment in higher education by offenses against human rights.[5] The counterproposal was rejected, and a process of collective guilt and punishment was instituted, which was unique in the history of university life in Germany.[6]

In 1990–1991, almost all university historians lost tenured appointments. They were pressured to accept altered contracts, which expired mostly in late 1991 (in a few cases some years later). These temporary appointments were justified only by the need to prevent the total collapse of education in the new East German federal states.[7] In 1992 the massive dismissals started.[8] It was obvious that history professors from the GDR-era were, at best, temporary placeholders for their successors, who, as at East Berlin's Humboldt University, were chosen almost without the involvement of GDR historians in the commissions that were responsible to appoint new professors.[9]

Moreover, other institutions of the historical profession ceased to exist or had largely lost their ability to function. The (East German) *Historiker-Gesellschaft* or Historical Association, which was in a transitional phase, was dissolved after the (West German) Historical Association declared that it rejected amalgamation and, moreover, demanded that "tainted" (*belastete*) East German historians should refrain from applying for membership.[10]

The collapse also meant a setback for the publication of ongoing and even completed research projects. Signed contracts for the publication of manuscripts were cancelled. Manuscripts ready for publication were halted because East German publishers, whether correctly or not hardly mattered, feared they would be "left sitting" on the books. This affected even such continuing ventures as the *German History* series, which had progressed to volume five, or an *Encyclopedia of German History* that was written largely by historians from the Academy of Sciences.[11] In many of such cases, it was by no means reservations with the manuscript's content that led to the decision. The publisher had to reconcile with the fact that the market for books in the new federal states was, from one day to the next, flooded with the enormous amount of West German books; moreover, among the declining number of former GDR residents who were able and willing to buy books, there was naturally a great demand for that literature that had previously been inaccessible. Like book publishers, journal editors struggled to find buyers and, even more so, subscribers. It is something of a miracle that the *Zeitschrift fur Geschichtswissenschaft* managed to survive. It is now published by Metropol-Verlag, Berlin.

Right after the collapse of their country, historians of the former GDR had begun to come to terms with their own scholarly accomplishments. They turned to subjects of research that either belonged to areas that were formerly taboo for publication or public discussion, or that could be pursued freely only to a very circumscribed extent. This was true, above all, of the forty-year history of the GDR, for research on which an extraordinary amount of archival material became available and was used by scholars from here and abroad. Interest had naturally turned, above all, to the neuralgic points of GDR history; for example, the period of its founding and programmatic foundations; the events during years of heightened social and political confrontation, such as 1953, 1956, and 1961; and the ousting of Walter Ulbricht and the fall of Erich Honecker.

The struggles of the quarter-century from the end of World War I through the end of World War II were interpreted as the immediate prehistory of the GDR, and the accomplishments and results of the communist movement in Germany were often unjustifiably vulgarized and magnified. More important and fateful, however, was the fact that the consequences of this stage of German and GDR history were viewed exclusively from the perspective of positive lines of tradition (or as lines of tradition that were interpreted as positive). Even when, in the 1980s, a growing (though small, in comparison to the Federal Republic) number of foreigners living in the GDR encountered clear expressions of hostility and xenophobia, and when youthful anti-Semites—very isolated, to be sure—"distinguished themselves," no one asked whether the lessons of German history had been learned. Indeed, everything negative was classified as a direct ideological import from the West; as a result, the majority within GDR society who had been unsettled by events was not mobilized intellectually and morally.

Preconditions and precedents exist for such attempts at mobilization because of diverse efforts within the profession. Whatever critical remarks can and must be made about the methods and results of GDR historical research on fascism and antifascism, since the 1970s, East German historians have produced respected studies and publications and have won for themselves indisputable international respect.

Important to this reputation was a group of historians, most of whom had entered the university as young students immediately after the end of the war (exceptions include Wolfgang Ruge and Kurt Gossweiler).[12] Some of them had been soldiers in the fascist *Wehrmacht,* others belonged to the younger generation that was later known under the rubric "Hitler Youth Generation." Even as students, they were united in practicing history with an expressly political purpose. Their intention was to use intellectual tools, about whose suitability they were still arguing, to ensure that events such as those of August 4, 1914, or September 1, 1939, did not repeat themselves in German or European history. Antifascism represented for them, above all, a strict antiwar position. These historians included Wolfgang Schumann, Joachim Petzold, Dietrich Eichholtz, Klaus Drobisch, Gerhart Hass, Karl Drechsler, Ludwig Nestler, Kurt Finker, and, as the youngest of this cohort, Manfred Weissbecker. Most of them had won recognition in West Germany, too. It remains a regrettable fact that none of their works have been translated into English.

The treatment of German fascism in historical writing in the GDR was in some respects convergent with historiography in the Federal Republic, but in other respects it diverged. Particular attention was paid to the question of why the Nazi Party could develop into a mass organization, indeed the largest party, in the Weimar Republic, and which factors finally secured the decisive success of January 30, 1933.[13] In a related matter, GDR historians analyzed the nature of the Nazi state and its goals. The regime was conceived of as a political system that from the outset (without even a brief "period of peace") prepared for war. This economic, political, and ideological preparation for war was the subject of intensive scholarly investigations, as was the course of the war itself. Indeed, the war years were more thoroughly researched than the period from 1933 to 1939. If one considers the connection between academic and political interests as understood and promulgated in the GDR, this emphasis contradicted the declared objective of avoiding future wars.

A number of researchers studied the ideological origins of Nazism. The philosopher Wolfgang Heise, who had been a victim of Nazi anti-Jewish persecution, produced the most important analysis. Similar to the works of Siegbert Kahn and Stefan Heymann, two older scholars who were also Holocaust survivors, Heise wrote that the "proclamation of Germanic-Aryan racial supremacy in association with the practice of anti-Semitism was—on the basis of the terror waged against all antifascist forces—the decisive ideological-political means of intimidation, corruption, and barbarism."[14]

The works of the historian Joachim Petzold also deserve attention: his examination of the relationship between Nazism and other authoritarian currents from the right as well as his analysis of the intellectual roots of Nazi ideology.[15] However, several contributors of a collection of essays that was published in 1980 lacked a comparative perspective. None of these studies dealt with Fascist ideologies from countries outside Germany.[16]

During the late 1980s it became clear among specialists that more energy should be spent researching the prewar years of the Nazi regime.[17] The topics that had barely been investigated included an explanation of the motivations and other factors that provided the Nazi regime with a mass following of unprecedented size.[18] One may wonder whether the extensive neglect of this particular topic did not arise from the intention of leading GDR politicians to suppress any suggestions of similarities between fascism and the GDR. One cannot conclusively answer this question on the archival record. Most East German party leaders discouraged any systematic inquiry into the mass base of German fascism, given the official Marxist-Leninist focus on elite support for Nazism.[19]

During the 1950s, under the circumstances of the Cold War, the intensity of the debate over the mass base of fascism abated. For pragmatic purposes of political acquiescence, the East German party leadership did not overemphasize the complicity of many rank-and-file East Germans with the Nazi regime. It was commonly understood that "one should not beat them on their heads with the past forever." None of this, however, justifies the gap in research that was allowed to open up, one that distorted and even rendered incomprehensible the overall picture of the Nazi regime. Downplaying the mass support for the Nazi system made it possible to focus more exclusively on the elite support for Nazism (specifically the political, economic, and cultural elites). Such an approach did not produce a balanced picture of German society during the Nazi period. Children and grandchildren in the GDR no longer found the lives of their parents' and grandparents' generations in history books, except in those cases where their ancestors were outright antifascists. The consequences are significant: they seriously limit the possibility of confronting the history of the masses within German history.

However, one should not overstate this. Historians who worked in the GDR should be granted a clean conscience in at least one area: they clearly exposed and rejected policies of imperialist expansion and the criminal, barbaric methods used to carry them out against the vital interests of other peoples.[20] Such euphemisms as crimes "in Germany's name" or "from Germany's hands" (as though they were not attached to a body in which a heartbeat and on which a head sat) were rejected as shameful. On the contrary, the responsibility of the German people as a whole was stressed, requiring that this responsibility be assessed and depicted. A distinction was made between the guilt of contemporaries and the responsibility of later generations to deal with the history of their own nation.

When, in the 1980s, Aufbau-Verlag, one of the major publishing houses in East Berlin published a critically edited collection of letters from the battlefield—written by a noncommissioned *Wehrmacht* officer who clearly thought and felt like a fascist and regularly reported his pro-Hitler reflections to his wife—a GDR cultural periodical inquired whether such publication that focused primarily on the reasons who one could become a Nazi, was really necessary.[21] East German history textbooks downplayed mass support for the Nazi regime as well.

This situation provoked a debate among GDR historians, but one, which, because it was internal, left no public record. At issue is the accuracy of the historical-materialist definition of fascism, which was at first promulgated at the Enlarged Plenary Session of the Comintern in December 1933.[22] Like every definition, this one is not fully adequate in understanding the full complexity of reality. Georgi Dimitrov's famous speech at the Seventh Congress of the Comintern in 1935, which repeated this definition, was incomparably more thoughtful.[23] Yet even this characterization is incomplete. First, it neglected entirely the mass basis of the regime; second, it explained nothing about the specific, immutable ideology of fascism.

With certain justification one may say that concrete research in the GDR had in many respects already surpassed this 1933 or 1935 definition. It has to be noted, however, that East German historians, myself included, did not go far enough in confronting the full force of the fascist experiences. This was also true on the subject of the persecution of Jews. GDR historiography described the crimes against German Jews step-by-step and stage-by-stage up to mass murder.[24] Yet, compared with the Federal Republic of Germany, the number of publications and in particular their attention paid to local and regional events was much smaller. Only in the mid-1980s did some East German historians' and grassroot researchers' efforts begin to remedy this imbalance. Some new and detailed studies on the persecution of Jews in the cities of Leipzig and Rostock and the towns of Plauen and Görlitz were published.

Just as efforts to explain the relationship between regime and masses were neglected, so, too, was any discussion of a connection between the majority of the population and anti-Jewish measures. One may make allowances for the extraordinarily fragmentary state of sources in this area (as in all similar cases, much room remains for conjecture and speculations). But even when one considers that only quite recently concrete evidence has been presented regarding how often non-Jewish Germans participated in and benefitted from the persecution of Jews, the picture presented remains unclear due to the range of behaviors, which went from complicity to acceptance and on to indifference. No official voice in the GDR ever made the case for restitution of the Jewish victims of Nazism.

This changed only in 1988, on the occasion of the fiftieth anniversary of the 1938 Pogrom, which was expressed, for example, by the restoration and care of Jewish cemeteries and the placement of memorial tablets. It is hard to assess how far this impulse spread. It originated with groups within the Protestant church, working groups in the East German *Kulturbund*, the Cultural Association, members of the Free German Youth, and individuals interested in local history.[25]

Another reason that complicated East German historians from fully confronting the fascist past was the German-Soviet non-aggression pact of August 1939 and its consequences which resulted in close cooperation between Nazi Germany and the Soviet Union. Until the period of *perestroika,* it was held that this topic, which included the shameful turning-over of German antifascist émigrés to the Nazi regime, should not be openly discussed until Soviet historians publicly admitted to this (which was unthinkable without a "green light" from the Kremlin). Nikita Khrushchev did not give this permission, even while courageously condemning the politics of Stalin and his associates. However, when the "green light" was finally turned on under Mikhail Gorbachev, GDR's political leadership distanced itself from the politics of renewal in the USSR by "waiting out" this supposed deviation from Marxism-Leninism. Only in January 1989, at a congress of the GDR's Historical Association, an open discussion took place on this dark chapter in German-Soviet relations, and its consequences for the German and international workers' movements and other anti-Nazi currents. At this late date, the schizophrenic situation established earlier came to an end: namely, in university lectures and seminars, this subject had long since been critically discussed, and at international forums GDR historians did not hesitate to debate that which was generally known. This led to the perception that some East German historians produced in their public presentations two versions of history: one for domestic consumption, one for the readership abroad.

This "tiptoeing" (a somewhat casual but appropriate expression) around the diplomatic documents signed by the governments of the Soviet Union and Germany in August and September 1939 demonstrates in extreme form how suppression and silencing affected East German party functionaries themselves, and the society as a whole. Being denied the possibility and capability of grappling with history, their view of the present was impeded, as was the sober recognition of their own successes and failures. Because the GDR historians continued this pattern into the final crisis of their state, rather than opposing it, they contributed to the inability of GDR society to reform it.

Extensive analyses of research and publications on the history of German antifascism substantiates this assertion. It is clear that specialists in this area have made significant contributions to the difficult reconstruction of the struggle of anti-Nazi opposition in Germany, and to research on Germans in political exile between 1933 and 1945. The contributions of GDR historians of literature on the struggle of writers, poets, and journalists against Hitler have also gained international respect.[26] Additional and internationally acknowledged research focused on the history of concentration camps, prisons, and other penal institutions and their inmates. The main focus of research was the antifascist struggle of the Communists, which was justified because the majority of antifascist opposition fighters came from their ranks. Top priority was given to research on the united and popular fronts against Hitler, but the fundamental differences between Communists and Social Democrats before 1933 that prevented united action against Nazism were often downplayed.[27]

Over a long period, GDR research on antifascism evolved a position counter to that in West Germany. While the latter concerned itself preferably with the conservative and military opposition that led to the assassination attempt of Hitler on July 20, 1944, and many Western historians tried to exclude the Communists from the true opposition to fascism as "totalitarian," GDR historians emphasized the inconsistencies of bourgeois and aristocratic opposition to Hitler. East German scholars tried to make this case largely by pointing to the "Great German Program" of the nationalist opposition leader Carl Goerdeler. In the 1980s the situation changed in both the GDR and the Federal Republic of Germany, and useful mutual discussions took place among specialists from both sides.[28]

Despite such progress and the high priority given research on antifascism by both the East German state and the SED, the results remained limited and extraordinarily spotty, even when judged by self-selected criteria. For decades, there was no general treatment of the non-communist German opposition to the Nazi regime, nor was there a biographical dictionary of antifascists. GDR historians produced hardly anything equivalent to offer alongside the detailed studies of Berlin Gestapo headquarters in Prinz Albrecht Street or on the level of the journal *Dachauer Hefte*, as produced by West German researchers, to mention but two examples.

This ideological straightjacket had many causes, which themselves need to be investigated. One—if not the primary—reason may have been that GDR research on antifascism, even after it revealed the breadth of the subject continued to operate under external restrictions or self-imposed handicaps. Most significant was the uncritical treatment that accorded the German Communist Party's (KPD) position on the rise of fascism, above all by the refusal to confront the long overdue need for detailed research into the real consequences of the Comintern's "Social Fascism" theory. This superficial approach continued to bypass internal conflicts in depicting the route to the 1935 Comintern and KPD decisions, which brought an abrupt correction of earlier positions. Yet no one inquired whether all leading Comintern functionaries supported the new general line. The impact of the Moscow show trials of 1936 to 1938 on the Comintern and the KPD were, at best, mentioned briefly.[29] The consequences of the German-Soviet treaties of August and September 1939 for Communist-Social Democratic relations (both nationally and internationally) were not seriously investigated either.

Tragically, many surviving communist antifascists, who fought courageously against the Nazis and their allies, now turned timid, apologists for the SED party line. They became, in Karl Marx's words, people "without eyes, without ears or teeth." How did this happen? There might be no satisfactory general answer inasmuch as human beings are motivated by a myriad of factors.

Given all accomplishments, which are substantiated in public research, East German scholarship and public research served above all to legitimize the authority of surviving antifascists who then occupied leading positions in the GDR.

This coincided with an ossified ritual in memory culture. A striking example of this was the cult that coalesced around the KPD leader Ernst Thälmann, who was killed on Hitler's personal order on August 18, 1944, in Buchenwald concentration camp. The most famous of innumerable Thälmann monuments was unveiled in 1986 in East Berlin's Prenzlauer Berg district. Without aid or context, schoolchildren stood before this gigantic bronze head, forming an architectonic ensemble that included Honecker's words, which praised the KPD leader uncritically, cast in metal. To be sure, historians were not directly responsible for this monstrosity, yet the authors of Thälmann's official biography, used for political propaganda, could not say that they had placed any intellectual barrier in the way of such celebrations. If anything, they had promoted this hagiographic treatment.[30]

The repulsive demonstrations by small groups of mostly young people, who, since 1990, pledged allegiance to neo-Nazism and celebrated "Hitler's birthday" in the cities of the former GDR, have led to critical questions and accusations.[31] The central question was as to what extent did East German antifascist education fail to reach young people? Even if one considers that some the expressions of neo-Nazism are part of a general dissatisfaction with current social and political conditions, they remain deeply disturbing.

Since 1990, when Germany unified, there is increasing pressure animating from Germany's leading opinion makers to sanitize German history and to finally draw a line under the past. This also resonated with many East Germans who wanted to distance themselves from their own involvement with the GDR dictatorship. "It was not me, it was Adolf Hitler" was a popular slogan of those who sought for exoneration after 1945. After 1990, one could hear such slogans throughout eastern Germany as well, except that the name Honecker had replaced Hitler. Moreover, in 1990 fewer barriers existed in the way of this escapism than did in 1945. The newly dominant discourse of Germany's two dictatorships, one being the Nazi regime and the other the SED system, served as a way for many East Germans to overlook their own culpability—East Germans could now see themselves most of all as victims and not as participants of the SED state. At first they were the hapless victims of Hitler and then the victims of Honecker. Just as many Germans after 1945 refused to confront their own complicity with the Nazi regime by delegating all responsibility to Hitler and his inner circle, many East Germans after 1990 tried to put all responsibility for the injustices of the GDR on Erich Honecker and the SED Politburo. "We just followed orders" was a popular slogan after 1945 as well as after 1990. In the words of the writer Ralph Giordano, this can produce something like a "third guilt," for no one can believe that this recent misinterpretation of the actual role of the majority of the East German population between 1949 and 1989, whatever its intent, will have no consequences.

At the same time, however, the leading West German media singled out those East Germans who were to be laid off from positions in academia and public life as personally responsible for the ills under communism. By doing so, they purposely downplayed the Cold War context that gave East Germans only limited options.

Many West German historians, who prior to 1990 cultivated cordial, if not friendly, relations with their East German colleagues, suddenly treated them as black sheep. While a smaller number participated directly in the large-scale purges of East German academics, the majority acquiesced by silence, a behavioral pattern that is unfortunately not atypical for German scholars.[32] Historians in the former GDR inevitably lost their prestige and Western connections overnight, almost exactly at the moment when their state collapsed.

The fate of East German historians was inevitably tied to the fate of the entire East German state and society. They shared in the experiences of many others, including all the new opportunities and obstacles that unification brought about. Christa Wolf's term *Wendehälse* (turncoats; literally, those with "flexible necks") applied only to a small number of historians, and not even any of those few could survive in the West German-designed academia. Thus, the issue is whether a group of historians who have been taught a bitter lesson by history, and who have been compelled to develop a new relationship with their discipline, can now bring their expertise to bear in the united Germany.[33]

Translated by Diana Loeser,
updated by Axel Fair-Schulz and Mario Kessler

Notes

1. This essay can be read as a sequel of the author's earlier article "Research on Fascism and Antifascism in the German Democratic Republic: A Critical Retrospective" that was published in *Radical History Review*, no. 54 (Fall 1992), 87 Friedrich-Wilhelms-University 109. Duke University Press, where *RHR* is published now, kindly acknowledged using passages from this publication. The author thanks his colleague, Professor Mario Kessler, particularly for bibliographical advice.

2. See, for the topic of fascism and antifascism in East German literary works, movies, and the media, Simone Barck, *Antifa-Geschichte(n): Eine literarische Spurensuche in der DDR der 1950er und 1960er Jahre* (Cologne, 2003); Christoph Classen, *Faschismus und Antifaschismus: Die nationalsozialistische Vergangenheit im ostdeutschen Hörfunk* (Cologne, 2004); Thomas Heimann, *Bilder von Buchenwald: Die Visualisierung des Antifaschismus in der DDR 1945–1990* (Cologne, 2005), and the extensive bibliographical annex by Renate Kirchner to Detlef Joseph, *Die DDR und die Juden: Eine kritische Untersuchung (*Berlin, 2010), 264–369. See also Werner Röhr, *Faschismus und Weltkrieg: Problemskizze zur historischen Faschismusforschung in der DDR* (Hamburg, 2001), and Thüringer Forum für Bildung und Wissenschaft (ed.), *Geschichtsschreibung in der DDR zum Zweiten Weltkrieg* (Jena, 2001). The most

extensive evaluation of East German historiography in English is Andreas Dorpalen, *German History in Marxist Perspective: The East German Approach* (Detroit, 1985). See also Georg G. Iggers's preface to his edited book *Marxist Historiography in Transformation: East German Social History in the 1980s* (New York and Oxford, 1991). For bibliographical references, see the special volumes of the *Zeitschrift für Geschichtswissenschaft* 1960, 1970, and 1980, published on the occasion of the International Historians' Congresses. The report for the years 1981 to 1990 was in print, but was never published (eds.).

3. The treaty between the Federal Republic of Germany and the German Democratic Republic concerning the restoration of German unity (31 August 1990), published in *Bundesgesetzblatt,* 2, 889 *et seq.*, Article 13, regulated the "liquidation." Its provisions were specified in a Protocol No. 905 to the treaty. According to a decision of the Federal Constitutional Court, an indeterminate number of cases were temporarily pending in labor and administrative courts. The rector of Humboldt University, Heinrich Fink, brought suit in Berlin's Administrative Court (*Verwaltungsgericht*) over a partial liquidation (*Teilabwicklung*) of academic institutions (Departments of Philosophy, History, Law, Economics, and Education). The Federal Constitutional Court in Karlsruhe, in a decision of April 24, 1991, ruled that "liquidation" was constitutional, but applied previously ignored restrictions on state governments in cases involving pregnant women, disabled persons, or maternal welfare laws. The court also ruled against "dummy liquidations" (*Scheinabwicklungen*), in which employees were fired from institutions or departments that were simply renamed and which then hired new appointees. See *Bundesverfassungsgericht* ruling 1 BvR 1341/90, on the "liquidation" of public servants. Some 600,000 persons were affected by the decision. See the text and argumentation in *Neues Deutschland*, April 29, 1991. Fink's own recollections can be read in his *Wie die Humboldt-Universität gewendet wurde* (Berlin, 2013).

4. For a nuanced discussion of the term "Unrechtsstaat,"see Robert Hansack, *Unrechtsstaat DDR: Zur Genesis des terminus politicus "Unrechtsstaat" nach der Transformation—Versuch einer historischen Bestandsaufnahme* (Frankfurt-Main, 2015), with extensive bibliography. For the international context, see Detlef Nakath and Dörte Putensen (ed.), *Unrechtsstaat DDR? Sichtweisen in europäischen Nachbarländern* (Potsdam, 2013), (eds.).

5. An early opposition to the undifferentiated historical view and the overall liquidation of East German scholarly institutions was expressed by the sociologist of literature, Hans Mayer, who himself had left the GDR in 1963 after being attacked for his nonconformist views. Mayer refuted the position that East German history could be judged entirely from the perspective of its demise. In his book *The Babel Tower* Mayer insisted that the GDR would remain a "German wound" for a long time. See Hans Mayer, *Der Turm von Babel: Erinnerung an eine Deutsche Demokratische Republik* (Frankfurt-Main, 1991).

6. In this regard, it is relevant to consider that the shameful expulsion of Jewish professors, lecturers, physicians, and other academics from German universities in 1933, during the initial phase of persecution of Jews, was proceeded

on the base of case-by-case reviews, so that, e.g., the contributions of "frontline combatants" in World War I were acknowledged. In 1935, after the decrees of the "Nuremberg Laws" were adopted, essentially wholesale mistreatment of the persecuted was institutionalized. See, for the case of Humboldt University, Konrad H. Jarausch, "Die Vertreibung der jüdischen Studenten und Professoren von der Berliner Universität unter dem NS-Regime," *Jahrbuch für Universitätsgeschichte*, vol. 1 (1998), 112–33. See also Jarausch's contribution to this volume. As a historic "rationale" for liquidation, it was asserted that in the Western Zones of Germany after 1945 a thoroughgoing change of personnel in public service (i.e., the dismissal of National Socialists) was avoided or unsuccessful. This "error," it was said after 1990, should not be repeated in regard to communists.

7. The beginning of the liquidation process and uncertainties regarding possibilities and conditions for study after October 1, 1991, caused student's protests. In particular, students could not anticipate what examination marks and certificates given by professors "in liquidation" might be worth in the future.

8. On April 8, 1991, at the outset of the spring semester, Humboldt University employees affected by "liquidation" were given a "choice": they could sign an alteration of their employment contract that changed their tenure status to one of terminating on 30 September 1991, thus relieving the employer of any need to give notice or to incur ensuing legal liabilities; or they could immediately be placed in provisional retirement (*Wartestand*, which in a literary turn of phrase was dubbed *Warteschleife* or waiting line). This status was de facto pre-unemployment; it continued for six months or nine for those over the age of fifty, and meant a reduction in gross income of 30 percent. Faced with this choice, most signed the untenured contracts while a minority brought their cases to labor courts and could prolong their appointments up to five years. See also the documentation: Ingrid Matschenz et al. (eds.), *Dokumente gegen Legenden: Chronik und Abwicklung [. . .] des Instituts für Geschichtswissenschaften an der Humboldt-Universität zu Berlin* (Berlin, 1996). For the author's personal reminiscences, see Kurt Pätzold, *Die Geschichte kennt kein Pardon: Erinnerungen eines deutschen Historikers* (Berlin, 2000), especially 260–85.

9. Reconstruction of the History Department of Humboldt University took place through a committee appointed by the Berlin Senate and headed by West German historian Gerhard A. Ritter. The only East German professorial member in that committee was Fritz Klein, formerly of the Academy of Sciences, but then retired. Klein resigned from the committee after an old contact to the East German *Staatssicherheit*, the Stasi, became known. See Fritz Klein, *Drinnen und Draußen: Ein Historiker in der DDR* (Frankfurt-Main, 2000), 353–59. The committee ordered the advertisement of all twelve existing professorships. See the advertisements in *Die Zeit*, April 12, 1991. Applications were due within fifteen days.

10. The East German Historical Association reorganized itself in March 1990, choosing a new presidium and a new chair, Günter Vogler, Professor of Early Modern History at Humboldt University. The process of renewal that had started very hesitantly occurred under pressure from the West German Historical Association; the argument that GDR historians were incapable of reforming their institutions

was thus disproven. The incapability thesis was also supported by the newly formed Independent Historical Association (*Unabhängiger Historiker-Verband*), which was founded on April 21, 1990, and gained a temporary degree of public attention. Members of this association included (mostly mid-aged) historians from East and West Germany. Some of its East German members were in the GDR in fact (or perception) disadvantaged and hindered in their academic careers. The West German Historical Association endorsed the harsh attacks of the Independent Historians against East German professors at its bi-annual meeting that was held in Bochum in 1990.

11. The Central Institute of German History at the Academy of sciences was publishing the projected twelve volume series of Deutsche Geschichte. Volumes 1 through 5 had been already published between 1982 and 1988. Volumes 6 and 7 (covering the periods 1871–1918 and 1918–1933) were at the publisher, Deutscher Verlag für Wissenschaften, ready for printing, but did not appear. The *Enzyklopädie für Deutsche Geschichte* was also at the publisher, Verlag Enzyklopädie (Leipzig), but was not published either. In a quick turnabout, the publisher's spokesman announced that they wished no longer to publish Marxist writings. The anti-Marxist attitude did not prevent Verlag Enzyklopädie from being "liquidated."

12. Ruge, a child of German antifascists, lived since 1933 in the USSR, and as a young ethnic German fell into a maelstrom of Stalinist persecution. He survived, and in 1956 was able to move to the GDR. A great number of books on the history of the Weimar Republic and the rise of German fascism came from his pen. His research interests included political biographies, a subject that was neglected in the GDR for a long time. He wrote biographies of the Weimar politicians Paul von Hindenburg, Gustav Stresemann, and Matthias Erzberger. Ruge was considered the forerunner of research on the Weimar Republic in the GDR and was awarded an honorary doctorate by the University of Jena. See his memoirs about his imprisonment in Stalin's camps, Wolfgang Ruge, *Berlin-Moskau-Sosswa: Stationen einer Emigration* (Cologne, 2003). See also the expanded version: *Gelobtes Land: Meine Jahre in Stalins Sowjetunion*, ed. by Eugen Ruge (Berlin, 2012). Gossweiler came from an antifascist family and grew up in Berlin. Forced into the Nazi army, he defected to the Soviet side and became an instructor in a German POW camp. His publications include a dissertation on the Röhm Affair, on banking in the Weimar Republic, connections between big business and Nazism, and the relationship between the *Reichswehr* and the Nazi Party. Berlin's Humboldt University awarded him an honorary doctorate.

13. For the history of the Nazi Party, see Kurt Pätzold and Manfred Weissbecker, *Hakenkreuz und Totenkopf: Die Partei des Verbrechens* ([East] Berlin, 1981). New and enlarged edition: *Geschichte der NSDAP, 1920–1945* (Cologne, 1998 and 2002). For Hitler's bid for power, see Wolfgang Ruge, *Das Ende von Weimar: Monopolkapital und Hitler* ([East] Berlin, 1983). West German edition: *Hitler, Weimarer Republik und Machtgergreifung* (Cologne, 1983).

14. Wolfgang Heise, *Aufbruch in die Illusion: Zur Kritik der bürgerlichen Philosophie in Deutschland* ([East] Berlin, 1964), 323. See the earlier works by

Siegbert Kahn, *Antisemitismus und Rassenhetze: Eine Übersicht über ihre Entwicklung in Deutschland* (Berlin, 1948), and Stefan Heymann, *Marxismus und Rassenfrage* (Berlin, 1948). Victor Klemperer's *LTI: Notizen eines Philologen* (Halle, 1947) was one of the most widely read testimonies of a survivor of the persecution and was re-published in several editions.

15. See Joachim Petzold, *Konservative Theoretiker des deutschen Faschismus: Jungkonservative Ideologien in der Weimarer Republik als geistige Wegbereiter der faschistischen Diktatur* ([East] Berlin, 1978): idem, *Die Demagogie des Hitlerfaschismus: Die politische Funktion der Naziideologie auf dem Wege zur faschistischen Diktatur* ([East] Berlin, 1982).

16. See Dietrich Eichholtz and Kurt Gossweiler (eds.), *Faschismusforschung: Positionen-Probleme-Polemik* ([East] Berlin, 1980).

17. For an attempt to examine the prewar years, see Dietrich Eichholtz and Kurt Pätzold (eds.), *Der Weg in den Krieg: Studien zur Geschichte der Vorkriegsjahre 1935/36–39* ([East] Berlin, 1989). For the war years, see the six-volume series *Deutschland im Zweiten Weltkrieg* that was published by a large group of authors under the direction of Wolfgang Schumann between 1974 and 1985 in East Berlin. Researchers from the Central Institute for German History at the Academy and the Institute for Military History at Potsdam were part of the project. On the other hand, there was no adequate book that could succeed the textbook *Deutschland von 1933 bis 1939* by Erich Paterna et al. ([East] Berlin, 1969).

18. The present author's theoretical approach towards this topic can be found in his essay "Die faschistische Manipulation des deutschen Volkes," *Grundlagen und Herrschaftsmechanismus des deutschen Faschismus*, vol. 1 (*Wissenschaftliche Beiträge der Martin-Luther-Universität Halle-Wittenberg*, vol. 42 [1980]). The essay's concerns include the regime's demagogic use of race, but also seemingly peaceful terms.

19. This was not the case in the very immediate postwar period, when the SED, along with other parties in east and west, turned against the position that was widespread in East (and West) Germany that rejected individual historical responsibility and guilt. Without this initial intellectual and moral debate over the role of the masses, it would have been impossible to accept the painful border in the East or to justify the reparation obligations, which brought much needed industrial capacities to the Soviet Union.

20. For a good example, see *Europa unterm Hakenkreuz*, an eight-volume series that was published through the particular efforts of Wolfgang Schumann and Ludwig Nestler. The series documents fascist occupation policy in different countries, such as Austria and Czechoslovakia (1988), Poland (1989), Belgium, Luxemburg, and the Netherlands (1990), France (1990), the occupied territories of the Soviet Union (1991), Yugoslavia, Greece, Albania, Italy, and Hungary (1992), Denmark and Norway (1994), and a summary volume on conceptions and practice of occupation policy (1994). While the six volumes that were published until 1991 came out at Deutscher Verlag der Wissenschaften, the following volumes were published under the direction of Werner Röhr at Hütig, a publishing house that is based in Berlin and Heidelberg. Many facts about the profiteers of Nazi rule

throughout occupied Europe can be found in Dietrich Eichholtz's three-volume study *Geschichte der deutschen Kriegswirtschaft* ([East] Berlin, 1969–1985; reprinted in five volumes, Munich, 2003). A special aspect of this research needs to be mentioned: the exploitation of foreign workers under Nazism. See the related chapters in Lothar Elsner and Joachim Lehmann, *Ausländische Arbeiter unter dem deutschen Imperialismus, 1900–1985* ([East] Berlin, 1988).

21. *Briefe des Soldaten Helmut N.*, ed. by Marlies Tremper, with a preface by Kurt Pätzold ([East] Berlin, 1988).

22. The Comintern definition of fascism as adopted by the 13th Plenary Session of the Executive Committee of the Comintern (ECCI) in December 1933 is as follows: "Fascism is the undisguised terrorist dictatorship of the most reactionary, most chauvinistic, most imperialistic elements of finance capital." Quoted from *Die Kommunistische Internationale: Auswahl von Dokumenten und Reden vom VI. Weltkongress bis zur Auflösung der Kommunistischen Internationale 1928–1943* ([East] Berlin, 1956), 226.

23. At the Seventh World Congress of the Comintern, Dimitrov characterized fascism as having two major features: it employed a demagogic ideology, which was able to mobilize the lower middle class, peasants, and the unemployed; and it utilized terror. Fascism, however, would become an option only at the point when big capitalists would fear their own expropriation by radicalized masses. In this case, they would turn to fascism in order to destroy all labor organizations as well as parliamentary institutions, which protected representation of the working class. Despite its self-criticism, Dimitrov's speech placed primary guilt for the defeat of the German working class in 1933 on "reactionary leaders" of the Social Democracy and their policy of a "united front with the bourgeoisie." *VII. Kongress der Kommunistischen Internationale: Referate und Resolutionen* ([East] Berlin, 1975), 14. For a more detailed discussion of the subject see Kurt Pätzold, *Faschismus-Diagnosen* (Berlin, 2015).

24. See the standard works by Helmut Eschwege (ed.), *Kennzeichen J: Bilder, Dokumente, Berichte zur Geschichte der Verbrechen des Hitlerfaschismus an den deutschen Juden 1933–1945*, with an introduction by Arnold Zweig ([East] Berlin, 1966) and by Klaus Drobisch, Rudi Goguel et al. (eds.), *Juden unterm Hakenkreuz: Verfolgung und Ausrottung der deutschen Juden 1933–1945* ([East] Berlin, 1973). Eschwege, a Holocaust survivor, who also contributed to the book about Jews under the Swastika, worked as a research librarian at Technical University of Dresden and was an academic outsider among GDR historians. See his memoirs *Fremd unter meinesgleichen: Erinnerungen eines Dresdner Juden* (Berlin, 1991). He was one of the few who managed to publish in the West. See his essay "Resistance of German Jews against the Nazi Regime," Leo Baeck Institute, *Year Book* (cited henceforth as: LBIYB), vol. XV (1970), 143–80. See also Kurt Pätzold, *Faschismus-Rassenwahn-Judenverfolgung: Eine Studie zur Strategie und Taktik des faschistischen deutschen Imperialismus 1933–1935* ([East] Berlin, 1975). For a detailed discussion of the topic, see Kurt Pätzold, "Persecution and the Holocaust: A Provisional Review of GDR Historiography," *LBIYB*, vol. XL (1995), 291–312.

25. For an overview of these initiatives, see Uwe Hecker, *Das historische Gedenken in der DDR zum 50. Jahrestag des Pogroms von 1938: Kommentierte Bibliographie* (Berlin, 1991). See also Kurt Pätzold and Irene Runge, *Pogromnacht 1938* ([East] Berlin, 1988).

26. See especially the seven-volume work *Kunst und Literatur im antifaschistischen Exil 1933–1945* (Leipzig, 1978–1983) that was published at the Academy Institute of the History of Literature, with Werner Mittenzwei, a renowned specialist on Brecht, as general editor.

27. In two books Klaus Mammach paid some attention to non-communist resistance. See his *Die deutsche antifaschistische Widerstandsbewegung 1933–1939* ([East] Berlin, 1974). The second edition came out under the title *Widerstand 1933–1939: Geschichte der deutschen antifaschistischen Widerstandsbewegung im Inland und in der Emigration* ([East] Berlin, 1984). See, by the same author, *Widerstand 1933–1945: Geschichte der deutschen antifaschistischen Widerstandsbewegung im Inland und in der Emigration* ([East] Berlin, 1987). These were the only overviews of the subjects that were published during the forty years of the history of the GDR, while there were many biographies of communist antifascists as well as books on local communist resistance. Karl Heinz Jahnke from the University of Rostock was particularly active in researching the youth resistance, even with reference to non-German resistance groups and currents. See, e.g., his *Jungkommunisten im Widerstand gegen den Hitlerfaschismus* ([East] Berlin, 1977).

28. The caesura was marked by East German commemorations of the fortieth anniversary of the attempt on Hitler's life on July 20, 1944. See Olaf Groehler and Klaus Drobisch, "Der 20. Juli 1944," *Einheit*, vol. 40 (1984), no. 7, 633–39. Of note are Kurt Finker's biographies of Count Stauffenberg (1967) and Count Moltke and the Kreisau Circle (1980). For self-critical evaluations, see Olaf Groehler, "Zur Geschichte des deutschen Widerstandes: Leistungen und Defizite," Reiner Eckert, Wolfgang Küttler, and Gustav Seeber (eds.), *Krise-Umbruch-Neubeginn: Eine kritische und selbstkritische Dokumentation der DDR-Geschichtswissenschaft* (Stuttgart, 1992), 408–18; *Werner Bramke, Freiräume und Grenzen eines Historikers* (Leipzig, 1998); Kurt Finker, *Zwischen Integration und Legitimation: Der antifaschistische Widerstand in Geschichtsbild und Geschichtsschreibung der DDR* (Leipzig, 1999).

29. The official eight-volume *Geschichte der deutschen Arbeiterbewegung* that was published in 1966 under the auspices of the SED Central Committee with Walter Ulbricht as general editor mentions the Moscow show trials only in brief. See vol. 5, 206–07.

30. See *Ernst Thälmann: Eine Biographie* ([East] Berlin, 1979), published by the Institute of Marxism-Leninism at the Central Committee of the SED. The book attained wide circulation with an inexpensive two-volume paperback edition.

31. See, among a vast amount of literature, Panikos Panayi, "Racial Violence in the new Germany," *Contemporary European History*, vol. 3(1994), no. 3, 265–87, and Mario Kessler, "The Extreme Right After German Unification: Is the Eastern Part of Germany a Special Case?" Krzysztof Glass et al. (eds.), *Fremde-Nachbarn-Partner wider Willen? Mitteleuropas alte/neue Stereotypen und Feindbilder* (Vienna and

Torun, 1995), 73–83. An enlarged version can be found under the title "The Fall of the Berlin Wall and the Radical Right in East Germany" in Mario Kessler, *On Anti-Semitism and Socialism: Selected Essays* (Berlin, 2005), 183–94. The English-language standard work on the subject is Gerard Braunthal, *Right-wing Extremism in Contemporary Germany* (Houndmills, 2010) (eds.).

32. No name but two examples: Wolfgang Schuller, then Professor of Ancient History at the University of Constance, remarked on the liquidation process that dismissed individuals who were not "tainted" by collaboration with the SED regime could apply as candidates for new academic appointments. In regard to the "politically tainted" he wrote: "Provided with a perhaps modest pension, they can do scholarly work." *Südkurier*, February 2, 1991. Even earlier, Jürgen Domes, Professor of Political Science at the University of Saarbrücken, congratulated the government on the liquidation decision and urged more thoroughgoing measures. See *Saarbrücker Zeitung*, December 29, 1990. Domes's condemnation of the East Germans included students who were involved in demonstrations, protest marches and hunger strikes in order to prevent wholesale measures against their teachers. For a critical review of the liquidation process and protests against it, see Karl Heinz Roth, "Anschlusshistoriker-Historikeranschluss," *1999: Zeitschrift für Sozialgeschichte des 20. und 21. Jahrhunderts*, vol. 16 (1991), no. 1, 8–12. See also Karl Heinz Roth's book *Anschließen, angleichen, abwickeln: Die westdeutschen Planungen zur Übernahme der DDR 1952 bis 1990* (Hamburg, 2000).

33. How East German historians continued working after being dismissed from universities and other academic institution, is the also subject of the essay by Stefan Berger, "Former GDR Historians in the Reunified Germany: An Alternative Historical Culture and its Attempts to Come to Terms with the GDR Past," *Journal of Contemporary History*, vol. 38 (2003), no. 1, 63–83. See also Marcus Aurin's essay in this volume (eds.).

8

Painful Transition and New Research on the History of Political Parties in Germany

MANFRED WEISSBECKER

When Mario Kessler and Axel Fair-Schulz suggested that I should report here as a historian of the GDR about my personal experiences from the time of "transformation," I was very delighted for the honorable offer. At the same time doubts tormented me. Those arose not only from my foreign-language inadequacies, for which I apologize. Even more, I was suspicious of my personal recollections and thoughts on the topic of my research: the history of political parties. I assumed that its results would not be very useful for the topic of the conference. However, my decision to participate was influenced by a *bon mot* of the French writer Albert Camus. In his novel *The Plague* he wrote of a generally well-known human behavior: if one speaks after catastrophes of different kind about a great number of victims, nobody is able to see the real extent. Hundred millions of corpses dispersed in the history are "nothing but smoke in the recollection," A dead person counts only if one has seen him dead. Above all, only a single, specific fate causes dismay and thoughtfulness.

The subject of our conference, however, hardly deals with dead people; you see me living and sitting in front of you. Yet, the quantitative aspect is of significance: after 1989–1990 as many as a million former GDR citizens have now lost their jobs largely for political reasons. Among them were many historians. This fact may fade away from contemporary awareness and is increasingly eclipsed by German unification as a supposed success story.

From another perspective one may come to very different conclusions, especially if one focuses on individual fates. In this sense, and as a historian who has been trained to think dialectically, I would like to elaborate on my own main subject of research: the history of political parties in Germany.

Let me start in 1945. The ten-year-old boy that I was at this time had witnessed the loss of many human lives at the end of the Second World War. The bombardment of Chemnitz, my hometown, let me to ask for the causes of war.

I found the first real answers when I came to Weimar in 1947. There I heard shocking facts about Buchenwald. I was told by former concentration camp inmates about the Oath of Buchenwald: "Never again war, never again Fascism!" This finally put me on a trajectory of critical scholarship and progressive political convictions. I wanted to contribute to the creation of a better Germany without war, oppression, and exploitation. For those idealistic reasons I joined the SED, the communist party in the GDR. I was outraged when I heard West German Chancellor Konrad Adenauer's statement that he prefers a half of Germany completely instead of 50 percent of a unified Germany. Basically Adenauer rejected the concept of a neutral but unified Germany in favor of a separate West German state that was fully integrated into NATO. As an alternative I supported the slogan "all Germans to a round-table" that the GDR offered in the 1950s, as a way to prepare a future reunification of the divided country. I was appalled by West Germany's reluctance to bring Nazi war criminals to justice, which was done much more systematically in the GDR.

Until 1958 I wished to become a high school history teacher, but was fortunate enough to end up as an assistant and later as a Professor of History at Friedrich Schiller University at Jena. There I started to research on communist antifascist resistance in Thuringia. Thus, I wrote a doctoral thesis on the subject dealing with the period of 1933 to 1935, which was followed by a Habilitation Thesis on German bourgeois parties at the end of the First World War and during the November Revolution of 1918. In 1972, I became full professor of German history and from 1983 to 1989 I was elected Dean (Provost in the American sense) of the School of Social Sciences at the University of Jena.

My everyday life was shaped by lectures, research projects, and administrative work. There was all conceivable joy as well as annoyance that are nowhere missing. I felt satisfied within the family and in my circle of friends, and also with the acquisitions that made life pleasant: a flat, a television set, a washing machine, and a car. With my family I also traveled a lot. Exciting holiday trips led to Eastern European countries. All-in-all it was a quite normal life. Nevertheless, since 1990 I hear again and again that my life was supposed to be a complete failure. I was not, and I am not now, willing to accept such judgments that demands my servility and subjugation.

The GDR was indeed a complex society with was characterized by a considerable degree of repression. In hindsight and compared with today's technical possibilities of surveillance and control East Germany's mechanism of repression were rather crude. My experiences make me very hesitant to label the GDR as nothing more but a repressive dictatorship while I do not want to belittle the dictatorial character of the regime.

Among the high point of my academic life was the publication and presentation of a multivolume collective project that dealt with political parties in Germany outside the labor parties. During the 1960s, I belonged to a large group of scholars that published a two-volume history of German bourgeois parties from the nineteenth century until 1945. A much larger version came out in four volumes between 1983 and 1986. All these books were reviewed in an overall positive way, including in West Germany. While our Marxist political premises were universally shared, the overall evaluations were increasingly professional and balanced. Even some West German historians considered our work as stimulating their own research. What followed were invitations for guest lectures, workshops, and discussions in West Germany. Without any exception, my colleagues and I felt accepted as partners and scholars, regardless of the fact that we were GDR citizens, Marxists, and Socialists. I still recall with great pleasure the joint research projects that leading West German professors Martin Broszat and later Hans-Erich Volkmann initiated and pursued with GDR historians.

Nobody could conceive of the watershed changes that were in store after 1989–1990, which were to turn our lives upside down. The worst-case scenario was for us the threat of a nuclear war, a war in which—as it was said—those would die second who had shot first. Preventing such a military disaster had priority in all thought and action; *Pro pace mundi*, hence, was the title of a series of publications of the University of Jena that I edited. This was part and parcel of the so-called "coalition of reason" which gathered antiwar activists from the political spectrum.

By the mid-1980s I became increasingly uneasy by the official tendency to replace a genuine commitment to social justice and peace with party conformity and opportunism. Discontent with the political and mental situation grew slowly within the GDR and even within the SED. I was still willing to partially accept certain restrictions that seemed to be an unavoidable consequence of the Cold War. Yet the utter lack of improvements within the GDR, particularly the selective and double-tongued information policy, struck me as unnecessary and even counter-productive. Within the relatively small realm that I could influence, I tried to improve the situation and help people in need. For example, I have tried to help the promotion of scholars based mainly on professional qualifications as opposed to mere party loyalty, sometimes with success.

It was a matter of reassurance that critical comments did not always fall on deaf ears. An example was the debate among GDR historians on the complexity of inheritance and tradition and also on the history of the German people and its contribution to world culture. That led to final renunciation of Erich Honecker's original thesis of a separate socialist German nation in the GDR. The last congress of GDR historians discussed in January 1989 openly the German-Soviet pact of August 1939 and its implications, although the Soviet magazine *Sputnik*, which dealt with this touchy issue, was confiscated and forbidden in East Germany just a few months ago, in November 1988.

The roundtable discussions of the congress focused on the shortcomings of official East German anti-fascism and its inability to effectively combat the growing underground neo-Nazi activities. It was the first time that this issue was problematized at an official symposium.

There was growing frustration with the paternalistic attitude of the SED leaders, their immobility and ossification. The party leader's refusal to accept the rising demands for an improved socialism in the time of "glasnost" and "perestroika" was astonishing and led, during the second half of the 1980s, to impatience and even outrage among the population and the rank-and-file party members. This outrage coincided with helplessness and paralysis on the part of the leadership while more and more East Germans fled to the West. Honecker's infamous sentence from August 1989 that those who leave the GDR deserve no tears let to widespread anger. On the other hand, the desire of many rank-and-file party members for structural reforms that would have made the GDR more attractive was not based on a coherent and realistic plan. There were no concrete ideas about how a transformation from the so-called democratic *centralism* to a viable *democratic socialism* could be carried out.

Thus I was personally disoriented about the "transformation" in the fall of 1989. In hindsight one cannot really justify or defend the party and state leadership. At that point it was far too late for any democratic renewal of the GDR. My personal reaction consisted of sullenness and discouragement. Dejection and resignation dominated my feelings and thinking for several weeks and months. For the first time, I began to fear for the future.

As someone who was born prior to the Cold War division of Germany into East and West, I welcomed peaceful German unification. On the other hand, I was very disturbed by the arrogant behavior of many West German politicians and opinion-makers who declared everything in East Germany as null and void. Many of East Germany's cultural and scholarly institutions were quickly and unilaterally dissolved by West German officials. According to the official announcement of the Federal Minister of Justice at that time, Klaus Kinkel, everything should be "de-legitimized" that characterized the GDR as an alternative to the bourgeois capitalist society. Those who had, in one way or the other, openly supported this alternative were fired from their positions. All-in-all, this concerned more than one million people.

For me, all this seemed to be the outcome of hatred, ignorance, and unscrupulous behavior of the conquerors that we could find often in history. The discrepancy between official slogans (such as "freedom of "scholarship," "pluralism," and "autonomy") and the reality—a discrepancy that was a character trait of the GDR—emerged anew. I found this new discrepancy as repulsive as the old one in the past. While a critical re-evaluation of the past was indeed necessary, an undifferentiated whole-scale dismissal resulted instead. 95 percent of the professors of the humanities and social sciences at the University of Jena lost their employment.

The dismissal caused a drastic turn in my life. It caused painful wounds. Without any consideration of my work as university teacher and scholar I was quickly dismissed and became unemployed. From that point on I lost the financial means to work systematically in archives and libraries. The new life was also characterized by a certain amount of opportunism on the part of some colleagues who looked for a chance to save their own careers at the expense of others. Some acquaintances even went to the other side of the street in order to avoid a conversation with me. Perhaps some were just afraid to be observed by the new West German professors when shaking hands with me. I was very hurt by this decline in the standards of civilized behavior. My relationship with social democratic, liberal, or conservative colleagues from West Germany deteriorated. It was only for a very brief period that East German historians had been considered as equal intellectual partners. The idea of the "ecumenism of historians," frequently invoked in the past, became obsolete quickly. West German colleagues who treated me with me respect until 1989 suddenly ignored me and my work altogether. Collegiality largely disappeared.

Until this day the history of the A*bwicklung* or dismissal of the GDR intelligentsia has not been examined thoroughly. Many of the files from that time period are still classified and thus not available to scholarly scrutiny. The legal basis for the sweeping dismissals of East German scholars is highly problematic.

The main purpose of those measures was to dismiss Marxist thinking and to exclude Marxists from academia. Careerists used their chances without scruples. The fact that many East German professors were approaching natural retirement within the next decade made their firings easier. Conveniently many East German professors were pushed into early retirement and their positions were immediately filled by West German candidates. Unfortunately, neither in the East nor the West was there any meaningful protest against the large-scale dismissal. If there was any protest at all it was primarily articulated by those scholars who themselves had experiences exile and professional marginalization after 1933.

I wonder how future historians may judge a policy that eliminated completely the educational system of the GDR, a system whose advantages of social security and universal access had been once considered positively by many West German intellectuals. East Germany was forced to accept the West German educational institutions and practices even though there was a growing consensus in West Germany prior to 1989 that the West German system itself was in need of structural reforms. German unification would have presented an opportunity to preserve and combine the best features of the West and the East German systems. Unfortunately, this opportunity was lost.

A few years after most East German scholars were pushed out of the historical profession, some key decision makers of this process stated that the main objective was not the destruction of people's careers, but the establishment of a new academic infrastructure. This does not correspond to reality, given the zeal of the *Abwicklung*. Such a line of argument purposely obscures the truth and misrepresents the essence of the transformation process and its inhumane aspects which, instead, was given the neutral-sounding term of *Elitenaustausch*, which translates literally as exchange of elites, but means in fact replacement of East German elites by West German ones. Dieter Simon, who, during the early 1990s was President of West Germany's *Wissenschaftsrat* (Supreme Academic Council) and thus mainly responsible for the procedures of *Abwicklung*, contested in 1995 that some West Germans who now taught as professors in the East hardly achieved the professional standards of their East German predecessors.

Incidentally, it was no East German professor but the West German liberal weekly newspaper *Die Zeit* that, as early as in the fall of 1990, characterized the methods of the large-scale dismissals as follows.

> Since the end of September, evaluation groups, comprised of scholars and bureaucrats from the Bonn Ministry of Science and Education, can be observed in [East German] academy institutes. In many places they left behind a virtual fright-trace like the one created by the envoys of the Holy Inquisition.

In this context one understands why the new "victors of history" have not yet presented a serious assessment of the transformation of academic institutions in East Germany. At this point most serious studies were published by the *Institut für Hochschulforschung* (Institute for the Research of Higher Learning) at the University of Halle-Wittenberg which is directed by Peer Pasternack, a renowned East German sociologist. Among those East German scholars who contributed to the research on *Abwicklung*, the historian Charles Melis, the literary historian Werner Mittenzwei, the neurologist Horst van der Meer, and the pathologist Arno Hecht, among others, should be mentioned.

The *Landesbüro Thüringen* (Thuringia Office) of the Luxemburg Foundation of which I was a co-founder has dealt thoroughly with the subject. Werner Röhr's impressive work on how the GDR historians have been treated still needs to be supplemented by works on other disciplines.[1]

Some of East Germany's dismissed university teachers and scientists fell into apathy and resignation. Figuratively speaking, they were buried by the ruins of the state socialism that failed. Others looked at how to navigate the new landscape. They tried to come to terms with the failure of the GDR. In some ways the now forcibly retired professors came to the conclusion, *De omnibus dubitandum est*, a conclusion at which they have arrived very late in life.

After my enforced retreat to the desk at home I continue, on my own, my work on the history and sociology of German political parties, primarily during the first half of the twentieth century. More than ever before I focus on the interconnections between political programs and political practice, especially vis-à-vis the concept of democracy.

Since the revolutions at the end of the First World War, the role of political parties could be interpreted as an intermediary element between state and society. They are constitutive factors for every modern political system in the West. From my viewpoint the twentieth century should not be exclusively seen as a century of political extremes, terrorist dictatorships, and murderous world wars, but should also be regarded as a century of a highly dynamic development of political parties and of divergent party systems. Basically, all modern political forms of party organizations have been tried out. It is impossible to understand the history of the twentieth and the early twenty-first centuries without a firm understanding of how political parties have shaped modern Western societies.

The primary function of political parties is to articulate and represent the political goals of specific interest groups and social classes within the context of capitalist competitive society.

In contrast to their claim to speak for the common interest—be it the state, the nation, the people, or the public good—political parties can, at least up to the present, not operate beyond their confined particular interests and egoism. Thus, particularistic interests triumph over common good, as parties compete over access to power and influence. As a consequence, party bureaucracies have grown in size and impact. In my understanding, healthy democracies also require the growth of institutions of civil society beyond the established form of party structures. Without a vibrant civil society, modern democracies can easily ossify under the weight of self-interested party bureaucracies.

It is regrettable that in today's discourse the research of East German experts, as it was particularly practiced by the Research Group of Comparative Party History at the University of Jena, is largely ignored. The website of the Institute of History at the University of Jena mentions East German research only briefly—after a long passage on how the SED policy instrumentalized historical scholarship. It is now the commonplace for West German scholars to assume that, if there was any serious research in the GDR it was achieved despite rather than because of the presence of the official East German state.

Contrary to the dominant present assumption that scholarship in the GDR was purely monolithic there were in fact lively and to some extent controversial debates among historians that concerned both methodological and conceptual issues. For example, more than fifty issues of *Jenaer Beiträge zur Parteiengeschichte*, a periodical that was devoted to comparative party history, demonstrate a distinctive variety of standpoints that were expressed by a great number of contributors. Such debates mainly focused on the role of single parties and their specific function within different party systems. A variety of approaches were articulated on topics, such as the history of German liberalism or the place of the Catholic Center Party in the history of Imperial and Weimar Germany. Particular emphasis was placed on the genesis and trajectory of the non-proletarian parties and their democratic legacy.

Considering my own work, I would mention the debates on the relationship of economic and policy issues in the Nazi Party. In addition, I should mention my essays on the party system and the leaders of bourgeois parties during the Weimar Republic. Some of those publications resulted from the annual Colloquiums on Fascism that were held in Jena between 1971 and 1990. These colloquia were well known for their undogmatic exchange of views among GDR scholars and some left-leaning historians from the Federal Republic of Germany.

East German scholars did not see the twelve years of Nazi rule as a "white spot" in history. Our works emphasized the role of the Nazi Party and its leadership as *the* power center of Nazi Germany. This approach differs from the conventional "Marxist-Leninist" line that the Nazi Party and its leaders were merely an instrument of monopoly capitalism. On the other hand, our studies illustrate how the Nazi Party during the Weimar Republic became increasingly integrated into the broader right-wing of the anti-democratic conservative spectrum. We emphasized the capitalist character of the Nazi Party despite its partial anti-capitalist rhetoric and, therefore, we used the term "German Fascism" instead of the misleading self-description as "National Socialism" in order to depict the social order in Germany between 1933 and 1945.

In retrospect a theoretical weakness can hardly be neglected. The term "*bürgerlich*" (bourgeois), as we used it in the GDR as a general category, included all political forces that were part of the capitalist system and could thus be identified with the "capitalist order." In short, this was an oversimplification of Marxist theoretical thought. The simplistic confrontation of "bourgeois" and "proletarian" parties in the historical narrative did not permit a broader approach toward the complexity of social reality.

It was a cardinal mistake to exclude the SPD, the German Social Democratic Party, and the KPD, the German Communist Party, from our research on the history of German political parties. This had to lead to selective and fragmentary results. It was impossible to discuss the political mistakes and shortcomings that characterized the KPD during the time of the Weimar Republic, particularly since Ernst Thälmann was made the party leader in late summer of 1925.

In the early stages of our research we considered political parties as a link between the state and the apparatus of economic rulers, while, when our work progressed, we came to emphasize increasingly the chances and limitations of mass support for bourgeois parties. In the final analysis we found that the dominant bourgeois parties, despite all their maneuvers and particularistic interests, worked toward stabilizing capitalist rule. Yet our analysis over-emphasized the degree to which bourgeois parties merely executed the political will of the capitalist class. Here we remained devoted to Lenin's theory of imperialism and even to the Procrustean bed in which an oversimplified Marxism-Leninism confined the mutual relationship between party, state, and class interests in the age of imperialism.

At the same time our approach toward the masses was contradictory. On the one hand, we saw their seduction (as we see it now in the time of an all-embracing manipulative advertisement). On the other hand, we followed the dogma according to which the masses are genuine agents of a predetermined and predictable historical process in which capitalism will inevitably succeeded by communism. The masses were not seen as an object *and* at the same time as a subject of policy. Only one aspect or the other was considered. As a consequence, there was a lack of research on party sociology. Social-psychological issues were only mentioned in brief. While we wrote about the desirability of an interdisciplinary approach, we failed to practice it. This resulted from our somewhat one-sided research plans that were limited to singly disciplines and also from traditional disciplinary divisions according to which historians should strictly do historical research without utilizing sociological or psychological methods.

A comprehensive Marxist theory of the party in and of itself (*Parteiwesen*) has yet to be developed. Historians still examine primarily the history of single parties, while sociologists and political scientists draw their attention mainly to party systems and to mechanisms of party democracy and the party state. Our own research project from the mid-1980s, the investigation of a complex problem that we called "the political organization of the bourgeois society," should be remembered as a contribution to a more complex approach of the interactions between parties and other components of bourgeois society. The primary aim of this project was to examine the totality of institutions and organizations that constitute the political life of society and is thus determined by the complexity of different interests.

Without the collapse of the GDR and the severe destruction of Marxist education and research after 1989–1990, what results of the research on the history of political parties in Jena are still valid today? The answer can only be speculative. But be it as it may, a critical approach of the capitalist party system is a greater necessity than ever before. Its structural deficits are only too visible. Corruption, patronage, unlawful policy, scandals, etc. seem only to be the tip of an iceberg. The fundament is rotten, in spite of seeming triumphs during the last decade of the twentieth century. *Parteienverdrossenheit* or open disgust with party politics and declining support for of political parties are widespread. For almost any traditional political party it becomes more and more difficult to recruit new and younger members, mainly young members.

More and more people are outraged about how politicians hide their true aims behind the smokescreen of pure propaganda slogans and the misuse of power. Around 50 percent of all Germans have expressed widespread disillusionment with the party system. Nearly 80 percent of the Germans consider their politicians as dishonest; many doubt their competence to solve crucial problems. On election days all this is confirmed by alarmingly high figures of non-voters, whose number has now become larger than that of the electorate of any political party. People criticize the growing uniformity of the various political programs as well as the pragmatic ignorance of programmatic principles, the routine break of promises, etc. The huge number and magnitude of such phenomena is indicative for the growing violation of democratic principles.

However, as long as political parties exist and continue to exist, critically minded research on the topic is a necessity. This perspective may be an overly optimistic outlook at the end of this essay. The society that has dismissed us East German scholars over two and a half decades ago still warrants to be critically analyzed. It is my hope that the scholarly efforts made by my GDR colleagues and myself will make a however modest contribution toward building a more just and inclusive society.

Translated by Axel Fair-Schulz and Mario Kessler

Note

1. Werner Röhr, *Abwicklung: Das Ende der Geschichtswissenschaft der DDR*, Vol. 1: *Analyse einer Zerstörung* (Berlin, 2011); Vol. 2: *Analyse ausgewählter Forschungen, Übersichten, Register* (Berlin, 2012).

9

Research on Conservatism in Jena

The Beginning and the End of an Interdisciplinary Research Project

LUDWIG ELM

Around 1970, a circle of right-wing intellectuals in West Germany started to revive a neo-conservative discourse. Their aim was to rehabilitate and to renew an ideological current that had been discredited and ended in disaster in 1945. For this purpose the *Deutschlandstiftung e. V.* was founded in 1966–67. Honorary chairman of this society was no other than Konrad Adenauer, the first Chancellor of the Federal Republic of Germany. He gave his name for the yearly award of the *Deutschlandstiftung* and attended its opening session in February 1967, just a few weeks before his death. West German scholars, such as Kurt Lenk, Helga Grebing, Martin Greiffenhagen, Hans-Gerd Schumann, and Kurt Sontheimer, a specialist of the history of the Weimar Republic, discussed the activities of the *Deutschlandstiftung* in critical perspective.

Authors from the GDR also discussed the neo-conservative publications, but after 1969, when the influence of Christian-conservative parties[1] in West Germany seemed to fade, they, and also the SED leadership, devoted less attention to these writings. This was, however, a superficial perception. In reaction to social democratic political and cultural dominance during the era of détente, a great number of conservative periodicals, foundations, associations, and publishing houses were established. They all were part of a conservative backlash. The main figure among conservative politicians and ideologists was Franz Josef Strauss, long-time chairman of the Christian Social Union and Minister-President of the State of Bavaria.[2]

There was a growing interest in conservative politics and ideology during the second half of the 1970s. The political revival of conservatism was marked by the victories of Margaret Thatcher and Ronald Reagan in the British and U.S. elections in 1979 and 1980, respectively. Even in France the Nouvelle Droite, represented by the Front National, achieved spectacular success in the election to the European Parliament in 1979. In West Germany, Social Democratic Chancellor Helmut Schmidt lost support in his own party, and the "social-liberal coalition" had to face a grave political crisis. But it was in October 1982, that the Free Democratic Party under Hans-Dietrich Genscher and Otto Graf Lambsdorff switched sides from their earlier coalition with the Social Democrats to support the CDU and CSU in their constructive vote of no confidence to have Schmidt replaced with Helmut Kohl (CDU) as West German Chancellor. Just at this time, the proceedings of the first colloquium on conservatism that had taken place on March 14 and 15, 1981, with participants from Bulgaria, Czechoslovakia, Poland, the Soviet Union, and East and West Germany were published.[3]

A reviewer overestimated the coincidence of the two events. "The timeline of research and the presentation of results show at a glance how carefully the authors watched the downfall of the social-liberal coalition, and it is no surprise that the book came out exactly during the 'turn' in Bonn."[4] The Institute for Society and Science (*Institut für Gesellschaft und Wissenschaft* or IGW) at the University of Erlangen-Nuremberg that specialized in research on the GDR, stated in a 1981 report "that the scholarly and intellectual level of GDR publications on conservative theory and politics has improved remarkably."[5]

In 1978, an interdisciplinary "Research Group on Conservatism" was founded in the GDR which promoted research on international and historical aspects of conservatism as an influential component of political thought. This group was initiated by a circle of researchers at the University of Jena that had already established a series of bi-annual workshops and publications.[6]

This emerging network included mainly historians, philosophers, economists, and legal experts from the universities of Jena, Halle, and Berlin, and also from the Academy of Sciences, the Academy of State and Law at Potsdam-Babelsberg, and the Academy of Social Sciences. Three international conferences were organized in Jena in May 1981, June 1986, and June 1990. Conference proceedings and further joint publications came out. Besides that, bi-annual German-Polish workshops resulted, in 1985, in the formation of a joint research group on "*Deutsche Problematik*" (German problems). Further international contacts have been established since then.

The main theoretical issues that were discussed in all these conferences and workshops included: social and economic foundations of modern conservatism, conservatism and neo-liberalism, political and intellectual traditions of conservatism since the eighteenth century in international perspective, progress and *Menschenbild* (concept of humankind) in conservative thought, modern authoritarian concepts of rule and its implications, conservative attitudes toward armament and military, war and peace, nationalism, anti-socialism and rightist theories of totalitarianism, conservatism and right-wing extremism, *Vergangenheitsbewältigung* (coming to terms with the past), historical revisionism, and politics of memory.

At the second conference in June 1986 the Inter-disciplinary Center for Research on Conservatism (*Interdisziplinäres Zentrum für Konservatismusforschung* or IZK) was constituted. It was one of three centers for social research at the University of Jena, which also included Centers for Classical Philosophy and Literature and for the History of German Bourgeois Parties until 1945. Scholars from twelve countries participated in the founding conference. In his keynote lecture Ludwig Elm emphasized that conservatism in the United States, the United Kingdom, West Germany, Japan, and other countries "had proven its ability to adapt to different political conditions and had demonstrated its durability. Its main analysis and social critique was, according to Elm, connected with "acute existential questions and future issues that humankind is dealing with," mainly the securing of peace.[7] Seven subgroups at this conference discussed themes that related to political problems of the United States and West Germany, as well as on the political right in the United Kingdom, France, Denmark, Austria, Greece, Turkey, Japan, India, Chile, and South Africa.

In 1985 an essay collection was published which dealt with Ronald Reagan's plan of a "New World Order." Within the context of the coming presidential elections in the United States, the IZK and other East German researchers on the United States organized a joint colloquium on November 24, 1988. Professor Claus Montag, head of the *Problemrat USA-Forschung*, an advisory council with the research focus on the United States attached to the Ministry of Higher Education, gave an inaugural lecture on American conservative politics on the eve of the 1990s. The report stated "that all participants agreed on the assumption that the coming decade would be determined by conservative governments in the US and most of capitalist countries. Since the East-West relations are at a turning point, socialist countries have to take this fact into account."[8] Only one year later the world at large came to a real turning point.

In 1988 the author of this paper was awarded a grant of the International Research and Exchange Program (IREX) and could visit Georgetown and Stanford Universities between March and July. In 1989 and 1990 he presented results of East German research on conservatism at West German universities in Tübingen and Bonn as well as at the Konrad Adenauer Foundation of the CDU and the social democratic Friedrich Ebert Foundation. He also offered a talk at the editorial office of *Criticón*, a conservative journal, in Munich.

A report noted "that East German scholars evaluate now the political right in the Federal Republic with more nuances than before. In a discussion at Friedrich Ebert Foundation [. . .] Professor Ludwig Elm, who leads a center for research on conservatism in Jena, refuted the once-popular assumption that the term 'Fascism' could be applied to diverse political movements in a broad sense."[9] In the GDR, political conservatism used to be seen, for too long, as a monolith. Today, the struggle for peace on the part of conservative currents is "generally acknowledged."[10] Another West German author empathized that East German scholars now include conservative partners in their ideological concept of a "coalition of reason."[11] This term referred to a pragmatic alliance of individuals and parties across the ideological spectrum. Furthermore, "most recent [East German] publications show a remarkably nuanced picture of the different currents within conservatism that correspond closely to reality." All-in-all, "Western conservatism is no longer perceived as a monolithic militaristic bloc. Instead, it is seen as differentiated forces, some of which promote and some of which hinder détente."[12]

In the beginning of September 1989 the 5th German-Polish Bilateral Conference took place at the College for Naval Sciences in Wustrow-Warnemünde at the Baltic Sea. The first section of the conference was organized jointly with the Mayor's Office of the City of Rostock and was devoted to the 50th anniversary of Nazi Germany's attack on Poland. Marian Rauszer, the Polish Consul-General in the GDR, attended the conference which dealt, in the light of historical experiences, with issues of European peace and security politics. It was inevitable that the conference had to deal with the crises, turns, new developments and their implications in the hitherto "socialist countries."

At the end of November of the same year the IZK organized a joint symposium with the West German *Vereinigung der Verfolgten des Naziregimes/Bund der Antifaschisten* (VVN/BdA), an association of former Nazi concentration camp inmates, in Jena. The symposium took place under the impact of the recent political changes in the East, as well as of the electoral successes of right-wing parties, mainly the nationalist Republikaner Party in the West. At the same time, there were also the first publicly acknowledged neo-Nazi activities in the GDR. A joint appeal of the IZK and the VVN/

BdA formulated as ultimate task "that it is most necessary to explore the roots of right-wing extremism in both [German] societies, even though the reasons for them may be different in the East and the West." Antifascism was defined as a "necessary component and guiding principle of democracy." It should be seen as a "litmus test of any group, organization, or party. What we need is a broad coalition of all democrats without the dominance of anyone group."[13]

From June 13 to 15, 1990, the 3rd IZR International Colloquium on "Conservatism and Progress" was held in Jena. It was devoted to the 200th anniversary of the publication of Edmund Burke's *Reflections on the Revolution in France* (London, 1790). Coincidentally, on the eve of this conference, the 175th anniversary of the foundation of the first student fraternity (*Urburschenschaft*) was celebrated in the university's main lecture hall. Until 1990, fraternities were banned in East Germany, while they had been reestablished in the West already in the 1950s. Their members attended this festivity in their original colored hats (red-black-gold with a golden oak leave's cluster) and were portrayed positively in the local press. However, this revival of the fraternities was also seen as part of the increasingly conservative atmosphere which developed during of the German unification process in 1990.

Around fifteen West German scholars participated at the IZR colloquium, among them were the professors Klaus Hornung, Hans-Hellmuth Knütter, Kurt Lenk, and Hans-Gerd Schumann, as well as participants from Austria, Bulgaria, Finland, France, Hungary, Poland (eight participants came from this country), Romania, the Soviet Union, Sweden, and the United States.

In his inaugural lecture Ludwig Elm compared the transformations of 1789 and 1989/90. "It is only consequent that the current conservative intellectual critique on Jacobinism and its implications and consequences, takes the fiasco of 'real existing socialism' as a proof for their general refutation of any revolutionary program. This critique implies a continuity from Jacobinism to Stalinism and suggests that 'real existing socialism' was developed directly out of the Enlightenment and the French Revolution. From a conservative perspective the historical failure of socialism between 1917 and 1990 has to be seen as the coming to an end of two and a half centuries of 'modernity.' The new era of 'post-modernity' is really a return to conservatism within the framework of global capitalism."[14]

Within this context Elm advocates a re-reading of conservative authors. "Some of their theoretical explications may be outdated but others have to be considered as relevant for contemporary scholarly work and its ethical, social, and methodological implications."[15] He came to reject self-critically the dogma that the contemporary epoch was supposed to be characterized by a global transition from capitalism to socialism as far too mechanistic. Instead, one should investigate similarities and differences between liberal, conservative, and Marxist critique of capitalism as recent East German research had already started to explore. "This requires an examination of the mutual relationships and overlapping of conservative and right-wing extremist currents and tendencies."[16] New trends in East and West had to be analyzed within the context of the experiences of the downfall of the Weimar Republic. A key question for the near future and the newly united Germany will be a reassurance of Germany's neighbors that past aggressions will not be repeated. The symposium stated that one of the next tasks would be a discussion about the issue what the term "progress" means in different social contexts.[17]

The reviews of the symposium in East and West were rather positive. Lisbeth Weihe-Lindenborg, a West German reporter, stressed the proficiency and openness of the symposium. She suggested that "Jena should become a center for the coordinating activities of European research on conservatism. Like no other place, Jena would provide participants in a European network with scholarly competence and with a great amount of publications in that field of research. That would be most relevant with regard to the unifying process of Europe."[18]

Even the rightist-conservative political scientist, Klaus Hornung (University of Stuttgart-Hohenheim), acknowledged an "open approach" on part of East German Marxist scholars that should not be excluded from public discourse. "Marxist research cannot be neglected without significant losses, especially during the process of unification."[19] Hornung published his contribution to the symposium in the journal *Mut* (No. 277, September 1990) and wrote a conference report in *Criticón*, where he considered "facets of new orientation" and a "remarkably high level of proficiency among younger [East German] scholars, especially in the field of the history of ideas." According to Hornung, Western "triumphalism is inappropriate and counter-productive. It is likewise incorrect to dismiss this [reorientation of East German researchers] only and everywhere in terms of opportunism." He diagnosed a "re-orientation even among party ideologists that should be considered as honest and serious."[20] The Western professors Kurt Lenk, Technical University of Aachen, and Karl Ucakar, University of Vienna, who had participated in the symposium, provided positive reviews of Ludwig Elm in the process of scholarly evaluation that the Academic Senate of the Jena University carried out. In September 1990, Hans-Joachim Meyer (CDU), Minister of Science and Education in the freely elected conservative government of Lothar de Maizière, gave his approval for Ludwig Elm's remaining at the university as full professor. He was nonetheless dismissed from his university position at the end of 1992, as new laws and regulations were introduced after German unification.

Due to the turmoil of the monetary union of June 1, 1990, the proceedings of the last IZR conference were never published. Likewise, the publication of the journal *Konservatismus-Forschung* with its workshop reports and reviews, was discontinued. Since October 3, 1990, the day of German unification, financial problems coincided with the mass dismissals of the personnel of East German universities, cultural institutions, and the media, who were replaced by West German newcomers.

This resulted in the discontinuation of the large-scale project *Handbook of Conservatism*, which began in 1987 and was slated to be published in 1993. The two last issues of *Konservatismus-Forschung* included preliminary articles that were planned for this handbook, such as entries on Franz Josef Strauss (by Manfred Behrend/No. 11) and on the Political Action Committees (by Gerhard Fischer), the Gesellschaft fur Deutschlandforschung or Society for Research on Germany (by Gustav Korner and Michael Sielaff), and the right-wing West German politician Hans-Christoph Seebohm (by Konstanze Tenner/all in No. 12).[21] A bibliography of research on conservatism in the GDR between 1971 and 1990 could still be published, as could be a collection of essays on conservative ideas and its representatives during the nineteenth and twentieth centuries.[22] The publisher, Akademie-Verlag, did not advertise or promote this publication.[23] The two-volume history of the university, which was published in 2008, dealing with the period between 1945 and 1990, did not mention a single page of research on conservatism in its more than eighty contributions on around 2,300 pages.[24]

The conservative writer Caspar von Schreck-Notzing, however, paid attention to East German research until its end and thereafter. As early as 1980 he had written a review article on the subject, in which he stated: "In 1972 Elm had started with a detailed study on West German universities and neo-Nazi tendencies (*Hochschule und Neofaschismus*). Several studies by [East German] authors on conservative anthropology, historical writing, pedagogy, etc. made adequate assessments. The exact source-based research by GDR authors needs particularly to be mentioned."[25]

Von Schreck-Notzing mentioned, in a short review of the last two issues of *Konservatismus-Forschung* and the abovementioned bibliography, that the end of the GDR also meant the end of a field of study that had no equivalent in the West: the comparative research on conservatism. "The more East German scholars had developed their research, the more they refrained from simplistic generalizations and from black-and-white clichés. From confrontation to serious scholarly approach was the leitmotif that Professor Ludwig Elm had propagated." These last publications illustrate this trend.[26]

Contrary to the expectations of Western participants in the last Jena symposium which was directed toward a fruitful cooperation and equal partnership, German unification was executed as an absorption of the GDR into the Federal Republic of Germany, and not as a merger of two equal partners. The primacy of politics dictated an unconditional surrender and a demand of the servility on the part of the East Germans toward their new Western overlords.

Ludwig Elm was a member of the Academic Senate of the University of Jena from 1971 until May 1991. Thus, he could observe the transformation of the university very closely. Most of the newly appointed professors from the West were full of prejudices vis-à-vis their East German colleagues. Contrary to their self-image as fair and open-minded, a rather large number of them exhibited prejudices and a high degree of paternalism. Equally distasteful was the old-new opportunism of some of those East German professors who were allowed to remain in their academic positions.

In the fall of 1990, the IZK, facing the coming dismissal of its members, reconstituted itself as a research group for the history and politics of comparative political ideas (*Abteilung Vergleichende Ideengeschichte*) at the University of Jena. It ceased to exist in September 1991. The interviews, or better, interrogations conducted by the Committee on Structure and Personnel with former East German members of the IZR, were only formal proceedings, and, as a predetermined result, all of them were sacked in a "post-unification purge." This large-scale dismissal contrasted remarkably with the rather indulgent treatment of former Nazi professors in West Germany after 1945. Thus, the character of German unification of October 3, 1990, under conservative auspices, confirmed much of the analysis made by East German scholars.

It was not least of all this situation that encouraged the author of this paper to continue and to broaden his research on trends in West German conservatism. This resulted in his book, *German Conservatism after Auschwitz*, which was published in 2007. It tried to demonstrate the interdependence of historical and contemporary issues that have shaped and still shape conservatism as a highly relevant current in politics.[27]

Translated by Axel Fair-Schulz and Mario Kessler

Notes

1. Christian Democratic Union (CDU) and Christian Social Union in Bavaria (CSU).

2. See Ludwig Elm, *Der 'neue' Konservatismus in der BRD* (East Berlin, 1974). A West German edition came out simultaneously; a Polish edition was published in Poznan in 1979 and a Russian edition in 1980 in Moscow.

3. Ludwig Elm (ed.), *Konservatismus in der BRD: Wesen, Erscheinungsformen, Traditionen* (East Berlin, 1982).

4. Manfred Wilke, "Zeitplan," *Capital*, no. 12 (1982), 181.

5. Dieter Walz, *Konservative Ideologie und Politik in der Bundesrepublik Deutschland: Jenaer Kolloquium vom 14. und 15. Mai 1981* (*Informationen zur Wissenschaftsentwicklung und politik in der DDR*, no. 6 (September 1982), front page.

6. In 1976, a special issue of *Beiträge der Friedrich-Schiller-Universität* (FSU) Jena: "Konservative Ideologie und Politik in der BRD," came out. In the same journal, in 1981 and 1983, edition under the same title were published (nos. 2–4), and between 1985 and 1990, nos. 5 to 12 were devoted to "Konservatismus-Forschung." Nos. 4 and 5 (1981) of the journal of the Friedrich Schiller University (*Wissenschaftliche Zeitschrift*) were also devoted to the subject and included more than fifty contributions. See Michael Eckardt, "Die Schriftenreihe 'Konservatismus-Forschung' der FSU Jena 1976–1990 [ed. by Ludwig Elm and Claus Remer]: Gesamtbibliographie)," *Hoffnungen, Enttäuschungen, Neue Erkundungen: Deutsche Hochschullandschaft in der "Wende." Das Beispiel Friedrich-Schiller-Universität. Protokollband* (Jena, 2007), 153–174.

7. Ludwig Elm, "Geschichtlicher Platz und soziales Wesen des Konservatismus der achtziger Jahre," *Deutsche Zeitschrift für Philosophie*, no. 2 (1987), 97.

8. Heidelinde Steinbrück, "Tagungsbericht," *Konservatismus-Forschung*, Nr. 11 (1990), S. 103. See the contributions of the conference, ibid., 6–79.

9. Helmut Lölhöffel, "DDR nähert sich Konservativen: Rechtes politisches Lager wird differenzierter gesehen," *Frankfurter Rundschau*, June 14, 1989. The article referred to a lecture of Ludwig Elm on the previous day.

10. Ibid.

11. Uwe Ziegler, "Die neue Sicht der DDR zur 'Systemauseinandersetzung,' " *Aus Politik und Zeitgeschichte. Beilage zur Wochenzeitung Das Parlament*, B 34/89, August 18, 1989, 33.

12. Ibid.

13. Resolution, as quoted in: *Konservatismus-Forschung*, no. 12 (1990), 109. See the report about the symposium ibid., 107 *et seq.*

14. Ludwig Elm, *Einführungsreferat auf dem III. Internationalen Konservatismus-Kolloquium* (Jena, June 1990), 7 (unpublished manuscript).

15. Ibid., 12.

16. Ibid.

17. See ibid.

18. Michael Schäf and Heidelinde Steinbrück, "Kritische Inventur und prinzipielle Neuansätze," *Alma mater Jenensis*, nos. 13/14 (July 11, 1990), 7.

19. "TLZ-Gespräch mit dem Stuttgarter Prof. Klaus Hornung über Konservatismus," *Thüringische Landeszeitung*, June 22, 1990, 5.

20. Klaus Hornung, "Beginn eines substantiellen Dialogs?" *Criticón*, no. 121 (September/October 1990), 228.

21. *Konservatismus-Forschung*, no. 11 (1990), 86–93 and no. 12 (1990), 79–95.

22. See Gabriele Winkel and Konstanze Tenner, *Konservatismusforschung in der DDR 1971–1990: Auswahlbibliographie* (Jena, 1990) (Bibliographische Mitteilungen der Universitätsbibliothek Jena, No. 53). This bibliography includes 1,755 items and a register of names. See also Ludwig Elm (ed.), *Falsche Propheten: Studien zum konservativ-antidemokratischen Denken im 19. und 20. Jahrhundert*. 2nd enl. ed. (Berlin, 1990). The authors of the chapters were Dorit Dirlam, Ludwig Elm, Eberhard Fromm, Herbert Gottwald, Heinz Malorny, Roland Meister, Joachim Petzold, and Günther Rudolph. The first East German edition was published in 1984 under the same title, while the West German edition came out as *Leitbilder des deutschen Konservatismus* in Cologne at the same year. The second edition included new chapters on clerical conservatism and on the ideologists Carl Schmitt and Ernst Jünger.

23. See the review of Hans-Martin Gerlach, in: *Konservatismus-Forschung*, no. 12 (1990), 119–121.

24. See Uwe Hoßfeld, Tobias Kaiser, and Heinz Mestrup (eds.), *Hochschule im Sozialismus: Studien zur Geschichte der Friedrich-Schiller-Universität Jena (1945–1990)*, 2 vols. (Cologne and Weimar, 2007).

25. [Caspar von Schreck-Notzing,] "CSN berichtet: Konservatismus-Forschung in der DDR," *Criticón*, no. 57 (January/February 1980), 8. The issue no. 34 (1976) of the same journal had reprinted an article by Ludwig Elm that was originally published in the East German newspaper *Sonntag*, January 25, 1976.

26. *Criticón*, no. 125 (May/June 1991), 152.

27. See Ludwig Elm, *Der deutsche Konservatismus nach Auschwitz: Von Adenauer und Strauss zu Stoiber und Merkel* (Cologne, 2007).

10

The Dissolution of East German Economic History at the Economic University in Berlin-Karlshorst

A Typical *Anschluss* Procedure

JÖRG ROESLER

In this paper I will first explore what happened to a group of economic historians, who taught at the GDR Economic University in Berlin-Karlshorst. Then I will make some comparisons about their fate, which was typical for GDR academics after the *Wende,* with university personnel in other countries and at other times, namely academics who were in similar situations. My aim is to explain by this approach the true reasons for their individual fate, which many scholars have had difficulties up to now in fully understanding.

The group of university teachers and researchers that I focus on was headed by the famous professor Hans Mottek, who, as a Jew and a communist, was forced into exile to Great Britain and Palestine at the beginning of the Nazi rule in Germany. He returned to East Germany after World War II and became the first professor of economic history at the Economic University of the GDR, which was founded in 1950.[1] His three textbooks about German economic history from the Stone Age to 1945 were not only used by GDR students but also at the universities of the Federal Republic of Germany.[2] He became the founder of what was called the "Mottek School" of economic history. Since the 1970s the team of professor Mottek, composed of three to four younger professors and six or seven younger lecturers, was mainly engaged in international economic history. The main focus was on Eastern Europe. At the center of their research were questions about the reasons for the economic backlog of Eastern European countries compared with Western European ones in the interwar period. In connection with this topic, research was conducted into the then ever-growing indebtedness of Eastern European countries to Western Europe.

The questions became relevant again during the 1970s and 1980s, and indebtedness has been a major problem of the Eastern European countries since then. Books pamphlets by the Mottek team were published about the economic history of Eastern Europe, as well as numerous articles in scholarly journals like the international well-known *Jahrbuch für Wirtschaftsgeschichte*. The Mottek group had close working contacts with the economic historians at the universities in the capitals of Czechoslovakia, Poland, Hungary, Romania, and Bulgaria. They also took part in numerous international conferences about East European economic history. During the first and second year of their curriculum all students at the Economic University had to take part in lectures on economic history offered by Mottek or his team.

At the beginning of the unification process around 1990 the members of the Mottek School felt relatively confident regarding their personal future. They assumed they would keep their jobs according to article 38 of the Treaty of Unification. They did not fear the West German criteria of academic qualification because of their high level of economic research and teaching, they had been highly respected by their West German colleagues until 1989, and they were well-known to economic historians in Western Europe and Japan. Even when East German scholars found out about the rigid criteria for evaluation that would be applied to them by West German commissions, the associates of the Mottek School still felt very confident.

The German Unification Treaty of 1990 outlined the criteria for individual reviews of civil servants, including university professors and lecturers, to determine whether they were qualified to keep their positions, in accordance with Western standards. The economic historians were convinced that they would get positive answers to the three central questions for the teaching personal at GDR universities, raised by the various appointed commissions and committees:

1. Professional achievement;
2. Victimization or degree of complicity;
3. Programmatic need (whether their research profile was still in demand).

However, the economic historians of the Mottek School were never formally evaluated. Yet, most of them lost their positions at the end of June 1991, half a year after the official dissolution (*Abwicklung*) of the Economic University at Berlin-Karlshorst by the Berlin regional government. The last scholars had to leave by the end of September 1991. Later on, the institution, while teaching continued, was transformed into a part of a West Berlin-based College (*Fachhochschule*) for Economy and Technology. Like most of the GDR academics, the Mottek scholars were replaced—if their lines were continued at all—by newly appointed Western professors.

Why did this happen? The answer seems simple: anybody who did not teach business or business administration-like subjects, was at that university part of the Department of Marxism-Leninism. This large department included a broad variety of scholars, ranging from philosophers and political economists to labor and economic historians. Researchers and teachers from this department would be automatically dismissed according to the German Unification Treaty that closed every Department of Marxism-Leninism at any institution of higher learning in East Germany without any recourse.

No scholar from the Mottek School would be able to find a professorial position later on. This was common for people from academic institutions that were dissolved "wholesale."[3] The quip that "the red oxen have to leave the farm" became widespread.

Seen superficially, the economic historians from Berlin-Karlshorst were simply unlucky and their fate could be interpreted as that of a small group of highly qualified scholars who, because of administrative decisions made during the GDR period, had been stuck among a group of people which was easily dismissed as mere ideologues. The question remains: Why did these economic historians not resist their dismissal which seemed to be based largely on an administrative miscategorization?

Or did they? Indeed, the professors—Mottek died in 1993—undertook a lot of initiatives in this direction. They wrote petitions to the Berlin State Senator for Science and Education, Manfred Erhardt, and also sent letters of protest to the Federal Ministry of Science and Education in Bonn. In addition, they even informed the President of the Federal Republic of Germany, Richard von Weizsäcker, the Foreign Minister, Hans-Dietrich Genscher (a native East German), and forwarded an appeal to the World Federation of Scientists. They also started to redesign the university according to Western standards. These efforts were supported by the students as well, many of whom protested, demonstrated, and even blockaded the road in front of the university buildings on one of the main streets of Berlin. However, all this proved to be in vain.

Some members of the Mottek School were allowed, after their dismissals, to teach at the refounded college in Berlin-Karlshorst as adjuncts. None of them got a permanent job in their fields again. Some went to the labor courts and sued against their "*Abwicklung*." Some started to write local or business history on their own, with impressive publications, while others withdrew from scholarly life altogether.

While some of their former colleagues in the Eastern European countries, one and a half decades later, finished their academic career at retirement age and were widely honored by the scholarly community, such as the economic historian and Professor at the Czech Economic University in Prague, Václav Prucha, the members of the Mottek School were pushed out of the German scholarly community and seemingly forgotten by the majority of West German economic historians.

The very different fate of their colleagues in Eastern Europe can be explained not by their different qualifications or their political engagement (more or less) before 1990, but with one word: *Anschluss*. *Anschluss* means an asymmetrical unification, when the dominating part (the "mainland") imposes its political, economic, legal, and educational structures over the other part (the "*Anschluss* area"). In 1990–1991, of all the former communist countries, an *Anschluss* only occurred in the case of East Germany.

As result of the *Anschluss* of GDR to the Federal Republic of Germany, the East German educational and university system was remodeled on the West German university system. The decisions about further professional careers of the East German university teaching staff were made mainly by West Germans, while, for example in the Czech Republic, Czechs decided the fate of Czech professors and lecturers. Those evaluations, contrary to the East German case—as can be judged easily in the case of economic historians—left talented and internationally well-known academics in their former positions, thus giving them the opportunity to further their academic careers.

If we not only compare the fate of the GDR university elites with the corresponding figures in Eastern Europe, but with those in other *Anschluss* areas at different historical periods, we will discover that the East German case was not an exception, but the rule. This is evident by comparing what happened at other universities in cases of asymmetrical unification. My own research addresses the *Anschluss* of Catalonia to Castilia (or Spain) in 1714, the *Anschluss* of Alsace-Lorraine (hitherto a province of France) to Imperial Germany in 1871, and the *Anschluss* of the Saarland (a French-dominated small territory that was cut off from Germany between 1919 and 1935 as well as between 1945 and 1957). If we take these three cases into account and compare them with the *Anschluss* of East Germany, one finds similarities in the stages and in the content of the *Anschluss* procedures.

The first stage: The defamation of the former university system and the depiction of the scholars in the *Anschluss* area as second- or third-class academics—if they were seen as academics at all.

In Catalonia the then-newly installed governor of Castilian origin, Patino, declared the Catalans to be a primitive tribe and similarly dismissed the abilities of the teaching staff at Catalonia's two universities.[4]

At the University of Straßburg, the only university in Alsace-Lorraine, the German evaluators, Lorenz and Scherer, wrote at the beginning of the evaluation process in the spring of 1871: "[t]here does not exist any freedom of teaching and learning. There does not exist any truly scientific teaching at all, there do not exist any real professors."[5]

After 1955, when the *Anschluss* procedure of the Saarland began, the Bonn Ministry of All-German Affairs (responsible as well for reviewing developments in East Germany and the Saarland from the point of view of the Federal Republic) defamed the Saarland University at Saarbrücken as follows: "[t]he freedom of teaching and research is limited. [. . .] It is a French orientated and manipulated institution, which serves only the interest of the French occupational forces" that were stationed in the Saarland.[6]

What happened during and after the *Anschluss* of East Germany? Some months before the winding up of the careers of the East German university elites began, during the summer of 1990, there was a campaign launched in the media, claiming that there was no real social science research in the GDR. Supported by the mainstream media, some West German professors of history proclaimed loudly that, concerning social sciences, there was nothing but a "research wasteland" or "research desert" in East Germany.[7]

The second stage: The evaluation itself, was always directed by administrative or university staffers of the "mainland," many of whom harbored deep-lying prejudices against the university personnel of the "*Anschluss* area." The evaluation, for the most part, did not focus on the individual's professional abilities or the academic demand for the individual professor. Instead, whole departments were judged *en bloc*. In 1871 Lorenz and Scherer came to the conclusion that there was only one department that deserved to be integrated into Imperial Germany's refounded Straßburg University, namely the Department of Protestant Theology.

The third stage: This usually includes the institutional change of the university structure, especially the closuring of the existing institutions and the founding of new universities—whether at the same spot, even situated within the existing buildings, or as completely newly created institutions in other towns. In May 1717, the newly appointed governor of Catalonia, Patino, ordered the closuring of the two existing Catalan universities at Lerida and Barcelona, which had been founded around 1300 and 1430. Instead, he created a new university at Cervera, which was a small town in Catalonia with 2,000 inhabitants. It had the advantage of having not resisted the Castilian occupation in 1714, and it could be reached relatively comfortably from the capital Madrid by mail coach.

In Alsace-Lorraine the traditional Straßburg University was dissolved at the end of 1871 and replaced by a new "German" university at the same place in April 1872. The same process happened to the Saarland University in March 1957, when a new university law and a new university constitution were approved, which made the Saarbrücken University compatible with the universities in the other parts of the Federal Republic of Germany.[8] In the East German case the Economic University in Berlin-Karlshorst was incorporated into a West Berlin college, as mentioned before.

The fourth stage: The transformation process consisted of the elimination of much of the existing university staff and its replacement by academics of the mainland. A 100 percent "exchange" of personnel took place in Catalonia. The professors and lecturers of the Lerida and Barcelona universities were all dismissed. At the newly founded Cervera University, the teaching staff, all of them Jesuits, were "imported" from Madrid and other Castilian university towns.

Under Lorenz and Scherer, those professors, who, in 1871, had evaluated Straßburg University, became professors at this new university themselves in 1872. Contrary to the former staff, which had been dismissed with the dissolution of the traditional institutions, Lorenz and Scherer did their utmost to change the Straßburg University into a "fortress of German culture in the West."[9]

In 1957, one-seventh of the professors of the School of Medicine at the Saarland University were forced to leave. One-fifth of the teachers at the Department of Philosophy, one-third of the professors and lecturers at the School of Law and the Department of Economics as well as half of the teaching personnel of the Department of Mathematics and Natural Science were also dismissed. All of the laid-off professors and lecturers were replaced by academics from universities in the Federal Republic of Germany.[10]

This fourth stage manifested itself also in the case of the Economic University in Berlin-Karlshorst.

The fifth stage—a stage of transformation: This was the de-professionalization and depreciation of the teaching staff who had been dismissed. The individual fate of former professors or lecturers had become only sporadically known to the public. A few of them reported on their experiences in their memoirs. It is fair to say that the fate of the dismissed university personnel in the *Anschluss* cases of Catalonia, Alsace-Lorraine, and the Saarland did not differ much from that which I have described, regarding the Mottek School of economic historians at the Economic University. Their qualifications were depreciated and denigrated. Much of their expertise is now permanently lost, even if some managed to continue some kind of scholarly work of their own expense and without any institutional support. In Berlin and in the whole of Eastern Germany exists an invisible wall between the "underground scientific community" and the official one. "If remnants are left, they do not influence our disciplines," wrote Jürgen Kocka, a prominent West German historian, with some degree of regret about the situation in historical and social sciences in East Germany four years after unification.[11]

Above all, one thing is obvious: if there was a chance of uniting the experiences of university teaching and research from two different educational systems, this chance had been, as in all the *Anschluss* cases that I referred to, completely dismissed. On the other hand, it may well be that the forces, which have preserved the universities of the mainland in their basis structure, have hardened their position of not reforming after the asymmetric unification, despite the "mainland" university system having proven to be far from perfect.

"By and large," as Jürgen Kocka argued, "the process of unification had not led to major innovations."[12] Others agreed on this point. About the transformation of the East German into the West German academic system, the American professor Kristie Macrakis wrote—and this will be the final sentence of my essay—that "[u]nification irrevocably missed to build up a new scientific and scholarly landscape shaped by Germans from both the East and from the West."[13]

Notes

1. On Mottek see Mario Kessler, *Exilerfahrung in Wissenschaft und Politik: Remigrierte Historiker in der frühen DDR* (Cologne, 2001), 146–62.

2. See Hans Mottek, *Wirtschaftsgeschichte Deutschlands*, 3 vols. (Berlin, 1957–1964).

3. Peter E. Quint, *The Imperfect Union: Constitutional Structures of German Unification* (Princeton, 1997), 178.

4. Jörg Roesler, "Die misslungene Intergration Elsaß-Lothringens in das Deutsche Reich nach 1871 als warnendes Beispiel," *Basler Zeitschrift für Geschichte und Altertumskunde*, no. 96 (1996), 134.

5. Ibid., 135.

6. Ibid., 136.

7. Quint, *The Imperfect Union*, 183.

8. See Wolfgang Müller, "Die Universität des Saarlandes in der politischen Umbruchsituation 1955/56," Rainer Hudemann et al. (eds.), *Grenzfall: Das Saarland zwischen Frankreich und Deutschland 1945–1960* (St. Ingbert, 1997), 424.

9. Roesler, "Die misslungene Integration," 135.

10. See Müller, "Die Universität des Saarlandes," 425.

11. Jürgen Kocka, "Überraschung und Erklärung: Was die Umbrüche von 1989/90 für die Gesellschaftsgeschichte bedeuten könnten," Manfred Hettling, et al. (eds.), *Was ist Gesellschaftsgeschichte? Positionen, Themen, Analysen* (Munich, 1995), 12.

12. Ibid., 11.

13. Quint, *The Imperfect Union*, 183.

11

The Dissolution of the Institute for Economic History at the Academy of Sciences

AXEL FAIR-SCHULZ

On September 25, 1990, Professor Thomas Kuczynski, the Director of the Institute of Economic History, informed the scholars and associates of his research institute that the evaluating committee of the German Higher Education Council, the *Wissenschaftsrat*, was coming to visit the Institute for the entire day of October 15, 1990. One can only imagine the impact of this news, given how much power this council and its verdicts could have on their collective future as an institute and their individual futures as scholars. Some associates of the Institute looked at this process of evaluation with some degree of hopefulness. After all, the institute had a reputation for producing serious research—not just in East-German academic circles but abroad as well. American historians like Georg Iggers, for example, had argued early on that this institute had earned its international reputation, irrespective of any explicit Marxist perspective, as a hub for innovative and engaging scholarship. As such, the Institute for Economic History occupied a unique place in the East-German academic landscape. Iggers pointed out that indeed no other group of East German historians had achieved so much recognition as the members of this Institute.

Of course, everybody involved understood that the watershed transformation of the former East Germany into a part of the Federal Republic of Germany would require significant changes in the discourse and substance of East German scholarship, including at the Institute for Economic History. The idea of schematic or dogmatic Marxist-Leninist phraseology was to be programmatically obsolete. New priorities were required, and it seemed that the Institute for Economic History was better prepared than most academic GDR institutions to survive this transition and adjust successfully to the new conditions and demands. Several associates of the Institute, including its former director and founder Jürgen Kuczynski, were well acquainted with the international scholarly currents and approaches. Consequently, there was great distress when then-institute director Thomas Kuczynski informed his colleagues that in all likelihood the Institute for Economic History would be dissolved and *abgewickelt*. To some observers—not only inside the Institute—this decision seemed arbitrary, motivated not by the Institute's actual performance and output but instead by ideological criteria. The decision to dissolve the institute is especially curious in light of the fact that about 70 percent of its research projects were evaluated positively by the Evaluation Commission of the *Wissenschaftsrat*—clearly far above average. The Institute's last director, agonizingly observed: one Kuczynski built it, and another Kuczynski was forced to tear it down.

At this point, it is impossible to present a comprehensive history of the dissolution of the Institute for Economic History. While there are hundreds of boxes filled with the papers, memos, reports, and other materials pertaining to East Germany's old Institute for Economic History, including its dissolution—which are currently stored at the Academy-Archives at Jägerstraße in Berlin—not all of them are yet accessible. Most of the material from the East German period can be viewed by scholars today, but this does not apply to the material since October 3, 1990. As soon as German unification took place on that day, the 30-year rule came into practice, meaning that the materials dated from October 1990 on cannot be examined by scholars or anyone else until 2020. In addition, even certain documents dated prior to the cutoff date of October 3, 1990, are off limits. This applies, for example, to travel papers created by members of the Institute who went to see Western colleagues and wrote reports. Those would contain not only information about the scholarly efforts of those Western colleagues but also more private information, such as their political leanings, interpersonal arrangements, and so on. In addition, there most likely would have been the occasional sentence about how those Western colleagues respected and appreciated certain East German scholars. Such complimentary statements very much collided with sweeping denigrations, like those of Hans F. Zacher (a former president of the then-West German Max Planck Society), who compared East Germany's social sciences and humanities to a desert, producing hardly anything of value. It is ultimately fruitless to speculate on what could be found in those reports at this point, and we will have to wait for a later date in order for the information to become available.

The Institute for Economic History is very much linked with its founder Jürgen Kuczynski. Until 1956, he was Professor for Economic History at Humboldt University and became the founding director of this internationally recognized Institute for Economic History from 1956 to 1968. Kuczynski continued to exert considerable influence within the institute during the tenure of his colleagues and successors Ernst Wolfgang Jonas (1968–1977), Helga Nussbaum (1977–1989), as well as his son Thomas Kuczynski, until its dissolution in 1991.[1] Jürgen Kuczynski built the Institute into one of East Germany's rare islands of genuine scholarly debate, a legacy that his successors continued. The institute was part of the East German Academy of Science, which was established in 1946 and grew out of the former Prussian Academy of Science (*Kurfürstlich Brandenburgische Societät der Wissenschaften*) as well as sectors of the *Kaiser-Wilhelm-Gesellschaft*. The GDR's Academy grew to over fifty institutes, eventually employing as many as 24,000 people. Given the size of the Academy and that its substructures that were located all over East Germany, the various institutes and centers were clustered into *Forschungsbereiche* (Research Divisions). Kuczynski's Institute for Economic History was part of the *Forschungsbereich Gesellschaftswissenschaften* (Research Division Social Science and Humanities), which included thirteen institutes and research centers. In addition to those research clusters, the Academy was also composed of the *Gelehrtengesellschaft*, a much smaller and highly select membership of scholars, encompassing in 1990 over 300 scholars from the GDR and abroad. Membership in this *Gelehrtengesellschaft* was based on scholarly qualifications at least as much as political and ideological reliability. Thus, the vast majority of members of the Academy's various institutes were not fellows of the Academy.[2] Kuczynski become a fully appointed fellow, or an *Ordentliches Mitglied*, of the Academy in 1955. Later on he was also invited to join the Soviet Academy of Science as well as the Royal Statistical Society in London as a fellow. These memberships speak to his growing scholarly reputation inside and outside of the GDR.

By August 1990, the Institute was composed of nine sections. They were:

1) the Section for Industrial History (*Abteilung Industriegeschichte*),

2) the Section for Economic History of Antiquity (*Abteilung Wirtschaftsgeschichte des Altertums*),

3) the Section for Economic History of the Middle Ages (*Abteilung Wirtschaftsgeschichte des Mittelalters*),

4) the Section of Mathematical and Quantitative Methodologies (*Abteilung Mathematische Methoden*),

5) the Section of Geographic Economic History (*Abteilung Geografische Wirtschaftsgeschichte*),

6) the Section for Agricultural History (*Abteilung Agrargeschichte*),

7) the Section for Comparative Economic History between East and West Germany (*Bereich Vergleichende Wirtschaftsgeschichte DDR-BRD*),

8) the Section Economic History of the 20th Century (*Abteilung Wirtschaftsgeschichte des 20. Jahrhunderts*),

9) the Section for Economic History of the Modern Period (*Bereich Wirtschaftsgeschichte der Neuzeit*).

During the tumultuous disintegration of the former GDR, the Institute for Economic History, as directed by Thomas Kuczynski with Bertold Puchert as the deputy director, had sixty-five people who worked for the Institute, forty-seven of them being research fellows, with eighteen technical support staff. The Institute's headquarters were located at Prenzlauer Promenade 149/152, in East Berlin. It also possessed a research library of about 170,000 volumes, including large parts of the old library of the *Statistische Reichsamt,* as well as a comprehensive collection of papers and *Festschriften* on industrial companies in the German-speaking realm. The Institute was well-connected with partner institutions in the GDR as well as abroad in East and West. In addition to other institutes of the GDR's Academy of Sciences, such as the Central Institute for Ancient History and Archeology, the Central Institute of History, as well as the Institute for Geography and Geo-Ecology, the Institute for Economic History was also closely linked with the Humboldt University in Berlin, the Economic University "Bruno Leuschner" in Berlin-Karlshorst, as well as the universities of Dresden, Jena, Greifswald, Leipzig, and Rostock. Foremost among the Institute's partner organizations from the Warsaw Pact countries were the Soviet, Polish, Czechoslovakian, and Hungarian Academies of Science. The Institute for Economic History also cooperated with Western institutions, including the Max Planck Institute for History in Göttingen and the universities of Mannheim, Siena, Amsterdam, Stockholm, Liverpool, as well as the State University of New York at Binghamton. There were also several others international institutions and associations with which the Institute for Economic History cooperated, such as the International Association of Agricultural Museums and the International

Association for the Research of Peasant Minute Books—headquartered in West Germany's Kiel.

The Institute for Economic History had a pronounced research profile on a very broad spectrum of topics, including the history of everyday life, the history of everyday life in the agricultural sphere, the history of foreign trade, the history of banking, population history, the history of economic elites, the history of capital exports, the history of the transfer of technologies, the history of urban centers, and the history of the development of territorial structures. Research on the history of economic crises, economic booms, and ecology and statistics were also part and parcel of its areas of special focus. In addition, the Institute for Economic History also researched themes like environmental history, industrial archeology, the history of technological innovations, as well as the social and economic history of industrialization, the social history of the poor and marginalized, the social history of elites, the comparative economic history of East and West Germany, and the economic history of rural areas.

One of the reasons why several of the Institute for Economic History's members were moderately hopeful about a positive evaluation of their institute and its potential survival was that its strengths consisted in being able to muster large scale research projects, which were too ambitious and broad for individual universities. Indeed, the uniqueness of the Institute cannot be overemphasized. Jürgen Kuczynski thus lamented with great sorrow: "the world's largest institute for economic history has been dissolved, despite its international reputation and many promising projects. This is such as loss for scholarship and science, here in Germany and internationally as well." Kuczynski, who also noted that Max Kaase from the evaluation committee had explicitly asked him not to participate at the meeting between the committee and the directorate of the Institute for Economic History, despite Kuczynski's role as a member of the board of directors, *the Institutsrat* to which he belonged by virtue of his membership in the Academy.

Of course, Jürgen Kuczynski's contributions to scholarship, especially scholarship in the GDR, are well known and despite his, occasional, kind of *Zettelkasten* methodology and overly schematic Marxism, were very well-respected. Nobody can ignore or belittle what he did for promoting *Alltagsgeschichte* and other methodological innovations, as evidenced in his *Geschichte des Alltages des deutschen Volkes* as well as his *Geschichte der Lage der Arbeiter im Kapitalismus*. In addition, other members of the Institute for Economic History have distinguished themselves as well. Foremost I want to mention—-and this list is by no means exhaustive or all-inclusive—Helga Nussbaum, Jan Peters, Jörg Roesler, and Hans-Heinrich Müller.

Helga Nussbaum, starting as early as 1966 with her solidly grounded, empirical, and seminal book, *Unternehmer gegen Monopole: Über Struktur und Aktionen antimonopolistischer bürgerlicher Gruppen zu Beginn des 20. Jahrhunderts*, contends that Marxist-Leninist assertions about how capitalists are automatically monopolistic, at the beginning of the twentieth century, does not reflect a more complex and contradictory reality. In fact, already in the introduction Nussbaum argues against grand and tidy generalizations, such as terms *Grandbourgeosie*, the middle-level bourgeoisie, and small-scale entrepreneurs. She is clear to point out that what might be true for some groups and individuals in different areas of Germany might not be valid elsewhere. In *Wirtschaft und Staat in Deutschland: Wirtschaftsgeschichte des staatsmonopolistischen Kapitalismus in Deutschland vom Ende des 19. Jahrhunderts bis 1945* (published in 1978), Nussbaum argues along similar differentiated and nuanced lines.

Jan Peters, with works such as his *Märkische Bauerntagebücher des 18. und 19. Jahrhunderts: Zeugnisse von Milchviehbauern aus Neuholland* and especially *Der Platz in der Kirche: Über soziales Rangdenken im Spätfeudalismus*, has also done much to introduce and proliferate an innovative methodological approach, seeking to combine Marxism with cultural history. Since the dissolution of the Institute for Economic History, Peters has continued to produce engaging books, such as *Ein Söldnerleben im Dreissigjährigen Krieg: Eine Quelle zur Sozialgeschichte* as well as his *Märkische Lebenswelten: Gesellschaftsgeschichte der Herrschaft Plattenburg-Wilsnack, Prignitz 1500–1800.*[3]

The productivity of Jörg Roesler, especially *Zwischen Plan und Markt: Die Wirtschaftsreform in der DDR zwischen 1963 and 1970* and his other diverse books since 1991, reflects well on his scholarly reputation as an economic historian.

Hans-Heinrich Müller's scholarly work as an agricultural historian also found the respect of tough critics, such as Hans-Ulrich Wehler, who had actually excluded East Germany's agricultural historians from his otherwise grim verdict that East German scholars produced little more than "tons of wasted paper." With books such as *Akademie und Wirtschaft im 18. Jahrhundert: Agrarökonomische Preisaufgaben und Preisschriften der Preussischen Akademie der Wissenschaften* (1975), *Herkules in der Wiege: Streiflichter zur Geschichte der industriellen Revolution* (1980), as well as *Im Dienste der Ceres: Streiflichter zu Leben und Geschichte bedeutender deutscher Landwirte und Wissenschaftler* (1988), Müller's scholarly efforts resonated well outside the GDR. And in 1982, for example, he was invited to join a newly created journal, titled *Food and Foodways*, published jointly by American and French scholars centered at Cornell University. Müller's work in fields such as "problems of nourishment in late Feudalism 1500–1850" in particular gained the attention of his Western colleagues.

In addition to countless monographs and other works, the Institute for Economic History distinguished itself by producing the *Jahrbuch für Wirtschaftsgeschichte*, which was edited by Jan Peters and published under the umbrella of the Institute between 1960 and 1991. Today the *Jahrbuch* still exists, but it has moved from its original place of publication in East Berlin to Frankfurt/Main. Over time this publication earned the esteem not only of critical East German Marxists but of some Western scholars as well. These included Western Marxists, like the British historian Eric Hobsbawm, as well as the non-Marxist Georg Iggers. Hobsbawm even joined the advisory council of this quarterly journal, while Iggers argued for a balanced understanding of the journal's contributions and limitations. To him the *Jahrbuch* was "taken at least half-seriously by Westerners because it was largely free of the usual formulaic [Marxist-Leninist] phraseology."[4] Already in 1982, the West Berlin economic historian Carl-Ludwig Holtfrerich considered the journal a serious academic venue, arguing that "within the boundaries of its ideologically predetermined scaffolding it achieved a high level of theoretical and empirical scholarship."[5] Others, such as the economic historian Wilfried Feldenkirchen from the Bavarian University of Erlangen-Nuremberg, arrived at a more directly critical assessment. To Feldenkirchen the *Jahrbuch* was characterized, until the very late 1980s, much more by polemics than analysis and penetrated by a "largely atavistic Marxist vocabulary."[6] However, the complexity and contradictory nature of Kuczynski's *Jahrbuch* cannot easily be explained by generalizations. Jörg Roesler himself, one of the editors of the journal between 1971 and 1989, concluded that despite the repressive nature of the SED regime, and its constant ideological interference into the ambit of scholarship, the *Jahrbuch* was able to carve out a space for academically serious as well as innovative contributions and discussions of new ideas, based, of course, on the discursive hegemony of Marxism. To Roesler this was made possible by the relatively marginalized place of the overtly technical and a-political discipline of economic history within the panorama of East German academia. He credits the authors, who provided consistently high-quality scholarship, as well as the editors' stamina and integrity, pushing for the actual publication of this scholarship—having to fight for the relative autonomy of the journal in each new installment. And finally, he praises the outside reviewers, who, like the editors themselves, were engaged in a skillfully negotiated dialogue with the censorship apparatus. They fought for each manuscript, while negotiating some degree of compromise in order to see things published. Keeping substance over phraseology, they would ultimately concede to modify ideologically problematic formulations if it would essentially preserve the core arguments. Roesler thus deemed this interplay of professionalism and tactical flexibility as one of the key strengths of the *Jahrbuch* in the GDR.[7]

Jürgen Kuczynski was the undisputed master of this interplay. He utilized the *Jahrbuch* as a venue to present and discuss his own ideas as well as the works of other Marxist scholars. In addition, he also used this forum to especially de-provincialize his East German readers (who were largely isolated from Western literature), familiarizing them with the broader currents of international scholarship, including the contributions of non-Marxist scholars. He reviewed works by Paul Kennedy, Vernon Lidtke, Brigitte Seebacher-Brandt, Ingeborg Weber-Kellermann, Karl S. Kramer, Ulrich Wilkens, and Hans-Ulrich Wehler, to mention just a few. Kuczynski praised the accomplishments of West German and French scholarship within the realm of *Alltagsgeschichte*, admitting that the methodological approach of history from below should have been most developed within Marxist scholarship but non-Marxist schools of thought had done more than East German Marxists.[8] In fact, Kuczynski used well-researched Western scholarship to directly criticize Marxist-Leninists' dogmatism from within the East German academic community. In his review of Charles Webster's *The Great Instauration: Science, Medicine, and Reform 1626–1660*, Kuczynski scolds GDR historians for endlessly repeating themselves—as well as Marx, Engels, and Lenin. Much should be learned, he insisted, from the empiricism and conceptual innovations of scholars like Webster.[9] He also used the *Jahrbuch* to display his debates and his Marxist scholarship. In a 1983 article, he observes, regarding Marx, that with "no figure from the past [other than Shakespeare] is there such diversity of views among Marxists."[10]

As mentioned, it is still impossible to sort out how and why evaluators, such as Max Kaase, arrived at their decision to dissolve the Institute for Economic History. Was this a forgone conclusion on their part, made prior to any serious appraisal of the of the institute's actual output, based largely on ideological grounds, as Jürgen Kuczynski and others have speculated? Did the assessors simply fail to understand the different cultural and discursive conditions, under which scholarship had to take place in the GDR? How contested was the ultimate sentence, of dissolving the Institute, among members of the committee, and what measures did they use to arrive at their decision? Progress on answering these questions cannot continue until 2020, when more of the archival material will be declassified. At this point, however, one cannot help but be saddened and disappointed, in regard to what has been lost by this dissolution in terms of German and international scholarship. While some of the Institute's former employees, such as Jan

Peters, have found new jobs at German universities, most did not. They have been pushed into early retirement or unemployment and been largely marginalized by the scholarly mainstream. German reunification brought with it much potential for genuine dialogue and cooperation between East and West German scholars, but that potential has gone unfulfilled, overlooked passively and/or actively. There are signs for some moderate hope, for example, the resurrection of the old *Robert René Kuczynski Prize* (since the end of the GDR) suggesting that there are better potential solutions in dealing with East German scholarly institutions and that new traditions can indeed be found and synthesized. What has been made possible for the RRK Prize should also be possible for working scholars, finding opportunities for them to function in their respective fields. Let us hope it is not too late.

Notes

1. Helga Nussbaum notes that, while she worked as director of the Institute, Kuczynski came into her office almost on a daily basis. He was interested not only in the general direction of the Institute but also in the day-to-day affairs. He used his connections within the upper levels of the Academy of Science to provide the Institute with hard-to-come-by items, such as new and top-of-the-line typewriters. Yet at times, his overly zealous efforts could backfire, when, for example, Kuczynski's lobbying on behalf of the Institute created resentment "higher up." Nussbaum eventually opted to pacify Kuczynski's enthusiasm with more general information and tried to keep him away from the day-to-day management of the Institutes' affairs. Helga Nussbaum, Winsen, to Axel Fair-Schulz, Fort Erie (February 28, 2004).

2. For a basic overview of the Academy of Science see Andreas Herbst, Winfried Ranke, and Jürgen Winkler, *So funktionierte die DDR: Lexikon der Organizationen und Institutionen*, vol. 1 (Reinbek, 1994), 35–40.

3. For Jan Peter's own view of the transformation, see his memoirs: *Menschen und Möglichkeiten: Ein Historikerleben in der DDR und anderen Traumländern* (Stuttgart, 2011), 457–98.

4. Georg Iggers, "Geschichte: Geschichtswissenschaft und autoritärer Staat. Ein deutsch-deutscher Vergleich (1933–1990)," *Berliner Debatte INITIAL*, no. 2 (1991), 129.

5. Carl-Ludwig Holtfrerich, "Zur Position und Entwicklung der Wirtschaftsgeschichte in der DDR seit 1960," *Geschichte und Gesellschaft*, 7 (1982), no. 1, 152–53.

6. Wilfried Feldenkirchen, "*Das Jahrbuch für Wirtschaftsgeschichte*," *Vierteljahresschrift für Sozial- und Wirtschaftsgeschichte*, 78 (1991), no. 4, 542.

7. Jörg Roesler, "Schon 1960 auf Westniveau? Das *Jahrbuch für Wirtschaftsgeschichte*," in Simone Barck, Martina Langermann, and Siegfried Lokatis, eds., *Zwischen "Mosaik" und "Einheit": Zeitschriften in der DDR*, 484–85.

8. Jürgen Kuczynski, Review of "*Volksleben in einem holsteinischen Gutsbezirk. Eine Untersuchung aufgrund archivalischer Quellen* by Karl S. Kramer and Ulrich Wilkens," *Jahrbuch für Wirtschaftsgeschichte*, 21 (1980), no. III, 141.

9. Idem, Review of "*The Great Instaration: Science, Medicine, and Reform 1626–1660*, by Charles Webster," *Jahrbuch für Wirtschaftsgeschichte*, 18 (1977), no. III, 201.

10. Idem, "Marx and Shakespeare," *Jahrbuch für Wirtschaftsgeschichte*, 22 (1983), no. I, 10.

12

Dismantling the GDR's Historical Scholarship

A Case Study of the University of Leipzig

WERNER RÖHR

I have selected the Department of History at the Karl Marx University in Leipzig for three main reasons, in order to illustrate, *pars pro toto*, some of the key problems and processes associated with the dismantling of the GDR's historical scholarship after 1990:

1) Out of all the university-based historical research institutions in the GDR, the History department at the University of Leipzig was the largest, the most productive, and the most innovative.[1]

2) The process of renewal did not go as far, at any other university in the GDR after 1989–1990, as at the University of Leipzig. Nowhere else did the democratic transformation of the department structures, its teaching, as well as scholarship programs proceed as far as in Leipzig. Then, a new and freely elected departmental council took the initiative and played, for some time, the most decisive role. The most important structural innovation was the reestablishment of the old and internationally respected Institute for Cultural and Universal History, which resulted from combining the subdivisions of General History of the Modern World as well as History of Historiography.[2]

3) The developments in the University of Leipzig's Department of History showcases how the process of self-renewal was ultimately thwarted, when whole subsections were summarily dissolved, on the orders of the new ministries, as the GDR was incorporated into West Germany and its academic structure. What happened in Leipzig also happened elsewhere in the former GDR, in terms of the mechanisms and procedures that led to a "cleansing" of East German scholars. Committees were established in order to announce new replacement job openings—without any consultation with the already existing faculty, whose legal rights were often ignored. Some of the best scholars were dismissed from their positions and not allowed to apply for any new openings, due to the simple fact that they had fulfilled university service obligations in the GDR in elected administrative positions. In addition, a campaign of blackmail and innuendo resulted in the circulation of anonymous, dubious, and deeply biased assessment reports of East German scholars that frequently called their qualifications and competency into question, both as scholars and as university citizens. There was also the very unfortunate tendency to divide and conquer, by enlisting some few GDR professors who had their contracts renewed to aid in disparaging their former colleagues and encourage their firings. Newly appointed West German professors were directed to force West German structures, procedures, and customs upon the University of Leipzig. As stated at the beginning, the fate of the History department at the University of Leipzig stands for what happened elsewhere in East Germany's History departments *pars pro toto.*

Selected Research Results by Leipzig Historians

In 1989, eighty-nine people taught and researched at the Department of History in Leipzig. This number included twenty-four full professors and nine associate professors. They trained and educated budding historians, classists, and high school history teachers, and each year, around 400 new history students were admitted into the program. My focus in this essay is not on teaching but on selected research accomplishments.

Leipzig historians have made significant contributions over the course of several decades in the research fields of German history as well as in international and comparative history. In German (and international academic circles), Leipzig's historians are known mainly for their contributions to comparative and world history. In fact, the colleagues from Leipzig have based much of their own case, for continued relevance after 1989–1990, on this reputation. Therefore, I want to stress their research and conceptual innovations in the field of German history.

Historical Scholarship on German History

Socioreligious Mass Movements of the High Middle Ages

Leipzig Medievalists, centered around Ernst Werner and Martin Erbstößer, have investigated the societal transformations during the eleventh century in Europe, especially regarding the connection between monastic reforms, reform popery, and the movements of socioreligious heretics. This circle of historians drew also on comparative studies in the field of Byzantine history, while exploring the social foundations and social stratification of heretical currents during the German Middle Ages.[3]

Heinrich Sproemberg and his research on Manichaeism in the Occident ignited this work.[4] He argued that economic and social forces largely fueled religious movements during the High Middle Ages, both within and outside the official Church. This argument stands in contrast to the conventional case made by the West German historian Herbert Grundmann, whose views on the matter are shared by many European scholars. Grundmann's interpretation rests on the supposition that medieval heretical movements cannot be explained primarily in terms of social unrest and class struggle. Instead, scholars should focus on new waves of religious piety and devotion that pulsed through all social layers—while acknowledging some connection between religious and social movements.[5]

The unique contribution of Leipzig's historians consists of looking at those heretical movements of the first half of the eleventh century within the context of the transformation of Early Feudalism to High Feudalism, which marked more general changes in the structure of the economy. Chief among those were the further accumulation of land on part of the nobility, demographic progression, increases in economic productivity, more social differentiation, and the developments of cities and artisan trade, especially long-distance trade. The coalescing of those developments generated a dynamic of fully unfolded Feudalism that was to last for about two hundred years. Yet, neither social power structures nor the dominant worldviews changed automatically. Restructuring and transforming the medieval world went hand in hand with long and complex class struggles. The power and prestige of the nobility increased further, as the monastic system enhanced its landed property as well. At the same time, the peasantry evolved into a more homogenous social layer. Feudal anarchy was pushed back in favor of more effective state-centered and intensified forms of exploitation.

These complex developments led not only to a questioning of the early feudal worldview but also became the basis for the three major ecclesiastical reform movements. First among those were the Gregorian papal reforms, second, the monastic reforms that emanated from the monastery of Cluny, Burgundy, and, third, the socioreligious mass movements. The Leipzig School of Medievalists around Ernst Werner focused methodically on how the ecclesiastical reform processes interacted with the socioreligious movements of heretics within the context of the transformations of the eleventh century, including the connections between more intensive forms of agrarian exploitation and populist eschatology, changes in land ownership and expressions of piety, heretical spiritualisms and social radicalization, as well as the increasing wealth and splendor of the mainstream church on the one hand and the "exaltation of *Sancta paupertas*" on the other.[6] Werner's key argument thus centers on how the causes for those socioreligious mass movements are explainable less in terms of a suddenly developing new wave of religiosity than in terms of social tensions and open conflict between the wealthy clergy and the impoverished peasants and agricultural day-laborers. The latter group searched for a *Via apostolica* to challenge and combat the dominant socioeconomic arrangements of the eleventh century, confronting the church hierarchy with the ideals of Christian poverty.[7] In the long run, the mainstream church succeeded in marginalizing and outmaneuvering the various movements of heretics. The ecclesiastic elites found allies among the feudal establishments who also felt threatened by the demands of the heretics.

The Study of Medieval Cities within the Context of Socioeconomic Struggles

Those Leipzig historians who focused on the history of the entire Saxon territory echoed the orientation of many East German medievalists toward city history.[8] The stability of the city required a communal spirit, which was ritualistically invoked by a so-called burgher oath. However, this oath could not cancel the opposing social interests of the different strata within the city, resulting in social tensions, between patricians and merchants, masters and apprentices, or the urban poor versus the ruling elite. The communal movements did not invent these struggles and conflicts but put them on a new foundation. There was much mutual interpenetration between the socioreligious communal movements on the one hand and the clashes among different social layers in the cities.

The GDR's experts on medieval city history focused on those social tensions during the High Middle Ages that foreshadowed the Early Modern Period in European history. Between 1300 and 1400 alone, around 160 such conflicts flared up in over 100 German cities. Especially Karl Czok from the University of Leipzig has contributed to breakthrough in scholarship here.[9] He was able to demonstrate that the social struggles of the second half of the thirteenth century; in the cities there were not only conflicts between different guilds but political and social struggles of the intracity opposition against the ruling patrician elite. Artisans, local merchants, coin-makers, money exchangers, brewers, owners of ships and city real estate, and even some members of the patrician class opposed the long-distance and large-scale merchants that dominated the city councils.

While the actual socioeconomic composition of the intracity opposition to the city councils changed, the main reason for discontent remained, namely the financial policies of the ruling families that dominated the city councils. Hence, specific fiscal decisions (such as new taxes, increased overall city debt, or the purchasing of new land), were also the catalysts for the flaring up of such confrontations. Financial mismanagement on the part of city councils led to ever-heavier burdens on the non-patrician layers of city dwellers. Protests against nepotism and cleptocracy evolved into more general demands for greater transparency of fiscal matters, including taxation. This implied greater power for the intracity opposition. Most East German medievalists were convinced by Czok's arguments, especially since he included the plebeian strata in the intracity opposition, even though they were not, in any legal sense, city citizens.

The "Early Bourgeois Revolution" in Germany

Max Steinmetz and his associates at the University of Leipzig developed the notion of the Protestant Reformation and the Peasant Wars as parts of the "Early Bourgeois Revolution" in Germany.[10] Originally developed by Steinmetz, Manfred Bensing, Gerhard Brendler, Gerhard Zschäbitz, Siegfried Hoyer, and others,[11] East German historians in Jena, Greifswald, Halle, and East Berlin also adopted this approach and developed it further.[12] They focused on how the German territories took the lead in the growing mining industry in Europe, at the end of the fifteenth and the beginning of the sixteenth centuries, especially in terms of mining for silver, lead, and copper ore. On one hand, the mining and processing of ore provided many new opportunities for investment on the part of rich merchants and speculators. While, on the other hand, social conflict and class struggle between hired miners and the owners of the mines increased. In addition, mining entrepreneurs and feudal landlords clashed over how to divide profit. Merchant capital began to penetrate metallurgy and textile production, thus dwarfing the leverage of artisans.

The simultaneity of a booming economy on the one side and the increasing socioeconomic contradictions between the various social layers in the cities, on the other, led to a serious of urban uprisings. Increases in agricultural output motivated the feudal landlords to appropriate an ever-larger amount of what the peasants produced for sale on the markets. This was done largely in the form of tax increases and other burdens, which took place especially in the southwest of the German territories, where feudal estates were fragmented. The result was frequent peasant uprisings. These two protest movements, in the cities and the countryside, were enhanced by further elements of crisis, including the decline of the lower nobility as a consequence of the expansion of the power of the territorial princes, the crisis of the Imperial constitutional system in the face of the growing power of the territorial princes, as well as the budding mass movement against the monopolies of the large-scale merchants.

All of these crises grew in intensity between 1509 and 1517 and shook the very foundations of feudalism. The Lutheran reformation gave those developments and movements a common direction and pushed against the power of the papacy. For a time, all of the various forces that challenged the status quo were unified in their opposition to Rome, despite their divergent social composition. The unifying umbrella of the Lutheran reformation was ultimately not large enough to accommodate the increasingly differentiated forces, movements, and interests in the long run.

Yet, for a while the Lutheran Reformation was in the interest of the urban patricians, who desired a church in accordance with their economic and religious sensibilities; it was also in the interests of the territorial princes who coveted the ecclesiastic estates and monasteries. Demands for social justice were channeled into the call for divine justice, which became a powerful tool in the hands of the downtrodden and protesting peasants.

The Reformation thus turned into the first act of the Early Bourgeois Revolution and unleashed mass discontent, on a scale not seen again until the Revolution of 1848.[13] The Protestant Reformation thus became the catalyst that burst open the feudal confines and enabled the eventual unfolding of bourgeois society. This is not to say that the Reformation created capitalism, as the very purpose of the term "Early Bourgeois" underscores that these developments mark merely the earliest stages of a much longer and more complex transition from feudalism to capitalism. The early bourgeoisie still thought and acted much more like a feudal estate rather than its own class.[14]

The Social History of the Proletariat

The research group "classes and social layers in bourgeois society" under the leadership of Hartmut Zwahr understood social history as the history of social classes. They sought to understand the genesis and the socioeconomic and sociocultural reproduction of the proletariat, as a social class, on an empirical foundation. Characteristic for this research approach were:

a) The correlative investigation of the beginnings of the bourgeois and the working classes;

b) The immediate connections between the history of classes to the history of territories, regions, and particular population centers, in this case with the principality of Saxony, the Saxon region of Lusatia, as well as the Saxon city of Leipzig;

c) A focus on the dawning of the social manifestations and compositions of the main classes, in terms of a typology of professional, family, and individual trajectories;

d) The systematic analysis of previously unused historical sources, such as address books, baptismal and death annals, as well as citizenship and other registries, in order to conduct group biographic research.

The Leipzig research team emphasized the origins of the social composition of the proletariat and, by implication, of the bourgeoisie as well.[15] Their research probed the development of working-class families as well as marital relationships, within the class of wage laborers and between this class and related subclasses.

In addition, the team explored the degrees of social mixing within those classes, subclasses, and groups. Among the conclusions of the Leipzig team was that it is not fully possible to speak of the proletariat as a distinct class, if it is still primarily constituted out of the remnants of feudal society. The proletariat must largely reproduce itself out of itself, in order to be a new class. Without ruling out the possibility of mobility, the proletariat evolved into a distinct class, as people began to be born into it. Proletarian marriages and family relationships, and connections between different social groups within the proletariat created a sense of social cohesion and stabilized the class position of workers.

The spectrum of those inquiries into social history encompassed:

- The coming into existence of proletarian families and their place within the constitution of the working class, including marriage strategies and the development of families within the proletariat of a large city;

- The evolution of urban middle-class layers, via the social constitution of a leadership layer of the bourgeoisie, vis-à-vis the vertical and the horizontal structure of the industrial, trade, and banking bourgeoisie of a whole country;

- The social structure of specific groups of employees, such as the journeymen and their patterns of migration, or of the higher bureaucrats in a state ministry, salaried technicians, teachers, natural scientists, and engineers within the overall reproduction of capital as well as the armies of the unemployed.

Most of those research projects focused on a whole country, region, or city. The systematic consideration of theoretical problems, within social history or neighboring fields, remained the exception.

Research About General and World History

Most often, East German historical scholarship in Leipzig is associated with the comparative studies of European revolutions during the early modern period. Those efforts are internationally recognized and thus will be my focus here.[16] Yet, in addition to European history, research divisions in African and Near Eastern Studies were augmented, and even within the context of medieval history; Ernst Werner and Klaus-Peter Matschke explored the Byzantine Empire.

Leipzig became most famous for its work on the Bourgeois Revolutions of the Modern Period, in particular with the books and articles by Walter Markov on the French Revolution, as well as Manfred Kossok's scholarship on the revolutions in the Iberian Peninsula as well as in Latin America. Those works, combined with the scholarship on the Dutch, English, and other European Revolutions, constituted the foundation of the University of Leipzig's comparative analyses of Bourgeois Revolutions between 1500 and 1917. This overall comparative approach led the Leipzig historians, in the late 1980s, to open themselves to the study of global history.

The University of Leipzig Department of History subdivision "General History" was the institutional successor of the famous Institute for Cultural and Universal History, which was dissolved in 1951. Karl Lamprecht created this Institute in 1909. In 1948, Walter Markov became its last director.[17] The new subdivision "General History" tried to free itself from the more Eurocentric tradition of Universal History by incorporating the study of the so-called Third World countries as well. They started to develop an interdisciplinary comparative history of revolutions research program.

The historians of the General History subdivision researched, by and large, in four fields, starting with the French Revolution and, building on its foundations, the bourgeois revolutions of Modern Europe. Those bourgeois revolutions were approached both individually as well as in a comparative fashion. The internationalization of the subdivision's research agenda was expressed especially in the new focus on the Iberian Peninsula during the Modern Period, as well as their colonial histories, particularly in Latin America. In addition, the national liberation movements and revolutions of Latin America, as well as the overall history of the continent all the way to the present age, were examined. African history was developed as a field of research and teaching as well.

In 1969, the Research Group for the Comparative Study of Revolutions during the Modern Period was established in Leipzig. Their focus was on comparative questions of the history of revolutions, including the involved social and class forces, all the way to the different types of revolutions and their trajectories. In 1976, the Interdisciplinary Center for the Comparative Study of Revolutions (IZR) was established under the directorship of Manfred Kossok.[18]

This Center was composed not only of the Research Group for the Comparative Study of Revolutions but also four other Research Groups. Together, those four research teams explored the cycle of European Bourgeois Revolutions of the Modern Period, the cycle of Socialist Revolutions in the twentieth century, the history of National Liberation Revolutions in the twentieth century, as well as the history of Revolutionary Movements within Contemporary Imperialism.[19]

The oldest research subject in Leipzig has been, since the 1950s, the French Revolution, as is manifest in the works of Walter Markov. He focused on the role of the people's movement, as well as the impact of the Radical Left in the form of the *Les Enragés* as well as the biography of the priest Jacques Roux.[20] Markov's research was not confined to France, as the French Revolution had an immense impact abroad as well. Markov focused on the international impact of the French Revolution long before it became fashionable to do so.[21] During the 1980s, Markov's team investigated especially the people's movements and the counterrevolution in France. Both the pre- and post-history of the French Revolution came into view as well, through the prism of

1) The problems of the primitive accumulation of capital, as well as the tax and economic policies of French Absolutism under the conditions of capital valorization at the end of the Ancient Regimes;

2) The mistakes, derelictions, and hesitations of the Revolution, especially regarding agrarian and economic policies;

3) The consequences of the Revolution for the development of France in the nineteenth century.

Markov's team conducted its research in cooperation with French experts on the French Revolution, foremost was Albert Soboul of the Sorbonne as well as historians from many other universities across Europe and beyond.[22]

Markov's foreign partners realized that comparative research requires very clear definitions of the criteria of comparison. Hence, methodological considerations were at the center of their efforts from the onset.

Thus, in the volumes that deal with the Study of the History of Revolutions, there are works that investigate different aspects of one specific revolution, such as the July Revolution of 1830 in France, as well as works that focus on one overarching subject matter, as for example the role of the peasants or of the proletariat during the era of the Bourgeois Revolutions. Beyond those parameters, the volume on the Revolutions of the Modern Period examines, in a comparative fashion, all previously explored bourgeois revolutions, while Manfred Kossok's book *In tyrannos* presents the bourgeois cycle of revolutions in form of a monograph.[23]

The research of Iberian history, including both Spanish and Portuguese colonial history, as well as revolutions for national independence in Latin America, started with the policies of the Holy Alliance (especially in the German principalities) toward Latin America after 1815. With regard to Spain, the focus of the Leipzig scholars was on this country on the brink of its bourgeois revolution, including the episodes of Enlightened Absolutism and the Iberian revolutionary cycle between 1789 and 1830.[24] Regarding Latin America, comparative studies of political, economic, and social structures were emphasized, including the period of national independence.[25]

Summary

1) The History Department at the University of Leipzig was one of the most productive in all of the GDR. Several of its members were among the best in their fields of specialty in the country. They were recognized as such both nationally and internationally.

2) With the traditions that were established by Walter Markov and Manfred Kossok, Leipzig's research capacity in international and cultural history was placed on very solid ground. The scholarship produced by this tradition of global history and comparative methodology was internationally acclaimed.

3) Historical scholarship from Leipzig manifested both in terms of content and methodology a discernible alternative to the West German professorial canon. Leipzig's best scholars combined a non-dogmatic Marxist approach with a comparative world history perspective. In addition, Leipzig had the GDR's only university-based professorship for historiography (chair: Werner Berthold).[26]

4) Historians in Leipzig were thus able to go beyond the confines of German and even European history, which contrasted well with the Eurocentric and German-centric conventions of the German historical profession. Leipzig established excellent cooperation with colleagues and universities in Latin American countries, as well as in Spain, France, the Soviet Union, Great Britain, the United States, Scandinavia, and the Netherlands.

The Democratic Renewal and its Derailment

Self-Directed Democratic Renewal

The Department of History at the University of Leipzig initiated a self-directed process of renewal that took stock of the department's work and led to a structural and substantive transformation. Between 1990 and 1992, those historians worked diligently to bring this about. They did so via:

First: A self-critical analysis of their own collective and individual scholarly efforts to date. These analyses are well documented in the third volume of the Selected Writings of Manfred Kossok, which were edited by Matthias Middell.[27]

Second: Beginning in 1990, the department established a committee that was to become the most important vehicle for the renewal of the entire department. The department chairs and division leaders submitted to a vote of confidence and new elections. The department evolved into a new structure that included different historical institutes. The committee coordinated the content-based renewal of teaching and those newly created institutes did research, while the bulk of the actual work.

The committee created a subcommittee that was to draft proposals for the new structure of the department. After long debates about what new structures should be implemented, the members of the subcommittee, as well as the entire coordinating committee, decided that institutes were to be the building blocks of the new departmental structure. In doing so they empathically rejected the more traditional German model of a hierarchical department, dominated by senior professors. Especially relevant in this regard are the minutes from the committee meeting of June 5, 1990, as they illustrate the vigorous debate and the various suggestions for a self-directed renewal. Unfortunately, all of this was later pushed aside by the forced implementation of the West German model.

- Chief among the recommendations for self-renewal was to privilege content over merely organizational considerations.
- The department was to be preserved as a recognizable teaching and research unit, given its international reputation.
- The unique profile of Leipzig was to be held onto, given the growing pressures to adopt the West German model wholesale.
- The already existing ties between teaching and researching German history with global history were to be enhanced.
- Established and effective research teams were not to be dismantled.[28]

Third: As a consequence of the conceptual and organizational process of renewal, as mandated by Professor Hans-Joachim Meyer, Minister of Science and Culture in the Free State of Saxony, structures were to be changed, within the department by September 30, 1992, so that the following institutes were to be established:

I) Institute for Pre, Early, and Ancient History (4 scholars);

II) Institute for Institute for Medieval History (3 scholars);

III) Institute for Universal and Cultural History of the Modern Period (10 scholars);

IV) Institute for Modern and Social History (6 scholars);

V) Institute for Contemporary History (7 scholars);

VI) Seminar for Regional History and the Study of Sources (2 scholars);

VII) Seminar for Didactic (2 scholars).

The largest of those new institutes did not fit within the previous structures and thus associates from different areas had to be recruited. This new structure, mandated by the Saxon Ministry for Science and Culture, did not cover all the subject matters and fields of inquiry that were addressed by the previous structure. For example, the histories of Eastern Europe as well as South-Eastern Europe were excluded. Out of all the newly created institutes, the one for Universal and Cultural History of the Modern Period was doubtlessly the strongest.

Since 1989–1990, there have been extensive efforts in Leipzig to put the study of universal/global history on a new foundation that would integrate it with the study of Western Europe, the Comparative Study of the History of Revolutions, the Study of Historical Transformations, Comparative Colonial History, as well as the History of Historiography, among others. Yet, the State Government of Saxony, as well as the new university leadership and the advisory commissions that were directed by West German professors, did everything in their power to undermine and prevent those efforts from succeeding.

Fourth: The self-directed renewal of teaching and research at the History Department in Leipzig was also manifest in several activities of its Institutes. Mid-level faculty members drafted a position paper for the regeneration of the department; parallel to it, an academic constitution was also drafted.[29]

Matthias Middell worked on a proposal for an Institute for the Universal and Cultural History of the Modern Period that would be affiliated with the university, while being partially independent as well. He called it the "Leipzig Model." At the same time, the Institute for Cultural and Universal History organized several conferences, including one on the French Revolution.[30]

Derailing and Ending the Process of Democratic Renewal

The attempts at democratic and self-directed renewal, on the part of the Leipzig historians encountered massive resistance. Emanating mainly from the State Government of Saxony, particularly from the Science Ministry under Hans Joachim Meyer, those attempts were undermined, blocked, and finally broken off. The new university administration adjusted to the directives from the ministry, and its decisions were implemented by freshly chosen East German professors, whose appointments were already based on the West German legal system that came to frame higher education in the East as well. West German university officials provided the justifications and guidelines for this process.

The administration of the University of Leipzig equally ignored all of the Leipzig historians' suggestions for self-renewal as well as the declarations of support, for their East German colleagues, on the part of the international scholarly community. The administrators failed to acknowledge not only any of the new publications produced by the Leipzig historians since 1990 but also any of the workshops and conferences organized by them.

It became increasingly clear that the administration, as well as the state government, wanted to adopt the West German model—of a university dominated by senior professors. Thus, any of the institutional innovations by the Leipzig historians were not recognized by the administration. Neither the administration nor the ministry sanctioned a single one of the newly established institutes, undermining the principles of academic autonomy and the democratic decision-making process. And in the fall semester of 1992, new professors were appointed, and only the scholars that were associated with the new professorial chairs continued to get any financing from the university. The administration did not even bother to dissolve the previously created institutes, as it had never recognized them in the first place.

Instead of Renewal: Destruction and Forced Transformation

A myriad of forces took part in dismantling the Department of History at the University of Leipzig, namely the conservative CDU Saxon State Government (especially Science Minister Meyer), the new university administration and its rector Cornelius Weiss, as well as other university councils and representatives from various West German institutions, such as the Science Council and other state ministries. In addition, some West German historians and the officials of different associations and learned societies played a role, as members of commissions, as evaluators, and/or as candidates for newly created professorships. Their roles were further convoluted by their natural interest in securing jobs in the East for their own West German academic associates. Some historians from Leipzig also participated in this process.

The Patterns of Disassembling Existing Scholarship

The main thrust of disassembling existing historical scholarship in Leipzig followed the same pattern as in Berlin, Halle, Rostock, Greifswald, and other East German university centers. The Historical Institutes were kept legally intact, while the state governments appointed commissions that developed a new professorial canon, recommending the right candidates for the new professorial positions. The state governments themselves appointed those candidates to their new positions, at which point, the previous East Germans holding those positions were dismissed.

East Germans enforced the political "cleansing" of East German academic personnel; there were no West Germans in those Personnel Commissions. The state ministries provided the norms and criteria. The subsequent mass layoffs were also put in the hands of East German representatives, namely those former East German professors who were reappointed according to the West German laws governing Higher Education. And as the newly appointed directors of the Historical Institutes, this fell under their jurisdiction.

Yet, when it came to deciding the new institutional and professorial structure, as well as the criteria for the job candidates, West German professors occupied all leading positions. Thus, the transformation of History departments was pushed largely along the lines of personnel policies. This resulted in two intended outcomes: first, it precluded any real engagement with the scholarly views of those former GDR historians about to lose their jobs; and second, the old German university tradition of dominance of the senior professors was reintroduced—undoing even some of the gains of the West German university reforms of the 1970s. None of these scholars had held a university chair before being appointed at the University of Leipzig.

Steps, Levels, Dimensions

When on December 12, 1990, State Minister Meyer informed the president of the University of Leipzig that the state government had decided to close several subsections, the History of the GDR (seven scholars) and the History of the USSR and the Socialist World System (eleven scholars), these eighteen scholars were summarily dismissed, without any consideration of their individual scholarly and political profiles. In addition, without any formal decision, the subsections of "the Methodology of the Teaching of History" (six scholars) and "Latin America Seminar" (five scholars) from the "General History of the Early Modern Period 1500–1789" were also disbanded.

The Saxon State Ministry for Science and Research created three personnel committees to assess the political reliability of all scholars at the University of Leipzig, and the Personnel Committee on Humanities and Social Sciences investigated the Leipzig historians between November 1991 and July 1992. The members of those committees were under oath to not divulge anything about their internal matters. The committees created dossiers for political reliability for each colleague, and a negative recommendation amounted to the scholar's dismissal. In the case of Professor Manfred Kossok, he was accused of political unreliability without any interviews or conversations conducted with him. The committee did not even officially inform him that his "unreliability" was due to his tenure as vice-rector between 1964 and 1968. Therefore, he was not allowed to apply for a new professorship because, twenty-five years earlier, he was relatively briefly part of the university administration, which was a reason for being deemed politically compromised.[31]

In the spring of 1992, the Saxon Science Ministry recommended gutting the academic and administrative personnel of the University of Leipzig from 24,000 to not more than 10,000. In the Humanities and the Social Sciences the planned reductions in personnel amounted to 67 percent. Manfred Kossok warned of the likely consequences of such a gutting in a memorandum from March 9, 1992, where he predicted that the reduction of Leipzig's History Department would undermine its reputation and quality. Leipzig was to become "a medium-sized department [. . .] just a little larger than Paderborn." The University of Paderborn was invoked as a symbol of an adequate but provincial West German university.[32]

In 1993 West German professor Ulrich von Hehl, previously funded by the conservative Adenauer Foundation, became the new department chair, and the entire department was given its pre-1945 name: "Historical Seminar." The freshly imported West German professors were apparently indifferent and/or—ironically, historically unaware—of the symbolic significance of this name, and what it suggested, vis-à-vis how pre-1945 professors in Leipzig had opposed any form of cultural, universal, as well as comparative history.

Epilogue

The leading force behind the dismantling of the Department of History at the University of Leipzig was the Saxon State Government under Professor Kurt Biedenkopf, especially the aforementioned State Minister for Science and Art, Professor Hans-Joachim Meyer. This Ministry provided the financial, as well as the political, ideological, and even the personnel-related criteria to the university committees. Furthermore, the Ministry involved itself directly with the undoing process, thus undermining its own official agenda, regarding the autonomy of institutions of higher education under its jurisdiction. As the process was accomplished largely via financial levers, the Saxon State Government used the hammer of cutting financial support to smash all those teaching and researching institutions that did not fit into West German conventions, enabling the perpetrators to remove scholarly considerations from the front lines of the debate.

Thus, financial restrictions became the main argument for the mass termination of employment in Leipzig. Of course, additional justifications were also utilized. The Saxon State Government, whose West German advisors were mainly imported from Bavaria, created a *tabula rasa* situation, which was intended to demoralize East German scholars and technical staff. The use of intimidation was exploited to keep the number of fired employees' lawsuits at a minimum, while the new university administration provided generously for defending against employment-related law suits in its overall budget.

The consequences of the mass firings were only too predictable: Leipzig's research profile decreased substantially both in depth and overall scope. The focus was narrowed toward German history and any subject matters beyond German history were severely limited. Leipzig's internationally respected tradition of universal and increasingly global history was cut off, the comparative history of historiography was sacrificed, and the international and interdisciplinary networks were ripped apart. The university administration's claim, to push for excellence, naturally rang hollow under these circumstances.

Yet one must note that in Leipzig at least a tiny minority of East German scholars were reappointed, while in other places of the former GDR, such as at Berlin's Humboldt University, not a single East German historian was allowed to keep his or her position. In Leipzig, two historians were reappointed to senior C-4 chairs (Hoyer and Zwahr) while three other scholars received lower-paid C-3 professorships (Held, Matschke, and Zeuske). Thus, the situation in Leipzig, at first glance, might not seem as severe as elsewhere, in the newly incorporated former East German territories. However, this image is somewhat misleading, inasmuch as there was no real integration of East German scholars. As some additional historians were kept on the payroll for a limited time (largely because no qualified West German candidate could be found to teach such unique fields as Saxon territorial history or historical didactics), this changed after 1993, as more and more West German scholars were hired on in Leipzig. The East

German professors, whose contracts had been renewed in 1992, left after they reached their mandatory retirement age within a few years.

Leipzig was purposely transformed from a world-class, historical-research site into a more provincial place, "not much bigger than Paderborn." This decline in profile, reputation, and quality was intentional. At the expense of Leipzig, the University of Dresden was supposed to become the show-horse of Saxon higher education. However, while the University of Leipzig was indeed destroyed as an internationally recognized research center, the University of Dresden never actually evolved into that alternative center of excellence—for original and innovative historical scholarship.

The dismantling of historical scholarship in Leipzig between 1991 and 1993 cannot be seen as some kind of transformation, let alone integration, of East German scholarship into the academic landscape of a united Germany. Instead, we see the purposeful destruction of what Leipzig represented and its replacement with a more provincial West German academic canon. This development cannot even be classified as a hostile takeover, inasmuch as what was unique and excellent about Leipzig was not "taken over," but obliterated. Historical scholarship in Leipzig lost its originality and its high academic standards. Its comparative, international, and global focus was sacrificed and its reputation in the international scientific community lost.

Translated by Axel Fair-Schulz

Notes

1. On the aims and criteria of a judgment of GDR historical scholarship, see Werner Röhr, "Entwicklung oder Abwicklung der Geschichtswissenschaft: Polemische Bemerkungen zu den Voraussetzungen einer Urteilsbildung über Historiker und historische Institutionen der DDR," *Berliner Debatte INITIAL*, 1 (1991), no. 4, 425–34, and no. 5, 542–50. For a full account of the destruction of East German historical scholarship, see Werner Röhr, *Abwicklung: Das Ende der Geschichtswissenschaft der DDR*, vol. 1: *Analyse einer Zerstörung*; vol. 2: *Analyse ausgewählter Forschungen, Übersichten, Register* (Berlin, 2011–2012), 1,141 (both volumes). For Leipzig, see especially vol. 1, 393–410.

2. On the history of this institute, see Matthias Middell, *Weltgeschichtsschreibung im Zeitalter der Verfachlichung und Professionalisierung: Das Leipziger Institut für Kultur- und Universalgeschichte 1890–1990*. 3 vols. (Leipzig, 2005), esp. vol. 1: *Das Institut unter Leitung Karl Lamprechts*. On Lamprecht, see also Roger Chickering, *Karl Lamprecht: A German Academic Life, 1856–1915* (Atlantic Highlands, NJ, 1993).

3. See Ernst Werner, *Die Geburt einer Großmacht: Die Osmanen (1300–1481). Ein Beitrag zur Genesis des türkischen Feudalismus* ([East] Berlin 1966, 4th

ed. 1985); Ernst Werner and Walter Markov, *Die Geschichte der Türken: Von den Anfängen bis zur Gegenwart* ([East] Berlin 1978, 2nd ed. 1979); Ernst Werner and Martin Erbstößer, *Ketzer und Heilige: Das religiöse Leben im Hochmittelalter* ([East] Berlin, 1986; Austrian edition: Vienna etc., 1986); Martin Erbstößer, *Die Kreuzzüge: Eine Kulturgeschichte* (Leipzig, 1977, 3rd ed. Bergisch-Gladbach 1998); English translation *The Crusades* (Newton Abbott, 1978, and New York, 1979); French translation *Les temps des croisades* (Paris, 1978). On Werner, see also Klaus-Peter Matschke and Sabine Tanz (eds.), *Der Mediävist Ernst Werner (1920–1993) und sein Platz in der internationalen Geschichtswissenschaft* (Leipzig, 2009). The following remarks are based on Röhr, *Abwicklung*, vol. 2, 715–48.

4. Heinrich Sproemberg, "Die Entstehung des Manichäismus im Abendland: Ein religiös-soziales Problem," Idem, *Mittelalter und demokratische Geschichtsschreibung: Ausgewählte Abhandlungen*, edited by Manfred Unger ([East] Berlin, 1971), 85–102. On Sproemberg, see Gerhard Heitz and Manfred Unger (eds.), *Liber memorabilis Heinrich Sproemberg: Etudes présentées à la Commission internationale pour l'histoire des assemblées d'états et du parlementarisme* (Rostock, 1966).

5. See Herbert Grundmann, *Religiöse Bewegungen im Mittelalter* (Leipzig, 1933); English translation *Religious Movements in the Middle Ages* (Notre Dame, 1996); Idem, *Ketzergeschichte des Mittelalters* (Göttingen, 1963). See also Walter Goetz, Herbert Grundmann, and Fritz Wagner (eds.), *Neue Beträge zur Geschichte der religiösen Bewegungen im Mittelalter, Archiv für Kulturgeschichte*, XXXVII (1955), Pt. 2.

6. See Klaus Peter Matschke and Ernst Werner (eds.), *Ideologie und Gesellschaft im hohen und späten Mittelalter: Studienbibliothek DDR-Geschichtswissenschaft: Forschungswege–Bilanz–Aufgaben*, vol. 8 ([East] Berlin, 1988).

7. See Ernst Werner's Habilitation work *Pauperes Christi: Studien zu den sozial-religiösen Bewegungen im Zeitalter des Reformpapsttums* (Leipzig, 1956).

8. See Evamaria Engel, "Stadtgeschichtsschreibung zum Mittelalter in der DDR: Ergebnisse, Probleme, Perspektiven," Fritz Mayrhofer (ed.), *Stadtgeschichtsforschung: Aspekte, Tendenzen, Perspektiven* (Linz, 1993), 81 *et seq*. See also Evamaria Engel, *Die deutsche Stadt im Mittelalter* (Düsseldorf, 2005), and Idem, *Städtisches Leben im Mittelalter: Schriftquellen und Bildzeugnisse* (Cologne, Weimar, and Vienna, 2006). The following remarks are based on Röhr, *Abwicklung*, vol. 2, 749–71.

9. See Karl Czok, "Bürgerkämpfe und Chronistik im deutschen Spätmittelalter," *Zeitschrift für Geschichtswissenschaft*, 10 (1962), no. 3, 637 *et seq*.; Idem, "Kommunale Bewegung und bürgerliche Opposition in Deutschland im 13. Jahrhundert," *Wisenschaftliche. Zeitschrift der Karl-Marx-Universität Leipzig: Gesellschafts- und sprachwissenschaftliche Reihe*, 14 (1965), no. 3, 413 *et seq*.; Idem, *Die Stadt: Ihre Stellung in der deutschen Geschichte* (Leipzig etc., 1969); Idem, "Die Bürgerkämpfe in Süd- und Westdeutschland im 14. Jahrhundert," Carl Haase (ed.), *Die Stadt des Mittelalters*, vol. 3 (Darmstadt, 1973), 303 *et seq*.; Idem, *Vorstädte: Zu ihrer Entstehung, Wirtschaft und Sozialentwicklung in der älteren deutschen Stadtgeschichte* ([East] Berlin, 1979. On Czok, see Helmut Bräuer and Elke Schlenkrich (eds.), *Die Stadt als Kommunikationsraum: Beiträge zur Stadtgeschichte vom Mittelalter bis ins 20. Jahrhundert. Festschrift für Karl Czok zum 75. Geburtstag* (Leipzig, 2001). See also

Erika Uitz, *Die Frau in der mittelalterlichen Stadt* (Leipzig and Stuttgart, 1988); 2nd ed. Freiburg im Breisgau, 1992; English edition: *Women in the Medieval Town* (London, 1990); Japanese edition: Tokyo, 1993; and many other publications by the same author. See Barbara Pätzold's obituary: "Nachruf auf Erika Uitz," *L'Homme*, 21 (2010), issue 1, 97–98. On East German historiography on medieval towns, see also Andreas Dorpalen, *German History in Marxist Perspective: The East German Approach* (Detroit, 1985), 93–98.

10. On the "early bourgeois revolution" concept and its implications, see Günter Vogler, "Das Konzept 'deutsche frühbürgerliche Revolution': Genese–Aspekte–kritische Bilanz," *Sitzungsberichte der Leibniz-Sozietät*, vol. 48 (2001), no. 5, 87–117.

11. See, e.g., from Leipzig historians, Manfred Bensing, *Thomas Müntzer und der Thüringer Aufstand 1525* ([East] Berlin, 1966); Manfred Bensing and Siegfried Hoyer, *Der deutsche Bauernkrieg 1524–1526*, 3rd ed. ([East] Berlin, 1973); Siegfried Bräuer, *Martin Luther in marxistischer Sicht von 1945 bis zum Beginn der achtziger Jahre* ([East] Berlin, 1983); Siegfried Hoyer, *Das Militärwesen im deutschen Bauernkrieg 1524–1526* ([East] Berlin, 1976); Siegfried Hoyer, "Die deutsche frühbürgerliche Revolution," Manfred Kossok (ed.), *Revolutionen der Neuzeit 1500–1917* ([East] Berlin, 1982); Max Steinmetz and Karl Czok, *Leipziger Land im Bauernkrieg* (Leipzig, 1975); Gerhard Zschäbitz, *Martin Luther: Größe und Grenzen*, vol. 1: 1483–1526 ([East] Berlin, 1967); Siegfried Hoyer (ed.), *Reform–Reformation–Revolution: Ausgewählte Beiträge einer wissenschaftlichen Konferenz in Leipzig am 10. und 11.10.1977* (Leipzig, 1980); Max Steinmetz and Gerhard Brendler (ed.), *Weltwirkung der Reformation: Internationales Symposium anlässlich der 450-Jahr-Feier der Reformation in Wittenberg vom 24.–26. 10. 1967, Referate und Diskussionen*, 2 vols. ([East] Berlin, 1969).

12. See Max Steinmetz (ed.), *Die frühbürgerliche Revolution in Deutschland: Studienbibliothek DDR-Geschichtswissenschaft: Forschungswege–Bilanz–Aufgaben*, vol. 5 ([East] Berlin, 1985), with an extensive bibliography. See also Adolf Laube, Max Steinmetz, and Günter Vogler, *Illustrierte Geschichte der deutschen frühbürgerlichen Revolution* ([East] Berlin, 1974). For fair judgments by Western historians, see Rainer Wohlfeil, "Entfremdung und Annäherung: Krise und Krisenbewältigung im Zeitalter von Reformation und Bauernkrieg, gespiegelt in Situationen deutsch-deutscher Diskussionen zur Deutung deutscher Geschichte des 16. Jahrhunderts," Monika Hagenmaier and Sabine Holtzt (eds.), *Krisenbewusstsein und Krisenbewältigung in der Frühen Neuzeit/Crisis in Early Modern Europe: Festschrift für Hans-Christoph Rublack* (Berlin and Bonn, 1992), 331–50, and also Dorpalen, *German History in Marxist Perspective*, 99–113. For the rare case of an American scholar who studied in the GDR, see Romwald Maczka, "Retheologizing Thomas Müntzer in the German Democratic Republic: 15 Years of Marxist and Non-Marxist Research," *Mennonite Quarterly Review*, 63 (October 1989), 345–66, and idem, *Thomas Muentzer Scholarship in the German Democratic Republic, 1949–1983*, PhD dissertation, Karl Marx University (Leipzig, 1987). *See* also the dissertation of the Swiss historian Laurenz Müller, *Diktatur und Revolution: Reformation und Bauernkrieg in der*

Geschichtsschreibung des "Dritten Reiches" und der DDR (Stuttgart, 2004). The young historian died tragically in an accident in the Alps immediately after the successful defense of the thesis.

13. An American scholar noted that, despite the "canonical" concept of early bourgeois revolution, even Max Steinmetz's "own students began to subject it to a threefold critique: First, they rejected Steinmetz's identification of pre-modern burghers as the forerunners of a modern bourgeoisie; second, they integrated Germany's reformation into European history via the theory of social revolutions; and third, they developed a new appreciation for the role of religion in the German Reformation. These revisions came to their peak during the Luther jubilee of 1983, which restored Martin Luther and his Reformation to a positive place in the official narrative of German history." Thomas A. Brady, Jr., *The Protestant Revolution in German History*, German Historical Institute, Occasional Paper No. 22 (Washington, DC, 1998), 21–22. See also Brent O. Peterson, " 'Workers of the World Unite—for God's Sake!': Recent Luther Scholarship in the German Democratic Republic," James D. Tracy (ed.), *Luther and the Modern State in Germany* (Kirksville, MO, 1986), 77–100 (*eds.*).

14. See *Deutsche Geschichte*, vol. 3: *Die Epoche des Übergangs vom Feudalismus zum Kapitalismus von den siebziger Jahren des 15. Jahrhunderts bis 1789* (Berlin, 1989), chapters 1 and 2.

15. See Hartmut Zwahr, *Zur Konstituierung des Proletariats als Klasse: Strukturuntersuchungen über das Leipziger Proletariat während der industriellen Revolution* (Berlin, 1978); West German edition: Munich, 1981; Idem, "Zur Klassenanalyse der deutschen Bourgeoisie in der bürgerlichen Umwälzung," *Jahrbuch für Geschichte*, vol. 18 ([East] Berlin, 1978). See also Georg G. Iggers (ed.), *Marxist Historiography in Transformation* (New York and Oxford, 1991), and idem (ed.), *Ein anderer historischer Blick: Beispiele ostdeutscher Sozialgeschichte* (Frankfurt-Main, 1991). See also Iggers's contribution to this volume.

16. See Manfred Kossok (ed.), *Revolutionen der Neuzeit 1500–1817* ([East] Berlin, 1982).

17. On Markov, see Manfred Neuhaus et al. (eds.), *"Wenn jemand seinen Kopf bewusst hinhält . . .": Beiträge zu Werk und Wirken von Walter Markov* (Leipzig, 1995); Sven Heitkamp, *Walter Markov: Ein DDR-Historiker zwischen Parteidoktrin und Profession* (Leipzig, 2003); Wolfgang Küttler and Matthias Middell (eds.), *Nation und Revolution: Beiträge eines wissenschaftlichen Kolloquiums der Leibniz-Sozietät aus Anlass des 100. Geburtstages von Ernst Engelberg und Walter Markov* (Leipzig, 2011); Matthias Middell (ed.), *Lust am Krimi: Beiträge zu Werk und Wirkung Walter Markovs* (Leipzig, 2011).

18. Between 1982 and 1990 the IZR edited in 29 parts the *Leipziger Beiträge zur Revolutionsforschung*.

19. Between 1971 and 1990 ten volumes of the *Studien zur Revolutionsgeschichte* were published. See Matthias Middell (ed.), *Vom Brasilienvertrag zur Globalgeschichte: In Erinnerung an Manfred Kossok anlässlich seines 70. Geburtstages* (Leipzig, 2002).

20. See Walter Markov, *Weltgeschichte im Revolutionsquadrat*, edited with an introduction by Manfred Kossok (Berlin, 1979); Idem, *Revolution im Zeugenstand: Frankreich 1789–1799*, 2 vols. (Leipzig, 1982); Idem *Jacques Roux oder vom Elend der Biographie* ([East] Berlin, 1966); Idem, *Die Freiheiten des Priesters Roux* ([East] Berlin 1967; new ed. Leipzig, 2009); Idem (ed.), *Jacques Roux: Scripta et acta* ([East] Berlin, 1967); Idem, *Exkurse zu Jacques Roux* ([East] Berlin, 1970). Markov and Kossok belonged to the very few GDR historians who established contacts with colleagues in Israel, namely with Walter Grab. See Walter Grab, *Meine vier Leben: Gedächtniskünstler–Emigrant–Jakobinerforscher–Demokrat* (Cologne, 1999), 169. See also Iris Nachum, "Es muss nicht immer Wiedergutmachung sein: Walter Grab und das Minerva Institut für deutsche Geschichte an der Universität Tel Aviv," José Brunner and Iris Nachum (eds.) *Tel Aviver Jahrbuch für deutsche Geschichte*, vol. 40 (Göttingen, 2012), 265–66 (*eds.*).

21. For an overview of the research and extensive bibliography on the topic, see Kurt Holzapfel and Matthias Middell (eds.), *Die Französische Revolution 1789: Geschichte und Wirkung. Studienbibliothek DDR-Geschichtswissenschaft: Forschungswege–Bilanz–Aufgaben*, vol. 10 ([East] Berlin, 1989).

22. See Walter Markov and Albert Soboul, *1789: Die große Revolution der Franzosen* ([East] Berlin, 1973), 4th ed. 1989; West German edition: Cologne 1980; Polish edition: Warsaw 1984; Slovenian edition.: Ljubljana 1989. See also Matthias Middell (ed.), *200. Jahrestag der Französischen Revolution: Kritische Bilanz der Forschungen zum Bicentennaire* (Leipzig, 1991). For an early cooperation between Markov and Soboul, see Walter Markov and Albert Soboul (eds.), *Die Sansculotten von Paris: Dokumente zur Geschichte der Volksbewegung, 1793–1794*, with preface by Georges Levebvre ([East] Berlin, 1957) (*eds.*).

23. Manfred Kossok, *In tyrannos: Revolutionen der Weltgeschichte. Von den Hussiten bis zur Commune* (Leipzig, 1989). See also his *Am Hofe Ludwigs XIV.* (Leipzig and Stuttgart, 1990); Dutch edition *Aan het hof van Lodewijk XIV* (Haarlem, 1993).

24. See Manfred Kossok, *Vergleichende Revolutionsgeschichte der Neuzeit. Ausgewählte Schriften*, vol. 2, ed. by Matthias Middell (Leipzig 2000).

25. Manfred Kossok, *Kolonialgeschichte und Unabhängigkeitsbewegung in Lateinamerika. Ausgewählte Schriften*, vol. 1, edited by Matthias Middell (Leipzig, 2000).

26. See Werner Berthold, *Zur Geschichte der Geschichtswissenschaft vom Altertum bis zum 20. Jahrhundert*, 2 vols. (Potsdam, 1989–1990).

27. See Manfred Kossok, *Zwischen Reform und Revolution: Übergänge von der Universal- zur Globalgeschichte. Ausgewählte Schriften*, vol. 3, edited by Matthias Middell (Leipzig, 2000).

28. Sektion Geschichte/Rat der Sektion, Beschlussprotokoll der Ratssitzung vom 5.6.1990 (author: Dr. W. Röke, Wiss. Sekretär, 8.6.1990). This and the documents that are quoted in the following are in possession of Werner Röhr.

29. See Fachbereich Geschichte, Positionspapier zur Neuprofilierung des Fachbereiches Geschichte der Universität Leipzig (Fassung vom 18.3.1991).

30. See Matthias Middell, Vorschlag zu einem Leipziger Modell für universitäre An-Institute (Anlage 2 zum Schreiben von Manfred Kossok an den Rektor der Universität Leipzig, Professor Cornelius Weiss, vom 9.3.1991), see fn. 32.

31. For a positive and nuanced evaluation of Kossok's life and work, see Michael Zeuske, "Manfred Kossok zum Gedenken," *Zeitschrift für Geschichtswissenschaft*, 41 (1993), no. 9, 821–23. See also Zeuske'e essay "Sozialgeschichte, Historismus und der Zykluscharakter von Revolutionen: Lateinamerikanische und spanische Geschichte im Werk von Manfred Kossok," Middell (ed.), *Vom Brasilienvertrag zur Globalgeschichte*, 49–84.

32. Letter of Professor Dr. Manfred Kossok to Professor Dr. Cornelius Weiss, Rector of the University of Leipzig, March 9, 1992. A copy of the letter is in possession of the author. It should be noted that Weiss sees the extent and form of *Abwicklung* in hindsight in a critical perspective. See Cornelius Weiss, *Risse in der Zeit: Ein Leben zwischen Ost und West* (Berlin, 2012), 307–42 (eds.).

13

From "Imperialist Class Enemy" to "Partners in Leadership" in 365 Days?

East German American Studies Since 1989

RAINER SCHNOOR

Prelude

Nearly twenty years after the "Fall of the Wall," the "Big Bang," and the *Wende*, scholars from the East and the West sat down together in the American town of Potsdam, New York, to discuss historiographical transformations in East Germany. This is an indication of the uniqueness of the changes that have happened over the past twenty years.

Whereas many previous revolutions resulted in the physical or social extermination of the former political and intellectual class, the process of German reunification was a superficially peaceful one. The very fact that scholars from the former GDR, all of them tied in one way or another to the *Ancien regime*, were able to attend this conference in the United States and had not ended at lamp posts, in front of a firing squad, in work camps, or in exile is evidence of this peculiarity.

Occasionally, one hears jeremiads by East German intellectuals about the *Abwicklung* (dismissal) of the East German academic system and sizeable numbers of its personnel. Yes, the laments are justified. However, rarely one hears an honest analysis of their part in the downfall of the GDR, as a result of their silence regarding the way the GDR leadership dealt with reality. Even less mention is made of the active participation of the GDR intelligentsia in this treatment of reality, and its substitution by ideology, here used in the Marxist double meaning of "preconceived sets of ideas" and "wrong consciousness." May everyone look at his or her own record by reviewing their publications and teaching!

Using Antonio Gramsci's concepts, the East German intellectuals survived the transformation of Marxism-Leninism from the "dominant" to a "residual" ideology, including the emergence of pluralist, multifaceted sets of ideas as the new "dominant" ideologies.[1] Although most of the East German participants of the conference mentioned above were "ejected" from the academic system, they succeeded in establishing a "second scholarly culture," existing parallel to the surprising strength of left-wing politics in East Germany and even in West Germany. This is a sign of the resilience of left politics and of dialectical and historical materialism, now freed from the fetters of real-existing socialism and its ideological guardians.

It appears to be worthwhile to look at how the "incoming" new and not-so-new ideologies eliminated, marginalized, or altered the structure of thought and action that had dominated the GDR and its academic system for forty years. (East) German novelist Ingo Schulze, in his novel *Neue Leben* aptly summarized the problem by asking: "*Auf welche Art und Weise kam der Westen in meinen Kopf? Und was hat er da angerichtet* [How did the West get into my head? And what did it do there]?"[2] How did East German scholars react to the "nouveau regime" after 1990? Did they put up stubborn resistance? Did they sing the praise of the new plurality? How did they change their approaches and their methodologies? What did they tell their students after the *Wende* (as long as they were able to teach in the transition period)—the same students they had known from the last GDR years?

The present writer will try to answer some of the questions raised from his personal, University of Potsdam (Germany)-based experience from 1990 to 2007. He was among the remaining eleven of sixty once permanently appointed East German Americanists who were able to continue research and teaching after the new system was established at the university in 1992–1993.[3]

The Status Quo Ante

At a talk in Berlin in January 2008, the (East) German writer Thomas Brussig said that it is convenient to talk or write about the GDR: its history seems to be over (at least chronologically), nothing new can be added, it is easily to be surveyed, and nearly everything is in the open. Elmar Faber, the former publisher of the East German Aufbau Verlag, contradicts this by saying that the case is *not* closed; it is still *open-ended*, but also open to fictionalization and distortion. It is comfortable, the joy of all historians, to be able to write its history from its end backwards in a finalistic "I've-known-it-all-before" tone.

Here is a case study: GDR American Studies was a small and relatively peripheral discipline up until the end of the GDR. Compared to, for example, History, Marxism-Leninism or German Studies as academic subjects, American Studies had always been marginal. From the very beginning, it had been firmly embedded in the framework of the Cold War, in the confrontation between the Soviet Union and the United States, as well as in the conflict between the Federal Republic and the GDR. Its mission was twofold: it was supposed to convey knowledge about the history, culture, and language of the United States and, at the same time, to de-mask the "true character of U.S. imperialism," as the "main enemy of mankind," and to refute American ideology. It was the critical, ideology-based study of *the* "imperialist superpower."

Although the discipline underwent transformations and partial differentiation between the "dangerous 1950s," the "narrow-minded 1960s," the "initially hopeful 1970s," and the "helpless 1980s," the political mission mentioned above remained the same.[4]

The actors in the discipline genuinely understood their research and teaching for a long time as a symbiosis of "Parteilichkeit und Professionalität," to use Konrad Jarausch's juxtaposition. The gap between "partiality/partisanship" and professionalism, characterized by Jarausch as a "Zwiespalt" (vicissitudes), had not existed from the beginning.[5]

It appeared later, initially after the infamous 11th plenary session of the Central Committee of the SED (the GDR Communist Party), in 1965, condemning all avant-garde art in East and West. It intensified in the aftermath of the expulsion from the GDR of dissident singer/songwriter Wolf Biermann in 1976 that caused an exodus of an important section of GDR writers and artists. It came to an apex when the SED leadership, in the late '80s, thwarted Gorbachevian hopes among the intelligentsia and lost its remaining credibility.

In American Studies, only then the rift between the "official," partisan view of the United States and the "professional" view became evident and was articulated, albeit in a disguised way. The underlying, exclusive philosophy and theory in the field was based on dialectical and historical materialism in the official GDR reading of Marx, Engels, and Lenin's analysis of "imperialism as the last and dying stage of capitalism." It was holistic, monistic, and, until the 1970s, very often economic-determinist. The documents of the Socialist Unity Party of Germany, the Communist Party of the Soviet Union, and the Communist Party of the USA, interpreted by the Institutes, later Sections of Marxism-Leninism, were the yardsticks and foundations of research and teaching. This, of course, structured and limited the American Studies curriculum.

In the 1970s, parallel to the hopes arising with, at that time, the new General Secretary Honecker, the influence of neo-Marxist and Euro-communist ideas made themselves felt in the intelligentsia. The direct contact with noncommunist scholars from the United States and the few study trips to the United States made possible after the U.S. recognition of the GDR in 1974, gradually softened and transformed the original, rigid representation of the United States. The expectations and the growing knowledge of a wider GDR audience and their increasing exposure to Western media, predominantly West German TV, gradually made a merely propagandist picture of the USA obsolete and doubtful. The limitation of the GDR American Studies "Geschichtsbild" (overall interpretation) to the history of progressive movements, the U.S. working class, the labor unions, and the CPUSA slowly gave way to a more comprehensive view. It began to include a more sophisticated social analysis. In the 1980s, East German senior economic historian Jürgen Kuczynski admitted the existence of xenophobic and reactionary tendencies in the U.S. working class and labor unions and undermined the exclusively idealized representation in GDR publications and curricula. However, despite tendencies of "*subtiler Entpolitisierung* [subtle de-politization]" (Manfred Jäger), GDR American Studies, up to the end, remained caught in what Max Weber called the "Gehäuse der Hörigkeit," the "cage of obedience," to the powers that be.[6] This does not exclude a good deal of interesting studies and honest teaching.

The Big Bang: Self-Reform, and "No Man's Land" for One Year

The rapid degeneration of the old regime and the fall of the Wall came unexpectedly for the majority of the GDR population, in general, and for the intelligentsia, in particular. Although sensing that something was in the air, the latter remained shut off in their cocoons. Many of them had hoped for a "biological solution," i.e., for the coming to power of a post-Honecker, pro-Gorbachov, younger leadership, genuinely opening the country to the rest of the world.

In academia, the fall of the Wall did not produce the November 9, Berlin-Kudamm champagne exuberance. Instead, it resulted in disbelief, shock, fear, numbness, and helplessness. Why?

The East German working class, on paper the ruling class, had begun to shake off the government and leading party that supposedly were their true representatives. The beginning opposition to the leading role of the SED and the Marxism-Leninism Departments in the universities did not come from the faculty, not even from the non-party faculty. It came from parts of the student body, supported by the increasing influence of the "Neues Forum," the first GDR-wide organized opposition group. At the same time, the SED organizations pulled up the drawbridges and began to prepare themselves for the role of opposition in a genuine multiparty "new" GDR. However, even the SED reformers had to accept the increasing wish for a quick unification that became increasingly popular among East Germans. The slogan "*Deutschland einig Vaterland*," the call for a rush to German unity, which was aggressively promoted by West German Chancellor Helmut Kohl and reluctantly accepted by East German Socialist Prime Minister Hans Modrow in February 1990, led to widespread disarray among the SED's "true believers." The small groups of the "Neues Forum" students successfully demanded the end of the Marxism-Leninist domination of the curricula and the end of the leading role of the SED within the university. In Potsdam, well-respected, non-party East German senior professors, mainly from the natural sciences, took over leading position in the administration, encouraging grassroots reform.

In American Studies, the new freedoms were used to their full extent: the ban of private contacts with colleagues in the West was lifted, the right to invite guest speakers without ministry permission was granted, new courses were added to the curriculum, and M.A. studies were introduced after consultation and with the assistance of West Berlin institutes. Formally, the cage of obedience was shattered, but mentally it was still intact. Nevertheless, the strong GDR "other-directedness" gave way to a quickly accepted, self-reforming "inner-directedness."

The student population was split: one third appeared to be as shockstruck as the faculty, another third was still undecided and waiting, and the last third welcomed the changes, cooperating creatively through newly elected committees outside the "Free German Youth," the official GDR youth organization. Apart from this, all students used the new opportunities to go to West Berlin for shopping, book buying, and culture. Many instantly used offers of study trips and *au pair* jobs in English-speaking countries and vanished from one day to the next. Nevertheless, the courses went on without any interruption—as did the train service and garbage removal. While the majority of the students at this time appeared to be pro GDR (visible in the demonstrative display of GDR flags in dorm windows during the unification process), they were open-minded and prepared for new developments. Quickly they spotted the "*Wendehälse*" (turncoats) on the faculty and challenged them.

The year 1990 was ambiguous: on the one hand, it was a creative "no man's land" between the "not-the-old-anymore" and the "not-yet-the-unknown-new." On the other hand, it was a period of deep existential insecurity and anxiety.

The Nouveau Regime: Change of Paradigms

This interlude ended with the formal unification on October 3, 1990. From then on the laws of the Federal Republic applied to the GDR. West German political structures, institutions, and, step-by-step, ways of thinking entered the new territories.

In higher education this marked the transition from a short-lived self-determination to new power structures dominated by West German academic elites. Peter Bender, Konrad H. Jarausch, Jürgen Kocka, Wolf Lepenies, Dieter Simon (in alphabetical order), and many others have written extensively about this process from the point of view of the West; Stefan Bollinger, Mario Kessler, Ulrich van der Heyden, Jörg Roesler, and others have written from the point of view of the East. Some of the former were not only observers but active participants in what Jürgen Kocka described as the "*Übertragung des westdeutschen Modells auf den Osten unter westdeutscher Regie* [the transfer of the West German model to the East under West German management]."[7]

This takeover was ambiguous; in the Potsdam Institute of English and American Studies a virtual Western flood rolled in: money, books, materials, photocopiers, and computers. Study trips, invitations to conferences, scholarships, guest lecturers, and exchange agreements were offered.

The same applied to all of the seven institutions in East Germany that had taught American Studies. Most of this came from the West German Federal Government, some from the European Union, some from the United States, and the (then-still existing) United States Information Agency, some from the partner West German state level, and, in the case of Potsdam, from the State of North Rhine-Westphalia and its universities. The first guest professors, sent and paid by their home universities as "development aid," came as early as the summer semester of 1990. Along with this gratefully accepted help, there came a "cargo" of administrators, in Potsdam from their partner Bundesland (state), abbreviated NRW, very soon dubbed "***Nun Regieren Wir***: [now *we* govern]. Most of them rigorously introduced the system they had known and worked in for decades, and the administrative and academic structures of the GDR were cut down very quickly.

Beginning with 1992, the first "*Berufungen*" (appointments) of West German professors or Privatdozenten (lecturers) to senior professorial posts took place. The East German faculty was confronted with a broad array of newcomers, ranging from competent and committed people with new ideas and good contacts to the not so competent, often merely career-oriented, often arrogant *conquistadores*—and also mixtures of both groups. This, of course, determined the character of the "contact zones" that developed between the East and West.

Unlike other West German professional organizations (historians, sociologists, political scientists), the "German Society for American Studies" (DGfA) welcomed East German Americanists as individual members without any checkups and entrance restrictions. On a human, subjective, professional level, the East Germans in the DGfA were generally treated without condescension. On an objective, structural level, the incoming West German colleagues had to act according to the political and ideological mission of the Federal Republic, which was to establish the West German political and academic system in the East, whether you call this "colonialist" or not.

West German Action and East German Personal Reactions

By the mid-1990s, a mere soccer team of eleven, out of the formerly sixty East German Americanists still worked in their field in universities. After the wave of checkups and investigations between 1991 and 1994, the majority had left or were told to resign: some left because of "smart" restructuring of the institutes that eliminated their positions, some went into early retirement or retirement; some, especially in the CDU-governed new *Bundesländer*, were sacked, because they had administrative or party functions. Some were fired because of Stasi connections or left because they were afraid that something might come to the surface.

The present writer was "evaluated" five times between 1991 and 1995: 1. Academic number one: degrees, publications, teaching; 2. Academic number two: recognition of GDR degrees and transfer to West German equivalents; 3. Structural: application for "*Überleitung*" (transfer) to new institute structure; 4. Political: laying open political past and "Systemnähe" (system conformity); and, 5. Investigation for possible complicity with the East German secret service, the Staatssicherheit or Stasi. In the Social Democrat-governed State of Brandenburg, famously nicknamed by Prime

Minister Stolpe as "Little GDR," the investigations were carried out with more patience and with consultation of students' and non-party colleagues' opinions.

Those few remaining East German professors and lecturers who were fortunate enough to keep their positions could rely on academic freedom. In essence they had three options. The first option was that in theory they could remain attached to parts of the old Marxist-Leninist dogma. In reality this was not a serious option and noone really pursued it, despite Brandenburg's exceptionally open political climate.

The second option was that they could change sides with flying banners and replace one set of gods with another. This would have meant to go seamlessly from Marxism into postmodernism, New Historicism, or any other of the "isms" offered. This would have meant to forget about Marx, Engels, and Lenin and go straight to Baudrillard, Deleuze, Derrida, and Foucault—no judgment intended. Noam Chomsky, Howard Zinn, and Richard Sennett would have been no option, because they were too suspiciously left-wing. Very few people in the East German American Studies environment engaged in this instant mimicry.

The third option was to review one's academic and intellectual record, analyzing where the strength and the weakness of one's work were, looking at the new intellectual opportunities, and engaging in dialogue and negotiations with them and their proponents. This was meant to maintain and extend your contacts to the people whose publications you knew and appreciated even in the "old times." It meant that you availed yourself of the new chances for exchange, travel, and communication. Most people did this, remaining in their Marxist matrix without carrying it around like a banner. As Richard Sennett said in a talk at Potsdam's Einstein Forum: "[y]ou know, we aging Marxists, we've never given up completely."[8]

Contact Zones: American Studies (East) Meets American Studies (West)

The contact and clash of two different sets of historiography (and literary studies) demands description and analysis. Here, it is hard to avoid the "them" and "us" dichotomy.

Whereas we, the East Germans, came from *one* school, the incoming West German faculty came from *many* schools. We had one master narrative: the Marxist-Leninist, mainly monolithic, linear, progress-oriented, rationalistic, holistic, teleological, chronological view of history as a sequence of "economic social formations," ending in communism. This was, in the

East German socialization, the "one and only truth." Lenin had stated: "Marxism is omnipotent because it is true."

It was said to be true because it was based on the ideology of the working class that did *not* have "limited" class interests and ideologies, as the preceding early class society, slave-owner, feudalist, and capitalist ideologies. The interest of the working class, however, was *not* the exploitation of lower classes but the liberation of all mankind. Related to the study of the United States, this meant that we, the socialist countries were supposed to be "one epoch ahead" of, for example, the USA (according to Lenin's theory of imperialism) in its contemporary, decaying, dying, and supposedly last stage of development.

This, of course, brought a doubtful smile onto the faces of many people inside and outside of academia. It was also a creative source for jokes of all kinds. Here an example: a GDR pensioner and party member, returning from a visit to the West, was asked in a party meeting whether it was true that capitalism was dying. His answer: "Comrades, this is true, but it is a beautiful death."

Marx's dictum that a social formation that had not yet reached its limits in the development of the productive forces was *not yet doomed to decline* was simply ignored. In the GDR this led to ludicrous party slogans like "Overtaking [West Germany] without catching up." Even the most orthodox of the ideologists had to admit privately that the West was far ahead in terms of technology and mass consumption.

Our new colleagues from the West had, in their majority, abandoned the enlightenment and Hegelian-Marxist notion of progress and truth—if they ever had it. They believed (if some of them believed anything at all) in various landscapes of theories and truths. The new slogan was "*die neue Beliebigkeit* [the new arbitrariness]," coined by Jürgen Habermas with critical intent. In order to "understand" our new colleagues, we very often had to engage in crash courses of various kinds: Niklas Luhmann today, Judith Butler tomorrow. Whereas *we* still thought within the concepts of class and class struggle, most of the older West German Americanists had either never used them or had given them up after the 1960s. They had seen, in the post-1960s theories and in their experience, that the working class in the West had abandoned the idea of a Communist world revolution. The Third World with its more visible class conflicts only began to appear on the horizon with the emergence of postcolonial studies.

We, however, still saw the American working class, albeit with beginning skepticism, as the agent of prospective socialist transformations in the U.S. Up to the end of the GDR some (a minority) of the Americanists thought that this revolution was going to happen under the leadership of the CPUSA. Most of the GDR scholars who had returned from study trips to the United States came to reject this, substituting an auxiliary construction of the concept of "new social forces," a conglomerate of class-conscious workers, left-wing intellectuals, disadvantaged minorities, Third-World sympathizers, etc.

In the 1980s, former orthodoxies made way to a nearly pragmatic representation of new realities without the abandonment of the basic creeds. Another important change after the *Wende* was the transformation of research and teaching approaches. Whereas *we* had to be generalists, due to the holistic Marxist orientation as well as to the lack of sources and literature, our new colleagues came with very specialized, sometimes overspecialized, segmented research and teaching interests. As we realized much later, this was caused not only by the academic imperative of "doing your own thing," but also by much better access to original sources and distrust of the "big picture."

Whereas *we*, in the tradition of Historical Materialism, emphasized, perhaps even overemphasized, the economic determinism in regard to U.S. society, many of our new colleagues arrived with "cargo" that was very often ignored or marginalized in GDR history/American studies: social, cultural, ethnic, women's, and other histories. In teaching, our rigid, survey-based curricula made way to the "neue Beliebigkeit" where everyone did his or her own specialty, often by riding their research hobby horses.

I do not want to indulge in "ostalgic" clichés, and I am well aware of the limitations we had in teaching and research. Still, no GDR student of English and American Studies left college without going through all of the survey courses in history, language, and literature. Most graduating students left our programs with a solid understanding of American society and culture. Politically the USA was seen as a danger to world peace and the enemy of worldwide social progress. (*Was this completely wrong and pure propaganda?*) Racial segregation, the prevention of progressive change all over the world, the atom bomb, the arms race, Korea and Vietnam served as evidence of this dictum. This posed problems for East German Americanists who knew that the United States was also a country with an astonishingly successful history and great democratic traditions. Two concepts could be applied to prevent the extreme "good and bad" dichotomy—one is Lenin's thesis about two cultures in every national culture: one reactionary and the other progressive and working class-oriented.

The second one was Jürgen Kuczynski's theory of the particularly progressive development of the United States until the end of the nineteenth century, ending with the Spanish-American War and its particularly reactionary development in the twentieth-century's imperialist phase.[9] This provided some leeway for research and teaching and led to remarkable publications on the "Other America," a field neglected in West German American Studies of the 1950s and 1960s.

After 1991 we met an older generation of West German Americanists who, although often with the academic-critical eye of a scholar, saw the Americans as liberators, re-educators, protectors, and friends. Suddenly, the ex-GDR Americanists were faced with an instant political switch from the underlying "bulwark of reaction" and "class enemy" orientation to the Kohl-Bush Sr. camaraderie of the USA and the new Germany as "partners in leadership." Fortunately, the relative autonomy of higher education, guaranteed by the German constitution, the *Grundgesetz*, did not demand from us (and our West German colleagues) that we indoctrinate our students with this "*Tagespolitik*" (daily political matters). These "contact zones" led to a gradual transformation of the institutes. In research and teaching this was predominantly a "Westernization," as the professorships and the academic administration were, which both are dominated by West Germans. I would like to propose that "we" learned more from "them" than most of "them" were prepared to learn from "us."

Very few of my colleagues gave up their Marxist socialization and went on in their work, guided by their lifelong ideas, purified from propaganda and excessive verbiage. To our astonishment, we found that many students, from West and East, appreciated the attempt at holistic explanations and a more or less clear-cut master narrative in the surrounding sea of the "*neue Beliebigkeit*." This was enhanced by the fact that (at least in Potsdam) the predominantly East German "*Mittelbau*," the non-senior faculty, became an anchor for many students in an academic landscape that was marked by massive, career-oriented fluctuation in the West German professoriate. In other words, if you wanted sustained tutoring, the chance to write papers and be examined, you had better to stay with the older faculty members from the East.

Exceptions Prove the Rule

The aging of the remaining Eastern "*Mittelbau*" will solve the question of the originally planned and failed "*Durchmischung*," the mixing of East and West faculty. The future development will lead to a further diversification of curricula after the abolition of the one standard curriculum in the GDR. It has led and will lead to more de-canonization and a plurality of contending canons. It has already led to pluralistic American Studies in the East of Germany.

To the dismay of many students, the introduction of the B.A./M.A. studies in recent years initiated a gradual erosion of the more "liberal arts"-oriented, old curricula. The developments of the last two decades have led (and I profoundly regret this not because of "*ostalgia*") to an over-fragmented faculty in once firmly established institutes with a long-term stable faculty. These were replaced by constantly changing, unstable setups and guest performances of a migratory academic proletariat, often not lasting longer than a semester or a year. Students are left alone with their problems of getting credit points, writing papers, and sitting for exams. Class sizes of sixty plus students in a seminar, i.e., discussion and presentation courses, adds to the problems in the field. Institutes increasingly become noncommunicating tubes held together by email and voicemail. East German colleagues, who were used to GDR standard class sizes of twenty to twenty-four students, were not alone in deploring this situation.

Conclusion and Postscript

This essay, which was not intended to be pessimistic, should end on an optimistic note.

Despite the obvious "You won—We lost" situation, the transformation of East German American Studies after 1991 has had positive results: a long impasse had ended, and petrification was overcome. Fruitful exchange, mutual help, and good cooperation between East and West appear on the sunny side of the balance sheet. Attempts of domination and condescending, arrogant behavior by the new masters are on the other side. Statements like the author's former, now deceased, West German colleague D. Sch., "my East German colleagues are incompetent and lazy," have not promoted an atmosphere of collegiality. The price for all the progress, however, was the end of East German American Studies.

More optimistically, despite all the problems, one considers the state of the student body. Students were and are a big source of hope and inspiration. They were in the GDR, and they are now, in their overwhelming majority committed, interested and hard-working. They are still predominantly antiracist, antixenophobic, anticonsumerist, antinationalistic, pro-Third World, and pro-environment. They were and are pro-USA. They were decidedly anti-Bush and are pro-Obama. They are on the side of the "Other America."

It was and is a privilege to work with them.

Notes

1. See Antonio Gramsci, *Zu Politik, Geschichte und Kultur* (Leipzig, 1980), 279.

2. Ingo Schulze, *Neue Leben* (Munich, 2007), 131.

3. See Rainer Schnoor (ed.), *Amerikanistik in der DDR: Geschichte-Analysen-Zeitzeugenberichte* (Berlin, 1999).

4. See Schnoor (ed.), *Amerikanistik in der DDR, passim.* See also Rainer Schnoor's chapters in: Detlef Junker (ed.), *The United States and Germany in the Era of the Cold War* (New York, 2004), vol. I, 618–26; vol. II, 519–25.

5. See Konrad H. Jarausch (ed.) *Zwischen Parteilichkeit und Professionalität: Bilanz der Geschichtswissenschaft der DDR* (Berlin 1991).

6. See Manfred Jäger, *Kultur und Politik in der DDR 1945–1990* (Cologne, 1995).

7. See Jürgen Kocka and Renate Mayntz (eds.), *Wissenschaft und Wiedervereinigung* (Berlin, 1998), 7.

8. Richard Sennett in a talk at the Potsdam Einstein-Forum, June 11, 1995.

9. See Jürgen Kuczynski, *Die Geschichte der Lage der Arbeiter unter dem Kapitalismus*, vols. 29 and 30 (Berlin, 1966).

14

Handling GDR Colonial Historiography

ULRICH VAN DER HEYDEN

The GDR's colonial historiography appeared toward the end of the 1950s, focusing primarily on the history of the German colonies on the African continent.[1] Four large colonial areas existed in Togo, Cameroon, Southwest Africa (today Namibia), and East Africa (today Tanzania, Burundi, and Rwanda), which were of greater interest than colonies in China (Tsingtao) or the South Pacific at least in terms of size, economy, and political importance. Another, not less important, fact that seemed to have furthered the GDR historians' focus on the history of German colonialism since the middle of the 1950s is that all the relevant files were stored on GDR territory. Moreover, in the 1950s an anticolonial liberation movement was rising throughout the African continent, sending clear signals to the communist countries.

The first, larger scholarly monograph on German colonialism published in the GDR that dealt critically with the German colonial legacy was, however, not concerned with a colony in Africa but with the history of a German colony in China.[2] It was the dissertation of Helmuth Stoecker who later became an internationally recognized colonial historian and whose book, with its several editions,[3] became the standard reference on German colonial history and was considered as such in Western Germany as well.

East and West German rivalry between acknowledged experts in political and social fields was well known; similarly, a competition between East and West German historians had developed regarding the interpretation of Germany's colonial past. Scholarly disputes between "bourgeois" and "Marxist-Leninist" historians, usually marked by the ideology of either side, arose at different times and on the most diverse issues revolving around the interpretation of the colonial past of Imperial Germany.[4]

For GDR historians it was a matter of course to deal critically with the German colonial past before World War I because up until then German historiography had lacked a particular academic discipline that addressed Germany's overseas colonialism in a critical way.

Neither the German historiography of the Weimar Republic, let alone the one of the Third Reich, nor the West German historiography up to the 1960s analyzed the colonial past of the German empire in a way that met scholarly standards. Thus, this fact alone proved to be a challenge for historians in the GDR, a then still young state.

Considered from the perspective of the research at the time it would have been the responsibility of Oriental or African Studies to analyze the challenges in the face of politics and academic policies emerging in the former colonial world. In the Western countries, handling this new situation obviously seemed to be difficult. In the Soviet Union and in the GDR as well as in other socialist European countries, however, politics and scholarship responded very quickly to the emergence of national liberation movements and their respective academic interpretations.[5]

The foundation for this had been laid quite early—soon after the end of World War II—by a few scholars in Germany's East who not only studied the history of the overseas world and the contemporaneous countries in Asia, Africa, and Latin America that at the time still suffered colonial oppressions but who also began to establish those academic fields at universities in the Soviet Zone of Occupation. Impulses came from faculty members who had dealt with overseas regions already in the Third Reich but were not overly involved in National Socialist ideology, such as Eduard Erkes and Walter Ruben who linked their former fields of study "with sustainable historical bridges to the political present."[6]

After World War II research on overseas history was actually not common; the primary objective was to account for Germany's very recent past of Nazi dictatorship and a world war with millions of dead. Similar importance was given to research on resistance against fascism, not in the least in order to show the world that not every German was a Nazi.

Thus it seems understandable that in the GDR more emphasis was placed on research of the recent past and the history of the workers' movement, which the anticolonial positions of the GDR were derived from, and maybe to an extent on research on the history of the new allies in Eastern Europe. Other historical disciplines developed only gradually.

However, the impetus to the systematic approach for overcoming Eurocentrism in research and academics was obviously not the result of scholarly realization but a response to the developments in the so-called Third World. After the military defeat of the fascist powers, the political and military decline of colonial powers in World War II, in particular Great Britain and France, and not least the emergence of socialist countries, the rebellion of the oppressed nations in the colonies became visible and was according to Marxism-Leninism a consequential development.

This spirit of rebellion was embraced by many humanities scholars in the early GDR, and thus a mood of solidarity evolved that dominated the lives of many a student and intellectual. The first historian after the *Wende*, the 1989 turnover, to point out this fact was the historian of colonialism, Peter Sebald, in his reminiscent article.[7]

Since the second higher educational reform in the middle of the 1950s the GDR government had provided funding for the relevant academic institutions in order to promote intensified non-European historical research. Already in 1951 the Modern History Branch at the History Department of Leipzig University received funding, which allowed it to focus on the history of the colonial exploitation of Africa and to begin the instruction of students.

In 1954, as a part of the principal reorientation of historical scholarship in the young GDR, which had been demanded from its historians since the seventh conference of the Central Committee of the GDR's leading party, the SED, in October 1951, a research team from Leipzig presented an authoritative contribution on the genesis of pre-imperialistic colonial systems for the first time to the public at an academic conference. The major presentation was given by one of the best-known and most influential exponents of GDR historiography, Leo Stern, and had the title "Present Tasks of German Historical Scholarship." This presentation, as well as the speech by the party leader, Walter Ulbricht, at that same time defined the tasks of historiography from the construction of a positive traditional progression of revolutionary struggles of the German people and promoted the establishment of Marxism-Leninism as the methodical basis for the entire teaching and research community of the GDR. Historical science was assigned an explicit function in establishing the legitimacy of the political power of the SED officials and the social scientists obligated to them.[8] This was, of course, also true for the historiography on colonialism and the non-European fields of historical studies. By comparing German and general history, a positive identification with the traditions of the "revolutionary German workers' movement" and other "progressive" developments in German history could be made that led to a departure from an up to then quite virulent portrayal of misery (*Miserekonzeption*).[9] From then on the demand of the GDR's party and state leadership for a critical discourse on the colonial past became an essential part of the new perspective on the German past.

The beginning of the analysis of colonial historiography in the GDR involved—as with later research on Asia, Africa, and Latin America—a close examination of the perceptions, views, and concepts of West German scholars because these in general still maintained a rather glorified view of the German colonial past. On the one hand, confronting these nationalistic and sometimes chauvinistic views was a necessity for GDR scholars; on the other hand, it was also an attempt—based on outlining the state of research—to showcase their Marxist-Leninist *Weltanschauung*.

This ideologically oriented research furthered exaggerations and one-sidedness when arguing against "Western based" views. For GDR scholars of the historiography of colonialism there were always enough reasons to deal with the West German historians' research, taking into account of these inglorious chapters of the German past. Not only because university teaching and research in the Federal Republic of Germany was for the most part controlled by experts from the "Third Reich," but also because in the academic world, in popular scientific journalism[10] and even in real politics[11] views that glorified the colonial politics or uncritically adopted those views were upheld until the 1980s.

The regional center of the young GDR's research on colonialism was established at the University of Leipzig where antifascist activist Walter Markov was responsible for a respective research assignment.[12] As early as in 1954–1955 he presented the first results.[13] Toward the end of this decade even some of his students were publishing their early research findings on the history of Africa.[14]

Publications on the history of colonialism were then released continually, most of all in the series *Studien zur Geschichte Asiens, Afrikas und Lateinamerikas* (Studies on the History of Asia, Africa, and Latin America) from Akademie-Verlag Berlin, and thus significantly helped to overcome the "petty-European conception of history," which dominated in West Germany until the 1960s, and to facilitate the concept of a "history of the wide spaces of Asia and Africa." According to the West German historian Erich Bayer, this led to an enforced "competition" between East and West German "Regional Sciences" as already predicted in 1962—in the West German opinion an inevitable competition.[15] Again and again the "competitors" in Germany's East were referred to "with proper seriousness."[16] In 1963, after the International Congress of African Studies in Accra, Rolf Italiaander, German-Dutch journalist in Africa, pleaded to West German scholars on Africa not to yield the floor to the GDR scholars, or else "the German studies on Africa might solely be represented by the Africa-Departments in Leipzig and East Berlin. [. . .] To allow that would mean another political ineptness."[17]

Already a few years before, the West German historian Wahrhold Drascher wanted to "evaluate the efforts of the Russian side accurately" and "to deal with the history of Africa much more intensely than before." He cautioned against the repercussions of ignoring his advice: "It could easily happen that Africa's junior academic elite will not go for our books but the Russian books in order to learn about their past."[18] Today's *nestor* of West German studies of African political sciences, Franz Ansprenger, saw at least the possibility that African Studies of the GDR could "be deemed to be prestigious for German research par excellence in certain foreign countries."[19]

Even in the field of the pre-colonial history of Africa West German scholars feared falling behind the GDR research, which the Frankfurt archeologist G. Smolla warned against in his speech at the German Africa Association in 1962.[20]

Hans-Ulrich Wehler's book *Bismarck und der Imperialismus* (Bismarck and Imperialism) from 1969[21] marked the point in time when West German scholars were finally convinced that "for the most part the GDR-research's lead seemed to have been caught up with."[22] However, there were only a few "Africa books" and academic essays with a political science orientation, mostly by Franz Ansprenger and Imanuel Geiss, who significantly distanced themselves from the hitherto dominant colonialist revisionist apologetics[23] in West German colonial historiography—on the GDR side, by the way, this was observed with reserve and lack of understanding, if not criticism.[24] Only Helmut Bley's work on colonial rule and social structure in German South-West Africa from 1968[25] was defined clearly as a critical book on colonial history.

The "historicization" of the regional studies in the GDR, which comprised studies on Africa and colonial historiography as well and were—unlike in the Federal Republic of Germany—taken up already at the end of the 1950s, was later assessed for the most part positively by West German experts. After visiting Leipzig in 1974 the West German Orientalist Ulrich Haarmann said about the Department of African and Middle Eastern Studies: "The Middle Eastern Studies, which for quite a while have been concentrated in one big department in Leipzig, are integrated into the Marxist historical scholarship and thus obtain a substantiated methodology. A scholar of Oriental studies becomes an expert historian; likewise, items from Africa or Asia will unquestionably be home in general history—still a strange idea for some West German historians." Referring to an analysis of the *Zeitschrift für Geschichtswissenschaft* (Journal for Historical Science) he conceded a "successful transformation of the Eurocentric world image" to his GDR counterparts; with contemporary issues, however, he recognized the tendency toward "partiality."[26]

In the system of the GDR's African Studies, German colonial history was considered an integral element of African history from its beginnings and its consolidation phase at the end of the 1950s until the 1960s and even in later years. This consideration did not exclude the awareness that colonial history was always defined as an element of research on imperialism. Consequently, GDR historians could in fact disregard the process in the West described by Munster historian Horst Gründer, that is, the conversion from old-style colonial history and overseas' history toward the history of the colonial period in the Third World at the beginning of the 1970s.[27] "Today, you are no longer a 'colonial historian' but a historian of South Asia, India, of the Arabian countries, of the Maghreb, or Black Africa," Rudolf von Albertini, one of the leading West German historians, said about this change.[28]

In comparison to the GDR's critical analysis of the European and in particular the German colonialism from the very beginning of its colonial research, West German scholars could recognize with relief the beginning of a trend commencing trend toward a "slow-growing (colonial) critical position" in the FRG only as late as in 1984.[29]

Alexandre Kum'a Ndumbe III., the Cameroon historian and political scientist, points out two thematic tendencies in the GDR's colonial historiography. One is characterized as an attempt to emphasize the imperial nature of German colonialism. The German bourgeoisie, which oppressed and exploited the German working class at home, expanded into the colonies and thus transferred exploitation to Africa in order to make the highest profits. Colonialism must therefore be considered capitalism in its imperialistic stage. The second tendency refers to the analysis of the resistance of the African people against the German colonial rule as part of African history.[30]

Due to the large number of doctoral theses by African students, who analyzed the colonial past of their countries in the GDR, and due to the international reputation of the GDR historians, GDR's historiography of colonialism produced a respectable amount of scholarship. However, quite a few topics and issues remained excluded from the research on the history of colonialism. They were not necessarily excluded because they should not or must not be worked on in the GDR because of political reasons. The main reasons seemed to be the scholars' subjective interests. Helmuth Stoecker, probably the most renowned GDR historian of colonialism, later declared that the greatest weakness of the GDR's research on colonialism was "that we did not attempt enough to compare the German colonial rule with those of other European powers. This is a kind of provincialism. [. . .] Also, we did too little work on the issue of the progressive component of modern colonial rule." Developments in the colonies that were initiated or influenced by colonialism had never been seriously analyzed. "Possibilities of alternative developments had not been paid sufficient attention to."[31]

Despite the recognition by GDR scholars of the gaps in their analysis of Germany's colonial past, it seems questionable that after the *Wende*, Heinrich Loth, one of the most productive historians in the GDR, found some "blank spots" not only in the GDR's historical scholarship but also in the GDR's general research on the Third World—which includes historical research—and stated them critically, but without any self-criticism.[32] Who else, if not professors of the GDR could have filled those "blank spots"? Loth's *post-factum* complaints hardly convinced anybody.

However, without doubt there are important achievements of the GDR historiography of colonialism, in particular with respect to the analysis of the anti-colonial resistance "beyond revanchist and apologetic facets,"[33] as a young scholar of the succeeding generation put it approvingly.[34]

The unanimously anti-colonial attitude of GDR historians—which is even today seen with amazement—is based on a state policy legitimizing itself through the so-called revolutionary traditions of the workers' movement.[35] This interpretation was not only propagated by the GDR scholars but also confirmed by foreign scholars like the Finnish colonial expert Juhani Koponen who wrote: "The GDR was the only one among the ex-colonial countries, in which 'anti-imperialism' was proclaimed as a part of an official ideology."[36]

The international recognition of publications on Germany's colonial past penned by GDR scholars can be attributed to their consistent anti-colonial partisanship on the one hand; on the other hand it was their clearly expressed, intense interpretation of the sources[37] that allowed an undeterred, satisfying, and critical discourse about European colonial rule in Africa and other regions overseas and its consequences. Thus, GDR scholars were in line with the main trends in international research on colonialism;[38] in fact, they set the trend since colonial history could hardly be considered a critical discipline up to this point.

This source-based research of GDR historians—which was also acknowledged as "very busy" by Western counterparts who did not approve of the developments in Germany's East[39]—was enabled when the archives of the *Reichskolonialamt* (Imperial Colonial Office), which had been confiscated after World War II, and the archives of the colonial department of the Foreign Office were returned from the Soviet Union to Potsdam in 1956. Only then the colonial files that before had been kept secret were opened for academic research. Besides performing other research, it was now possible—based on Marxist views—to find substantiated proof for the close and manifold connections between the colonial ambitions of single representatives or entire interest groups and the central apparatus of state of the former German Reich or Prussia, respectively, and even large companies.[40]

To enable the colonial historians to deal with the huge amount of relevant files in the GDR's *Zentrales Staatsarchiv* (Central State Archives) the individual German colonial regions—excluding the South Pacific regions—were "distributed" among the GDR historians interested in them.[41] This "distribution," however, was not performed by order of a superior authority, as could be assumed in a centralized state. In fact, several younger colonial historians partitioned the German colonies among themselves: South-West Africa: Horst Drechsler, Cameroon: Adolf Rüger, Togo: Peter Sebald and Manfred Nussbaum. Heinrich Loth, who later taught in Magdeburg, found international recognition with a large number of books and essays on German colonial policy. Kurt Büttner and Fritz Ferdinand Müller dealt with German East Africa. After a relatively short time at the end of the 1950s the latter published his findings in an internationally renowned book.[42]

The general aim was to compile a historical overview for each German colony on the basis of the accessible sources; however, it could only be accomplished for the period of the anti-colonial war of the Herero and Nama in German South-West Africa.[43] A chronologically and systematically comprehensive history of a former German colony has been published only for Togo.[44] Whereas a monograph about the colonial rule in East Africa from Kurt Büttner was harshly criticized,[45] Müller's publications, and especially his book *Deutschland-Zanzibar-Ostafrika*, a history of German colonial rule in Eastern Africa, found better reviews. One critic praised Müller's "combination of strong anti-imperialist commitment and meticulous historical research written in an animated style."[46]

George Hallgarten, the prominent German-American historian on imperialism, criticized in his overall positive review of Müller's book the East German author for tending to overestimate the anti-colonial ambitions and intentions of some African individuals. Hallgarten criticized in particular Müller for "following the scheme of communist historiography" and thus attempting "to transform the slave trader Bushiri into a black Nasser or Fidel Castro, who he surely was not."[47] Whether that was Müller's intention or it is the impression one could infer from his book will never be known for sure. However, despite occasional or even generally positively assessments, other Western scholars also criticized that the GDR scholars'—see Kurt Büttner[48] and Klaus Klauß[49] in particular—attempts "to substantiate Marxist-Leninist theories on the basis of the colonial developments."[50] This critique may indeed be the case; however, it by no means compromises the GDR scholars' work, achievement by on their interpretation of sources.

Brückenkopf's critique that was mentioned earlier shows two aspects of the critique itself: on the one hand, that the GDR scholars' internalized anti-colonialism could lead to exaggerations and unscientific comparisons and on the other hand that the West German scholar's internalized anti-communism led to exaggerations when criticizing their Eastern counterparts' academic accomplishments.

There can be no doubt that GDR historians dealing with colonial and African historiography allowed themselves to be guided by Marxism-Leninism. Nor that this perspective compromised scholarly objectivity—in particular when dealing with ideological issues—as was clearly stated by the West German scholars on African Mission History, Erhard Kamphausen and Werner Ustorf, in their 1977 analysis of the historiography on German missions. Historiography on Christian Missions during GDR times was basically always considered in the context of the history of colonialism and Africa. Both the abovementioned authors are right when they state that "there is no doubt that the Marxist-Leninist analysis [. . .] elicits its positive function by uncovering ideological positions and the corresponding praxis of bourgeois missionary thought from the solidarity with the peoples in the colonies, it, however, comes itself under the 'suspicion of ideology' by claiming to command a universal and complete historical-philosophical emancipation theory."[51]

In fact, in other areas as well GDR scholars tried to insert Marxism in its dogmatic form into their African and Colonial historiography. They particularly attempted to apply the Marxist formation theory to Africa.[52] However, all colonial historical depictions—no matter how partisan, ideologically marked, or Marxism-Leninism worshipping—did not lead to falsifications of objective historical events.

Admittedly, since almost exclusively European sources were used for the colonial historiography, and since field studies in Africa were practically impossible due to the pretense of a lack of foreign currency, indigenous developments were almost completely ignored and, up to a certain degree, a Eurocentric perspective and a reduced focus on the relationships between the colonial power and the African societies were maintained. This, consequently, led to a certain imbalance in the GDR's historiography on Africa.[53] Yet in the 1960s and at the beginning of the 1970s, the heyday of historiography on Africa in the GDR, this imbalance concerning the relationship between the colonial power and African societies was hardly a feature of the GDR academics alone but also of the Western research on overseas history.[54] The African developments and initiatives have not until much later become an academic subject of study worldwide, although in the GDR there were already disputes about them.

GDR publications often attributed the active part solely to the European colonial conquerors; the Africans were thus the passively responding party. Of course, this discrepancy was obvious to the academic officials in the SED party apparatus, and thus a controversy about the institutional classification of colonial history, which was not argued out in the open, flared up: Should it be considered African History or History of Imperialism?

Eventually the view prevailed that the colonial historiography could only serve as a support for the Leninist theory on imperialism, which consequently proved to be a disadvantage for the autonomy of colonial history. Thus, colonial history remained a component of the history of the colonial powers.

Moreover, the GDR's historiography of colonialism as part of the research on imperialism suffered from a certain deficit in theory. Historians in the GDR hardly ever absorbed the discourse on imperialism and the colonialism inherent in it that was going on in the FRG and the remaining Western countries and thus ignored its substantial content.[55] Put in a simple way, Düsseldorf historian Wolfgang J. Mommsen assumed that due to the government's control over public discourse, the majority of GDR historians were immune to serious criticism and thus believed that they could afford to maintain "the old forms of the imperialistic nature of capitalism in an utmost generalized form."[56]

However, achievements from different special areas of colonial analysis have been accepted worldwide, as, for example the GDR historians' first discourse on colonial ideology and the war objectives of World War II.[57] Still, from the mid-1970s on, research on colonialism increasingly lost its privileged position within East German scholarship. One reason for the declining significance of historical research was the emergence of several disciplines and sub-disciplines of African Studies, such as ethnography, sociology, and linguistics, in academic research and teaching. Another reason was that political studies on present-day liberation movements seemed to be more useful for the practitioners of East German foreign policy. Despite the establishment of a historically orientated *Interdisziplinäres Zentrum für Vergleichende Revolutionsforschung* (Interdisciplinary Center for Comparative Research on Revolutions) at Karl Marx University in Leipzig, the primacy of colonial history in Leipzig in scholarly research and publishing was abandoned, and colonial history gradually lost its function as a link to area studies.[58]

Nevertheless, works on colonial history never left the spectrum of the GDR's research on the Third World.[59] In later years, though, GDR scholars failed—for whatever reasons—to put stronger emphasis on documentary collections, which were rightly referred to as "an extraordinarily neglected area" by Thea Büttner, one of the most important GDR historians of African studies, at a conference of the Berlin-Brandenburg Academy of Sciences and Humanities in October 1995.[60]

Yet, during the entire time when the GDR and its historiography existed, West German historians attentively observed the activities and achievements of GDR scholars in their research on the history of colonialism and in particular on the academic research on and teaching of African Studies at the University of Leipzig.[61] Other foreign scholars of African and colonial studies as well acknowledged that the "Leipzig Initiative" was a trailblazer on analogous research in other countries.[62] Since the 1960s historians of African and colonial studies in West Germany, the United States, and some other West European countries increasingly began to follow Markov and focused on European colonialism and German colonial rule in Africa as well, which, for example, can be concluded from the great number of users of the GDR's national archive in Potsdam. Working in this archive seemed to have been less complicated for users from abroad, such as the United States or Great Britain, than for historians from West Germany.

However inexorably and determined the GDR scholarship presented the interpretation of Germany's colonial past in Africa or dealt with the West German academic "defenders" of German colonial politics, they only verbally argued about the racist past of West German diplomats and German citizens in Africa.[63] Contrary to the fear of the Federal Foreign Office in Bonn, the GDR never attempted to use the colonial files from the Potsdam national archive as incriminating material against West German diplomats in Africa and other representatives of the German federal state or its economy who were active in particular in Tanganyika or Tanzania.[64] The GDR only made quite a few general accusations with regard to the politics in Bonn being the neo-colonial successor of the expansionist politics of the Nazis.[65]

Concerning those historians who dealt with German colonial history, it can be stated that interactions between East and West German counterparts had already existed before the *Wende*. Thus, a fruitful cooperation between colonial historians of both German states would have been possible after the *Wende* and the unification in 1990. However, as is well known, that did not happen; instead of cooperating in this and other fields of study, East German scholars were more or less superseded by their West German counterparts.[66]

After the *Wende*, some West German scholars have not only simply refused to acknowledge or selectively criticized the analyses in East German scholars of colonial and Africa studies but have quite often ignored them entirely.[67] This colonial-like[68] suppression of the East German historians and other scholars seems to be based on the fact that all GDR scholars of the humanities per se would have cleaved to Marxist ideology and therefore no reasonable work could have been elicited. Up to now those allegations have been made, though often refuted. Although more recent publications on German colonial history have quietly incorporated research findings from GDR historians, the almost entire eradication of GDR historiography after the *Wende* is still explained more or less directly with its cleaving to Marxism.

Karl Marx, however, according to Franz Ansprenger in his article on the "reunification of African Studies in Germany" (that unfortunately has not come true), has left an analytical tool, "which is not a shame to use. And this is also true for exploring Africa."[69] Also, Juhani Koponen, the Finnish historian of African and Colonial Studies who focuses on the history of German colonialism in East Africa, does not reject Marx's theory on the exploration of Africa's history and concedes its innovative impact.[70] That sounds like an homage. Today, a critical historiography of colonialism in the tradition of the GDR does not exist anymore. At the time of the German unification in 1990 the generation of professors dealing with this topic had already retired or was close to retirement, so that even in the case of a positive evaluation and their employment in a unified Germany their resigning and making way for younger scholars would have been the natural consequence. During the last two decades several of them died and cannot respond to the criticism of their works that has arisen in the meantime. Besides the often undifferentiated and inappropriate criticism of publications of individual GDR scholars, keeping quiet about the literature published in the GDR is the latest trend to dominate the field.

Translated by Beate Schiller

Notes

1. See Thea Büttner, "The Development of African Historical Studies in East Germany: An Outline and Selected Bibliography," *History in Africa*, vol. 19 (East Lansing, 1992), 133–46.

2. Helmuth Stoecker, *Deutschland und China im 19. Jahrhundert: Das Eindringen des deutschen Kolonialismus* (Berlin, 1958).

3. See idem (ed.), *Drang nach Afrika: Die koloniale Expansionspolitik und Herrschaft des deutschen Imperialismus in Afrika von den Anfängen bis zum Ende des Zweiten Weltkrieges* (Berlin, 1977). 2nd ed. as: *Drang nach Afrika: Die deutsche koloniale Expansionspolitik und Herrschaft in Afrika von den Anfängen bis zum Verlust der Kolonien* (Berlin, 1999). Engl. transl.: *German Imperialism in Africa: From the Beginnings until the Second World War* (London, 1987).

4. See Ulrich van der Heyden, *Die Afrikawissenschaften in der DDR: Eine akademische Disziplin zwischen Exotik und Exempel, eine wissenschaftliche Untersuchung* (Munster etc., 1999), esp. 66–76.

5. See, with reference to ethnographic studies, Chris Hann et al. (eds.), *Studying Peoples in the People's Democracies: Socialist Era Anthropology in East-Central Europe* (Munster, etc., 2005), here esp. Ulrich van der Heyden, "Africanist Anthropology in the German Democratic Republic," 303–30.

6. Walter Markov, "Zu einigen Ergebnissen und Problemen der Erforschung der Geschichte der nationalen Befreiungsbewegung," *Historiker-Gesellschaft der DDR: Wissenschaftliche Mitteilungen*, no. 2 (Berlin, 1974), 49.

7. See Peter Sebald, "Völkerfreundschaft oder Auslandsinformation: Impressionen zum Wirken der Deutsch-Afrikanischen Gesellschaft," Ulrich van der Heyden et al. (eds.), *Die DDR und Afrika: Zwischen Klassenkampf und neuem Denken* (Munster and Hamburg, 1993), 79–94.

8. See Fritz Kopp, *Die Wendung zur "nationalen" Geschichtsbetrachtung in der Sowjetzone* (Munich, 1955).

9. See Matthias Middell, "Jenseits unserer Grenzen? Zur Trennung von deutscher und allgemeiner Geschichte in der Geschichtswissenschaft und Geschichtskultur der DDR," Konrad H. Jarausch and Matthias Middell (eds.), *Nach dem Erdbeben: (Re-)Konstruktion ostdeutscher Geschichte und Geschichtswissenschaft* (Leipzig, 1994), 100–01.

10. See, e.g., Hellmuth Hecker, *Kolonialforschung und Studentenschaft an der "Hansischen Universität" im Zweiten Weltkrieg: Die NSDStB-Kameradschaft "Hermann von Wissmann" und die "Übersee- und Kolonial-Arbeitsgemeinschaft"* (Baden-Baden, 1986). See also Wolfgang Höpcker (ed.), *Hundert Jahre Afrika und die Deutschen* (Pfullingen, 1984).

11. See Helmut Bley and Rainer Tetzlaff (eds.), *Afrika und Bonn: Versäumnisse und Zwänge deutscher Afrikapolitik* (Hamburg, 1978).

12. See van der Heyden, *Die Afrikawissenschaften*, 160–203.

13. Walter Markov, "Fragen der Genesis und Bedeutung der vorimperialistischen Kolonialsysteme," *Wissenschaftliche Zeitschrift der Karl-Marx-Universität Leipzig: Gesellschafts- und sprachwissenschaftliche Reihe*, nos. 1–2 (1959/60), 43–46.

14. See ibid., from the issue No. 3 (1959/60): Kurt Büttner, "Restaurierungsversuche eines 'Kolonialhelden': Bemerkungen zur Einschätzung Carl Peters'," Siegfried Krebs, "Zwangsarbeit in der ehemaligen deutschen Kolonie Ostafrika," Heinrich Loth, "Die Ketzerbewegung in Südwestafrika, ihre Vorgeschichte und ihre Grenzen im Freiheitskrieg 1904 bis 1906," Modilim Achufusi, "Die Herausbildung des Ful-Hausa-Staates Sokoto unter Usman dan Fodio 1802/04 bis 1910."

15. See Erich Bayer, "Historik und Geschichtsunterricht," *Geschichte in Wissenschaft und Unterricht*, vol. 13 (1962), no. 6, 352–53.

16. See Franz Ansprenger, *Aufgaben der deutschen politischen und historischen Wissenschaft in Bezug auf Afrika* (Hannover, 1964), 107.

17. Rolf Italiaander, "Diesmal schlief der Westen nicht: Schwarze und weiße Afrikanisten. Welche Möglichkeiten bleiben dem Westen? Ein Kongress in Ghana," *Die Welt*, February 5, 1963.

18. Warhold Drascher, “Russische Forschungen zur Geschichte Afrikas,” *Historische Zeitschrift*, vol. 186 (1958), 723–33.

19. Franz Ansprenger, “Neuere Geschichte und politische Wissenschaft,” Herbert Abel (ed.), *Deutsche Afrikawissenschaft: Stand und Aufgabe. Vorträge einer Tagung* (Cologne, 1962), 139.

20. G. Smolla, “Vor- und Frühgeschichte,” Ibid., 145.

21. Hans-Ulrich Wehler, *Bismarck und der Imperialismus* (Cologne and Berlin, 1969).

22. Wolfgang Zorn, Review of Wehler, Bismarck und der Imperialismus, *Vierteljahresschrift für Sozial- und Wirtschaftsgeschichte*, vol. 57 (1970), 130.

23. Jutta Bückendorf, *“Schwarz-weiß-rot über Ostafrika!” Deutsche Kolonialpläne und afrikanische Realität* (Münster, 1977), 12, emphasized that early West German historiography on colonialism followed “almost seamless” pro-colonialist writers of the 1920s. She acknowledged criticism from the GDR as basically correct.

24. See Adolf Rüger, “Zu modernisierungs- und elitetheoretischen Aspekten in Schriften von Franz Ansprenger und Imanuel Geiss über Afrika,” *Asien-Afrika-Lateinamerika*, vol. 7 (1979), no. 3, 487–96.

25. Helmut Bley, *Kolonialherrschaft und Sozialstruktur in Deutsch Südwestafrika 1894–1914* (Hamburg, 1968). Engl. transl.: *South-West Africa under German Rule, 1894–1914* (London, 1971).

26. Ulrich Haarmann, “Die islamische Moderne bei den deutschen Orientalisten,” Hans Kochwasser and Hans Robert Roemer (eds.), *Araber und Deutsche: Begegnung in einem Jahrtausend* (Tübingen, 1974), 56–91, here p. 82.

27. Horst Gründer, *Geschichte der deutschen Kolonien*, 2nd ed. (Paderborn, etc., 1991), 11.

28. Rudolf von Albertini, in cooperation with Albert Wirtz, *Europäische Kolonialherrschaft 1880–1940* (Zurich and Freiburg im Breisgau, 1976), 9.

29. Henning Melber in cooperation with Mary Melber and Werner Hillebrecht, *In Treue fest, Südwest! Eine ideologiekritische Dokumentation von der Eroberung Namibias über die deutsche Fremdherrschaft bis zur Kolonialapologie der Gegenwart* (Bonn, 1984), VI.

30. See Alexandre Kum'a Ndumbe III., *Was will Bonn in Afrika? Zur Afrikapolitik der Bundesrepublik Deutschland* (Pfaffenweiler, 1992), 3.

31. Helmuth Stoecker, as quoted in: Ulrich van der Heyden, “Sichten auf die historische Afrikawissenschaft in der DDR: Ein Rundtischgespräch mit Afrikawissenschaftlern,” *Asien-Afrika-Lateinamerika*, vol. 22 (1994), no. 5, 549–50.

32. Heinrich Loth, *Weiße Flecken im Geschichtsbuch: Altlasten sozialistischer Geschichtsschreibung* (Magdeburg, 1990).

33. Jigal Belz, *Geschosse zu Wassertropfen: Sozio-religiöse Aspekte des Maji-Maji-Krieges in Deutsch-Ostafrika 1905–1907* (Cologne, 2003), 46.

34. For anti-colonial resistance in East Africa, see, e.g., Helmuth Stoecker, “Deutsch-Ostafrika 1885–1906,” and “Deutsch-Ostafrika 1906–1914,” Idem, *Drang nach Afrika*, 84–101 and 131–41; Thea Büttner, *Die Geschichte Afrikas*, Bd. 2: *Afrika von den Anfängen bis zur* territorialen *Aufteilung Afrikas durch die*

imperialistischen Kolonialmächte (Berlin, 1976), 86–89; Heinrich Loth, *Griff nach Ostafrika: Politik des deutschen Imperialismus und antikolonialer Kampf—Legende und Wirklichkeit* (Berlin, 1968); Idem, "Die 'neue Politik' des deutschen Imperialismus und der Widerstandskampf in Tanganyika (1906–1918)," Horst Krüger (ed.), *Nationalismus und Sozialismus im Befreiungskampf der Völker Asiens und Afrikas* (Berlin, 1970), 151–61; Horst Bernhard, "Der Maji-Maji-Aufstand als Kulminationspunkt im bewaffneten Widerstandskampf gegen koloniale Unterdrückung und Ausbeutung in der deutschen Kolonie Ostafrika," Kurt Büttner and Heinrich Loth (eds.), *Philosophie der Eroberer und koloniale Wirklichkeit*, 251–302; Klaus Helbig, "Die ostafrikanische Widerstandskampf während des Ersten Weltkrieges," Ibid., 303–49.

35. See Hans Piazza/Lothar Rathmann, "Zur Kontinuität des antikolonialen Kampfes der revolutionären deutschen Arbeiterbewegung und zur Entwicklung der Asien-, Afrika- und Lateinamerikawissenschaften in der DDR," *Partei—Tradition—Wissenschaft: Beiträge von Gesellschaftswissenschaftlern der Karl-Marx-Universität Leipzig* (Berlin, 1976), 207–22.

36. Juhani Koponen, *Development for Exploitation, German Colonial Policies in Mainland Tanzania, 1884–1914* (Helsinki and Hamburg, 1995), 17.

37. See Brückendorf, "Schwarz-weiß-rot [. . .]," 12.

38. See Juhani Koponen, "Knowledge, Power and History: German Colonial Studies in Tanzania," Ulrich van der Heyden and Achim von Oppen (eds.), *Tanzania: Koloniale Vergangenheit und neuer Aufbruch* (Munster, 1996), 118–39.

39. Hans Georg Steltzer, *Die Deutschen und ihr Kolonialreich* (Frankfurt-Main, 1984), 9.

40. See Kurt Metschies, "Quellen im Zentralen Staatsarchiv in Potsdam zur kolonialen Politik Deutschlands in Afrika und Nahost," *Archivmitteilungen*, no. 4 (1990), 134–39.

41. See Günter Raue, "Die Aufteilung der Welt als Parteiauftrag: Protokoll zur Sache und Person," *Neues Deutschland*, January 27, 1973.

42. Fritz Ferdinand Müller, *Deutschland-Zanzibar-Ostafrika: Geschichte einer deutschen Kolonialeroberung 1884–1890* (Berlin, 1959).

43. Horst Drechsler, *Südwestafrika unter deutscher Kolonialherrschaft* (Berlin, 1966). See also idem, *Let Us Die Fighting: The Struggle of the Hero and Nama against German Imperialism, 1884–1915* (London, 1980).

44. Peter Sebald, *Togo 1884–1914: Eine Geschichte der deutschen "Musterkolonie" auf der Grundlage amtlicher Quellen* (Berlin, 1988).

45. See, e.g., Ernst Dammann, Review of Kurt Büttner, *Die Anfänge der deutschen Kolonialpolitik in Ostafrika*, *Orientalistische Literaturzeitung*, nos. 7/8 (1960), cols. 424–26.

46. Koponen, *Development*, 17–18.

47. George W. F. Hallgarten, *Imperialismus vor 1914: Die soziologischen Grundlagen der Außenpolitik europäischer Großmächte vor dem ersten Weltkrieg*, 2nd ed., vol. 1 (Munich, 1963), 352, fn. 3.

48. Büttner, *Die Anfänge* [. . .], *passim*.

49. Klaus Klauß, *Die deutsche Kolonialherrschaft und die deutsche Kolonialpolitik von den Anfängen bis 1895,* unpubl. dissertation, Humboldt University (Berlin, 1966).

50. Brückendorf, "Schwarz-weiß-rot," 12.

51. Erhard Kamphausen and Werner Ustorf, "Deutsche Meistergeschichtsschreibung: Anamnese einer Fehlentwicklung," *Verkündigung und Forschung* (Beihefte zu "Evangelische Theologie"), no. 2 (Munich, 1977), 53.

52. Thea Büttner, "Das präkoloniale Afrika und die Diskussionen zur asiatischen Produktionsweise," *Jahrbuch für Wirtschaftsgeschichte*, Pt. IV (Berlin, 1967), 287–312; Idem, "The Feudal and Semifeudal Aristocracy in Africa in Historical Development up to the Present Time: A Case Study from Zanzibar," *African Studies* (Leipzig, 1978) 10–18; Irmgard Sellnow, *Grundprinzipien einer Periodisierung der Urgeschichte: Ein Beitrag auf Grundlage ethnographischen Materials* (Berlin, 1961). See also Markus Oberlack, *Das präkoloniale Afrika und die Kontroverse um die "Asiatische Produktionsweise" in der DDR-Historiographie* (Munster and Hamburg, 1994).

53. See Horst Gründer, "Kolonialismus und Marxismus: Der deutsche Kolonialismus in der Geschichtsschreibung der DDR," Alexander Fischer and Günther Heydemann (ed.), *Geschichtswissenschaft in der DDR*, vol. 2: *Vor- und Frühgeschichte bis Neueste Geschichte* (Berlin, 1990), 671–79.

54. Vgl. Helmut Bley, "Schwerpunkte in der Afrikageschichtsschreibung," Brigitte Benzing and Reinhardt Bolz (eds.), *Methoden der afrikanistischen Forschung und Lehre in der BRD: Eine kritische Bilanz*, 5. Jahrestagung der Vereinigung von Afrikanisten in Deutschland (VAD) 1973 (Hamburg, 1976), 41–58.

55. See Jürgen Herzog/Peter Sebald, "Kolonialismus 'von innen': Überlegungen zur Bedeutung der Kolonialherrschaft für die Entwicklung afrikanischer Gesellschaften," *Asien-Afrika-Lateinamerika*, vol. 19 (1991), no. 4, 731.

56. Wolfgang J. Mommsen *Imperialismustheorien: Ein Überblick über die neueren Imperialismusinterpretationen* (Göttingen, 1987), 95.

57. See Horst Kühne, *Faschistische Kolonialideologie und zweiter Weltkrieg* (Berlin, 1962); Richard Lakowski, *Die Kriegsziele des faschistischen Deutschland im transsaharischen Afrika*, unpubl. dissertation, Humboldt University (Berlin, 1970).

58. See Kai Hafez, *Orientwissenschaft in der DDR: Zwischen Dogma und Anpassung, 1969–1989* (Hamburg, 1995), 31.

59. See Autorenkollektiv unter Leitung von Walter Markov, "Arbeiten zur Geschichte des Kolonialismus und zur nationalen Befreiungsbewegung der kolonialunterdrückten Völker," *Historische Forschungen in der DDR: Analysen und Berichte zum XI. Internationalen Historikerkongress in Stockholm, August 1960*, Sonderheft der Zeitschrift für Geschichtswissenschaft (Berlin, 1960), 544–62; Walter Markov et al, "Forschungen zur Geschichte Afrikas," *Historische Forschungen in der DDR: Analysen und Berichte zum XIII. Internationalen Historikerkongress in Moskau 1970*, Sonderband der Zeitschrift für Geschichtswissenschaft (Berlin, 1970), 746–62; Thea Büttner and Helmuth Stoecker, "Forschungen zur Geschichte des subsaharischen Afrika," *Historisce Forschungen in der DDR 1970–1980: Analysen und Berichte zum*

XV. Internationalen Historikerkongress in Bukarest, Sonderband der Zeitschrift für Geschichtswissenschaft (Berlin, 1980), 493–501.

60. Thea Büttner, "Die Afrikawissenschaften in der DDR: Überlegungen für eine weiterführende Analyse. Kommentar zum Vortrag von Ulrich van der Heyden," Wolf-Hagen Krauth and Ralf Wolz (eds.), *Wissenschaft und Wiedervereinigung: Asien- und Afrikawissenschaften im Umbruch* (Berlin, 1998), 467–79.

61. So, for example, a literary report in one of the most important West German magazines on relevant GDR research on Africa said: "We already mentioned that the West German historiography still neglects colonial history. [. . .] Our passivity is in particular precarious with respect to the activities of professor Markov (university of Leipzig) and his team of anti-colonial historians who have already submitted several analyses, attracted the attention at different conferences, and have taken charge of educating junior scholars in the developing countries." See Heinz Lehmann, "Literaturberichte Entwicklungsländer, besonders Afrika," *Geschichte in Wissenschaft und Unterricht*, vol. 13 (1962), no. 3, 197.

62. Lothar Rathmann, "Walter Markov und die 'farbigen Kontinente': Persönliche Reminiszenzen," Manfred Neuhaus und Helmut Seidel in Verbindung mit Gerald Diesener, Gerald und Matthias Middell (Hg.), *"Wenn jemand seinen Kopf bewußt hinhielt . . .": Beiträge zu Werk und Wirken von Walter Markov* (Leipzig, 1995), 183.

63. See Victor Grossman, "The Starling List of Guilty Men: West German Ambassadors who Served Hitler," *Democratic German Report*, XI (1962), no. 2, 18. See also Nationalrat der Nationalen Front (ed.), *Graubuch: Expansionspolitik und Neonazismus in Westdeutschland. Hintergründe—Ziele—Methoden* (Berlin, 1967), esp. 105–17.

64. See Werner Kilian, *Die Hallstein-Doktrin: Der diplomatische Krieg zwischen der BRD und der DDR 1955–1973. Aus den Akten der beiden deutschen Außenministerien* (Berlin, 2001), 192.

65. See, e.g., Heinrich Sperker, *Zur Afrikapolitik der deutschen Imperialisten: Tatsachen und Argumente No. 21*, ed. by SED Central Committee, Department for Agitation and Propaganda (Berlin, 1960); Kurt Büttner and Christian Rachel, *Zehn Lügen über Afrika* (Berlin, 1974).

66. See Ulrich van der Heyden, "Wie die Afrikawissenschaft in Ostdeutschland durch eine 'päte Abwicklung' beseitigt wurde," Stefan Bollinger and Ulrich van der Heyden (Hg.), *Deutsche Einheit und Elitenwechsel in* Ostdeutschland (Berlin, 2002), 113–54; Stefan Bollinger, Ulrich van der Heyden, and Mario Kessler (eds.), *Ausgrenzung oder Integration? Ostdeutsche Sozialwissenschaftler zwischen Isolierung und Selbstbehauptung* (Berlin, 2004).

67. See for example the statements in the following article, in which the accomplishments of the GDR scholars were mentioned briefly only after one of the historians concerned had intervened: Anna-Maria Brandstätter, "*Kolonialismus: Wider den vereinfachenden Dichotomien,*" Jan-Georg Deutsch and Albert Wirtz (eds.), *Geschichte in Afrika: Einführung in Probleme und Debatten* (Berlin, 1997), 75–105.

68. See the more detailed theory from Wolfgang Dümcke and Frith Vilmar (eds.), *Die Kolonisierung der DDR: Kritische Analysen und Alternativen des Einigungsprozesses* (Münster, 1995).

69. Franz Ansprenger, "Zur Wiedervereinigung der deutschen Afrikawissenschaft," *Internationales Afrikaforum*, no. 1 (1991), 71.

70. See Juhani Koponen, *People and Production in Late Precolonial Tanzania: History and Structures* (Jyväskylä, 1988), 39.

15

Obscuring East Germany

The Phantom Menace of East Germany to Social Scientific Understanding of Post-Reunified Germany

MARCUS AURIN

During the *Wendezeit*, or "turning time" between the fall of the Berlin Wall on November 9, 1989, and official reunification on October 3, 1990, the overwhelming majority of East Germans thought of themselves simply as Germans, rallying under the popular slogan "we are one people." This is no longer the case. In 2001, roughly 70 percent of East Germans identified themselves as more East German than German—as citizens of the so-called *Neue Länder* or "new (East) German states" first, and as German nationals second.[1] In a 1999 survey, 75 percent of East German respondents claimed they felt like "second-class citizens" in reunified Germany.[2] It appears that reunification of the two postwar German states has given rise to a *new* national minority in Germany: East Germans. However, one of the most striking features of post-*Wende* social science research focused on eastern Germany is its role in the apparent displacement of East Germans from the emerging national imaginary of the reunified State. Reunification has lead to the production of a wave of "Unification Literature," "Transformation Studies," and a new national discourse describing post-socialist Germany without East Germans. This has become a problem not only for the coherence German social science, but also for the integrity of Germany's reunification itself.

When I began fieldwork in Berlin, I quickly discovered that the historicity of Germany's reunification is sharply divided. In the beginning, I approached a number of faculty members at universities and institutes in what had been East Germany, asking them about their experiences of reunification, and what sorts of institutional changes they had witnessed. I was baffled by the repeated claim that they had had little or no direct experience of reunification, despite the fact that they were ensconced in institutions that had been at the center of large-scale reforms. They had come after reunification, they explained, and had not been personally involved in the "transformation."

Durchmischung and *Abwicklung*

What was it like working with East German colleagues? I asked. There would generally be a pause at this point, and then they would reply that they could not really say, because they did not personally work with any—not directly, anyway. I had specifically chosen Humboldt University, which had been East Germany's leading social science university, as one of my primary sites because I had read that post-reunification reformers had singled it out to be an exemplar of an experimental policy called *Durchmischung* (intermixture), which was intended to preserve a balanced mix of East and West Germans on the faculty. Most of the West Germans I talked to at Humboldt had never heard of *Durchmischung*. The first East German faculty member I came across at Humboldt turned out not to actually be on the faculty. Dr. habil. Detlef Nakath lectured on the history of socialist Berlin in a summer program I attended at Humboldt for foreign graduate students. Although he had been the acting director of Humboldt's Department of History during the *Wende*, when I met him he was lecturing as a temporary *Dozent* (lecturer) for the summer semester, with no attachment to any university department. When I asked him after class one day about *Durchmischung* at the university and what it was like going through all the post-reunification changes there, he laughed nervously and said he could tell me a little about it, but not on campus because there were people around, "who did not like to hear about some of these things."

This, I found, is certainly the case: many German academics do not like to hear about the *Abwicklung* or reunification any more. In Berlin I talked to many West Germans who had recently moved to eastern Germany, but felt that they had no direct personal connection to the reunification process. As they would tell it, they had come to the East because reunification had (already) happened, "opening things up" for them there, which were more restricted in the West—including cheap apartments and, for my informants in particular, new academic job openings. They talked about reunification abstractly, as historical events that had essentially unfolded elsewhere (i.e., in the East). Indeed, when I first arrived in 2004, there was a pervading sense of boredom with the topic of reunification among many West Germans I talked to. As one West German who had joined the faculty at (the formerly East German) Humboldt University put it:

> [t]here was so much endless discussion [about reunification] in the 1990s that went around and around and never went anywhere. You really get tired of it after a while! I think a lot of people, especially academics, think the whole discussion—transformation, *Abwicklung*, whatever—is pointless at this point—that it has not been productive; it's not taken very seriously anymore.[3]

When asked by an interviewer from the American journal *Nature* about the fate of the tens of thousands of East German scientists who lost their jobs through the reforms following 1990, Dagmar Schipanski, the former president of the *Wissenschaftsrat* (the national Science Council) from 1996–1998, replied that little was known: "No one talks any more about the fate of these people, most of whom were very highly qualified."[4] Considering that between 1991 and 2000, the *Wissenschaftsrat* had commissioned between 1,000 and 1,600 research projects focused on the transformation of eastern Germany, and had compiled ca. 12,000 publications under the rubric of "unification literature" in their databases, Schipanski's statement is quite striking.[5] There is clearly something unusual going on within reunified Germany's social sciences if, despite the blizzard of well-funded research focused on developments in the *Neue Länder* produced throughout the 1990s, the plight of vast numbers of East German professionals remains shrouded in scholarly silence.

Outside the universities, however, I eventually found East German scholars willing and eager to talk to me about reunification and how it is affecting eastern Germany. These avowed *East* Germans tell a different reunification story. For them, reunification *is* an ongoing process that has impacted their personal lives, which they are continually forced to grapple with. Over time I discovered a wide network of East German scholars who are preoccupied with the direction reunification is going, and who spend a great deal of effort articulating—through books, newspaper and journal articles, lectures, seminars—an alternative East German perspective on the reunification process. Most of this activity takes place outside Germany's mainstream academic institutions, and has been largely overlooked by mainstream German academics.[6]

East German Intellectuals: Losing Their Legitimating Constituency

For many East Germans, particularly the academics I worked with, reunification has been a traumatic and very personal experience that is far from over. According to some estimates, 85 percent of East German faculties throughout the scientific disciplines have lost their academic positions since reunification; in the social and political sciences the figure is 95 percent.[7] A 1999 study commissioned by the scientific journal *Nature* found that 70 percent of full professors at universities and technical schools in eastern Germany were held by West German academics, an increase from around 50 percent in 1994.[8] For the East German social scientists I spoke with in Berlin, the ambiguity of their status as working scientists is inextricable from the ambivalence of their national identity within reunified Germany. As one put it, many East German intellectuals share a personal experience of "conscious and unconscious exclusion [as] citizens of a different species [*anders geartete Landsleute*—a phrase that resonates with the Nazi term *entartet*, meaning having lost membership in the (human) species], with the wrong biography in the wrong country."[9]

Following reunification, many East German intellectuals feel they have lost their legitimating constituency: under the new state, they have been largely excluded from the public sphere and are no longer recognizable as fully German. They have self-consciously become East German, a nationality belonging to another and former state. This feeling was powerfully confirmed during the 2005 national election campaigns when Edmund Stoiber, then head of the conservative CSU party (the Bavarian branch of Angela Merkel's CDU party) declared, in reference to polls indicating widespread support in eastern Germany for the PDS (successor party to the East German Socialist Unity Party [SED]), "I can not accept East Germans determining who the next chancellor will be. The frustrated can not be allowed to determine Germany's future."[10] In 2005, the East German Angela Merkel became Chancellor of the Federal Republic of Germany.

Mainstream social scientific discussions of eastern Germany in terms of economic development (as an immature or lagging region destined to catch up with the rest of Germany) or in terms of the end of the Cold War (as a population slowly and painfully learning the ways of liberal democracy so long denied them) have tended to erase East Germany as a socioculturally (self) determinate place, and disrupt the coherence of East German narratives at the level of national public discourse. The *Wissenschaftsrat*'s "Commission for the Study of Social and Political Change in the New Federal States" (*Kommission fuer die Erforschung des sozialen und politischen Wandels in den neuen Bundeslaendern* [KSPW]), which focused largely on the deconstruction of East Germany's scientific institutional apparatus, provides an illuminating example. In a sense, the *Wissenschaftsrat* had commissioned an autopsy of East Germany's scientific infrastructure as it was being dismembered. Through a process of apparently objective ("non-ideological") assessing, cataloging and (re-)archiving of defunct GDR social science, these large-scale studies and research projects lead to the establishment of the field of German Transformation Studies. Completed in 1997 (most of the actual field research ended several years earlier),[11] the KSPW programs generated a raft of published material, and facilitated the establishment of a professional network of social scientists expert in the field of East Germany's "transformation," who constituted a sub-discipline of their own, largely disbursed among many of the same academic institutions that were the focus of their own research.

After a formative boom-period in the early- to mid-1990s, East German Transformation Studies had reached a dead end by the end of the decade. By 2000, empirical, mainstream social scientific research focused on post-socialist eastern Germany had dropped to less than 1 percent of what it had been at its peak in the early 1990s: the discussion of transformation seemed to be closing.[12] German scholars now widely agree that German Transformation Studies, despite the thousands of research projects undertaken and the large amount of literature produced, largely failed to improve social scientific understanding of contemporary eastern Germany. At a conference on the future of social scientific research focused on East Germany in 2005, Berlin's former Senator of Science, Research and Culture, Dr. Thomas Flierl, declared that, "there has been a paradigm shift; Transformation Studies is over," while stressing the need to develop a new program of "East German Studies" (*Ostdeutschlandforschung*).[13]

At the same conference, Professor Rolf Reißig pointed out that Transformation Studies cannot provide new data because, "its presuppositions have been achieved."[14] Although Reißig was careful to couch his claims in terms of the theoretical and methodological problems of the field, I believe a deeper, and possibly more disturbing, significance can be attributed to the "achievements" of Transformation Studies he referred to. The end of Transformation Studies was, in effect, the institutionalization of a new, West German-dominated sub-discipline upon the site of its (now extinct) object of study. If Transformation Studies ultimately failed to deliver better scientific understanding of the current situation in East Germany, it did manage to achieve the study of reunified Germany without East Germans: the work of Transformation Studies enabled a new cadre of predominantly West German-trained scholars to emerge as experts in a new field, and they have survived the apparent death of that field to this day within universities and research institutions throughout East Germany. The social scientific discussion of reunified Germany continues to be dominated by West Germans.

The legitimacy of current mainstream social scientific knowledge of eastern Germany depends, in fact, on the active erasure of East German scholars from the discourse. West German leaders of transformation studies have steadfastly neglected to respond directly to critics from the second East German scientific culture. For example, Hans Bertram, chairman of the former KSPW project that was the forerunner to transformation studies (and now head of the micro-sociology program at Humboldt University in East Berlin), published a highly technical study that attempts to refute, "the idea which has recently been spread around, mostly by older East German social scientists, that East German social scientists are, according to their catchphrase, the 'losers of unification.' "[15] In their article entitled *"Das fünfte Rad am Wagen? Die (ost)deutschen Sozialwissenschaften im Vereinigungsprozes"* [The wagon's fifth wheel? (East) German social scientists in the reunification process], Bertram and Kollmorgen (a former student of his) argue that the elimination of East German social scientists was the inevitable result of bringing the *neue Länder* into line with the current conditions of global capitalism, emphasizing cross-German cutbacks in education and research which lead to higher redundancy rates in the East because the socialist system was more "bloated" and "top-heavy" (i.e., there were more academics per capita) than West Germany's.

However, Bertram and Kollmorgen fail to mention that the "catchphrase" they refer to be in fact the title of an article published in the East German scholarly journal *Hochschule Ost* (which is, now as *Die Hochschule*, devoted to developments within higher education in eastern Germany from an eastern perspective). That article was written by then-younger East German social scientists (*Nachwuchswissenschaftler*), a group with which the original KSPW studies were purportedly concerned.[16] The oblique reference to "mostly older East German social scientists" is particularly ironic: the social scientists in question were indeed ten years older than they were when transformation studies began. The Kollmorgen and Bertram piece, published in a ponderous follow-up to the KSPW transformation studies reports Bertram headed, pointedly avoids reference to any of the critical second scientific culture literature being "spread around" by these now "older East German social scientists." They allude to new, East German "independent [social scientific] research institutes" (which publish and actively promote the work of these so-called "losers of reunification") without mentioning any by name.

Like most of their colleagues in the academy, Kollmorgen and Bertram are loath to acknowledge their East German critics as really existing interlocutors.[17] Mainstream transformation studies, it would seem, is being pushed into an awkwardly defensive position by unnamable critics coming from out-of-bounds—namely, East German scholars who were "about 30 or 40 years old at the time of the opening of the Wall, and now around 40 or 50 years old, [but] not really considered scholars of the new generation."[18] Since their own scientific and professional positions have become emblematic of a particular ideological image of the successfully reunified German nation-state, West German social scientists now ensconced in the *neue Länder* are not in a position to openly recognize the formation of a second, East German scientific culture by the very scientists they have effectively replaced. The implication is that the "older East German social scientists" they mention are by definition *former* scientists who must be excluded from mainstream discourses at all costs. The boundary mainstream transformation studies is at pains to maintain between scientific and public discourse is, as such defensive actions indicate, showing signs of leakage.[19]

The new discipline of *Ostdeutschlandforschung* (East German Studies) being proposed today in place of a failed East German Transformation Studies remains disturbing precisely because it would require, at minimum, the inclusion of East Germans. As Stefan Bollinger has argued, what is currently glaringly missing from German research is the "particular knowledge of East German specificity [and] its historical and mental conditions *from those who themselves are the product of this society*, [so that their] knowledge and subjective experience of the processes of transformation can become usable for reunified Germany."[20] This is, and will remain, a disturbing research proposal because it would ultimately need to reveal that East Germany's "transformation," as demonstrated by mainstream social scientists, is not, and was never, synonymous with a real or meaningful "reunification" of East and West Germany. As long as East Germans remain almost totally excluded from state-sponsored academia in Germany, there can be no scientific conceptualization or understanding of a reunified German state without systematically erasing East Germans from the discourse. This erasure currently provides what semblance of coherence may exist in mainstream discussions of a successfully reunified Germany. To acknowledge the existence of—not to mention engage with—East Germans is to recognize that their national identity is a product of their institutionalized alienation from the German State, giving the lie to "reunification" as a coherent national principle.

How German Is Reunified Germany's Social Science?

The exclusion of East Germans—and a specifically East German experience of reunification—from mainstream social scientific discourse, can be interpreted as a rejection of the quintessentially German tradition of *Geisteswissenschaft*. This tradition is grounded in a rigorous methodological emphasis on subjective experience and knowledge systematically informing scientific understanding. Social scientific understanding is explicitly placed in a dialectical relationship with society, and is grounded in *Bildung*, understood as a form of insight into society based on the cultivated, self-conscious social empathy derived from lived experience, or *Erleben*.[21] According to this methodological approach, *Geisteswissenschaft* plays an important formative role in modern society, where, as Mannheim puts it, "theorizing is a prerequisite of [social] cohesion."[22] Ironically, the failure of East German Transformation Studies seems to demonstrate Mannheim's dictum in reverse: theories of transformation premised on the disappearance of East Germany presuppose a fundamental lack of social cohesion within reunified Germany.

W. E. B. DuBois, one of America's greatest practitioners of the *Geisteswissenschaft* methodology, famously described the problem of racial exclusion in the recently "reunified," post-Civil War, U.S. in terms of the "double-consciousness" produced by the exclusion of a national minority from full citizenship in the State: The Negro is a sort of seventh son, born with a veil, and gifted with second-sight in this American world—a world which yields him no true self-consciousness, but only lets him see himself through the revelation of the other world. It is a peculiar sensation, this double consciousness, this sense of always looking at one's self through the eyes of others, of measuring one's soul by the tape of a world that looks on in amused contempt and pity. One ever feels his two-ness—an American, a Negro; two souls, two thoughts, two un-reconciled strivings; two warring ideals in one dark body, whose dogged strength alone keeps it from being torn asunder.[23]

I do not wish to claim that East Germans have become an ethnic minority within Germany. But I do believe that those committed to developing an effective *Ostdeutschlandforschung* will need to confront a similarly—if less severely—disturbing national problem at the heart of their research: the threat East German exclusion poses to the integrity of German democracy.

Notes

1. See Laurence McFall and Lothar Probst, "After the GDR: New Perspectives on the Old GDR and the Young Länder," *German Monitor* (2001), no. 54.

2. See Raj Kollmorgen and Hans Bertram, "Das fünfte Rad am Wagen? Die (ost)deutschen Sozialwissenschaften im Vereinigungsprozess," Idem (eds.), *Die Transformation Ostdeutschlands: Berichte zum sozialen und politischen Wandel in den neuen Bundesländern* (Opladen, 2002), 389–424.

3. This was from a private interview in 2004. I have translated all quotations from interviews and German texts into English myself.

4. See Allison Abbott, "Tough Measures Bring a Scarred Science Back to the World Stage: Ten Years After the Fall of the Berlin Wall, East German Scientists are Putting the Pain of Reunification Behind Them," *Nature*, 401 (1999), no. 14, 635–39.

5. See Kollmorgen and Bertram, "Das fünfte Rad am Wagen?," *passim*.

6. I use "mainstream academia" to refer to Germany's national (public) system of higher education. The "mainstream academics" are faculty at these institutions, who officially hold the status of civil servants. Private colleges and universities are an extremely insignificant part of Germany's academic landscape. There are, however, a number of independent research institutes.

7. Arno Hecht, *Die Wissenschaftselite Ostdeutschlands: Feindliche Übernahme oder Integration?* (Leipzig, 2002), 60–61.

8. See Abbott, "Tough Measures."

9. See Stefan Bollinger, "Deutschland braucht die ostdeutschen Sozialwissenschaftlerinnen und Sozialwissenschaftler," paper presented at the conference "Ostdeutsche Sozialwissenschafter—Wege der Reintegration" at Wissenschaftszentrum Berlin, November 30, 2002. A revised version of the paper can be found in: Idem et al. (eds.), *Ausgrenzung oder Integration: Ostdeutsche Sozialwissenschaftler zwischen Isolierung und Selbstbehauptung* (Berlin, 2004), 49–65.

10. "Ich akzeptiere nicht, dass der Osten bestimmt, wer in Deutschland Kanzler wird. Die Frustrierten dürfen nicht Deutschlands Zukunft bestimmen," as quoted from *Frankfurter Allgemeine Zeitung*, August 11, 2005.

11. Hans Bertram, *Soziologie und Soziologen im Übergang: Beiträge zur Transformation der außeruniversitären soziologischen Forschung in Ostdeutschland* (Opladen, 1997).

12. See Kollmorgen and Bertram, "Das fünfte Rad am Wagen?" *passim*.

13. Initiativgruppe Netzwerk Ostdeutschlandforschung, *Ostdeutschlandfroschung: Befunde, offene Fragen, Perspectiven*, transcripts of conference held at Haus der IG Metall, Berlin, August 4 and October 6, 2005.

14. Ibid.

15. Kollmorgen and Bertram, "Das fünfte Rad am Wagen?" 411.

16. Stefan Bollinger, Ulrich van der Heyden, and Mario Kessler, "Verlierer der Einheit: Die Geisteswissenschaften aus der DDR," *Hochschule Ost*, nos. 3–4 (2000), 195–203.

17. The degree to which the burgeoning Second Culture, East German social scientific literature is ignored by Germany's mainstream academia is endemic; much of this literature is more readily available in the University of Chicago Library than in the Humboldt University libraries or even the *Staatsbibliothek zu Berlin*.

18. Bollinger et al., "Verlierer der Einheit," 8.

19. See T. F. Gieryn, "Boundary-Work and the Demarcation of Science from Non-Science," *American Sociological Review*, 48 (1983), no. 6, 781–95.

20. See Bollinger, "Deutschland braucht die ostdeutschen Sozialwissenschaftlerinnen und Sozialwissenschaftler," *passim*.

21. See the standard works of Karl Mannheim: *Ideology and Utopia* (1929, first Engl. ed. 1936), Wilhelm Dilthey: *Einleitung in die Geisteswissenschaften* (1887),

Fritz Ringer: *The Decline of the German Mandarins* (1969), and Norbert Elias: *Über den Prozess der Zivilisation* (1937/1939).

22. Karl Mannheim, *Ideology and Utopia: An Introduction to the Sociology of Knowledge* (London, 1963), 131.

23. W. E. B. Du Bois, *The Souls of Black Folk* [1903] (New York, 1990), 8–9.

Conclusion

A Note on Research Directions and Literature

AXEL FAIR-SCHULZ AND MARIO KESSLER

The collapse of the German Democratic Republic and the unification of Germany provoked deep and thorough social and institutional transformations. Between 1990 and 1992 the structures of GDR historiography were dismantled. The evaluation process of the historical institutes of the universities and the Academy of Sciences resulted, as this book informs, in the disbandment of most of these institutions and the large-scale dismissal of East German historians from their workplaces.[1] As it is shown here, only very few East German historians found a place in the scholarly landscape of unified Germany.

For the jobless majority, especially for those who remained committed to working within a Marxist-conceptual and analytical framework, the only other alternatives were to leave the profession or to take part in the building of the academic "counter-culture" that is discussed in this book.[2]

In consequence, East German historians and their biographies were seemingly relegated to obscurity. After 1990, established German historians rarely cited the monographs, essay collections, or articles created during the forty years of the GDR in the footnotes of current academic literature, even when it would seem pertinent. Most of the exceptions to this trend stem from the works of historians trained in the former GDR. Some of those who remained scholarly active, after 1990, contributed to this volume.

For those critically reflective historians, allegiant to Marxist historical thought, one consequence emerged out of the failure of the Soviet model of socialism: that any formulaic and/or predictable notions of a linear historical process toward socialism—as insisted upon by the former-state's *version* of "Marxism-Leninism"—had to be abandoned. Inasmuch as East German Marxist historians made significant contributions to international debates, they did it primarily as they departed from the rigid demands of a state-canonized and anti-pluralistic understanding of historical work.[3]

After the end of the GDR, East German historians were forced to confront the reality that most of them were, before 1989 and the disintegration of East Germany, resistant to the insights and research from disciplines—that the nineteenth-century founding generations of Marxist thinkers could not have been familiar with. Thus East German historians, contrary to many Western Marxists such as Herbert Marcuse, failed to open themselves to the new and differentiating understanding of personal and mass psychology.[4] This led to a narrower perspective, which was particularly harmful in the analysis of Fascism. These differences are also to blame for the relatively negligible contributions of East-German research to our understanding of the Holocaust.[5]

Given these circumstances, it is remarkable that GDR historiography enjoys growing attention among the community of researchers. One reason for this fact is that "the varied career progression, choice of topic, and published output of East German academics tell us a lot about the complex relationship between history writing and politics in a communist dictatorship."[6] Another reason is that the history of West German historiography is only fully comprehensible when placed within a German-German context.[7] East German historiography, on the other hand, must also be seen as part of a Soviet-styled model of science and scholarship.[8]

Thus, scholarly literature on GDR historians in German is abundant and has proliferated since 1989–90. Historians, journalists, and other interested parties now have unprecedented access to archives. Debates about the legacy and contributions of GDR historians have been infused with no small degree of polemics, particularly in the 1990s and early 2000s. It became fashionable to call into doubt the "scientificity" (*Wissenschaftlichkeit*) of East-German historical research as such and to label it as pure party propaganda.[9]

But as the GDR and its community of historians fade into history, more balanced and less partisan assessments are emerging, as the publications of Konrad H. Jarausch, Matthias Middell, and Martin Sabrow (to name but three researchers) demonstrate. Their objective is to critically examine East German historical scholarship as embedded within its discursive culture.[10]

In recent years, an increasing number of English-language publications have addressed the legacy of the GDR in post-unification Germany.[11] They are based on a large number of British and North American studies, devoted to the politics and culture of the GDR during the last decades.[12] New works in English on the social history of the GDR made extensive use of the archival material that is now accessible for research,[13] with special attention devoted to the early history of the country.[14] Deserving mention among these books, discussing the *Wende* and its immediate effects, are Konrad H. Jarausch's *The Rush to German Unity* and Charles Maier's *Dissolution*.[15]

However, with the exception of Rosalind M. O. Pritchard's instructive overview and the unpublished dissertation about Leipzig of Rosita Munger, no study of the transformation of East-German historical scholarship has been written in English.[16] And none of these books pays special attention to historians. Moreover, only a few books deal with East German historiography at all.[17] Among those authors, Georg G. Iggers in particular focuses on the innovative potential of some sections of GDR historiography, as does Stefan Berger, who taught at Glamorgan and Manchester universities before accepting a professorship at Bochum University, Germany.[18]

It is easy to predict that the transformation of East German historical scholarship will continue to be a subject of controversy and research. First-hand sources include the growing numbers of reminiscences by East German historians, peaking in the year 2000.[19] Some of these were published since 2008, when the conference in Potsdam, New York, was held.[20] One of the conference participants, Werner Röhr, published a massive two-volume study of the transformation of East German historical sciences.[21] A circle of dismissed East German Scholars, mostly working in the social sciences and humanities, documented the transformation of the University of Jena in a collection of essays.[22]

The present book attempts to question the oversimplified concepts of either *Ostalgie* or the indiscriminate and undifferentiated condemnation of the GDR. It also tries to show that the almost wholesale dissolution of East German research institutions and the dismissal of East German historians from academic posts following unification have caused the anomalous absence in a "reunified" Germany of a Marxist historiographical tradition that is well established elsewhere in Europe. As stated in this book, the West German historians' guild never offered Marxist Scholars full citizenship.[23] Had it been otherwise, would some decisions about the liquidation and the continued existence of GDR institutions after 1990 have turned out differently? It is arguable that a more inclusive approach, on the part of West Germany's historical profession as a whole, would have led to more constructive decisions about the institutional and academic legacy of East German historical scholarship in a now reunified country.

Notes

1. For an early account see Ingrid Matschenz et al. (eds.), *Dokumente gegen Legenden: Chronik und Abwicklung [. . .] des Instituts für Geschichtswissenschaften an der Humboldt-Universität zu Berlin* (Berlin, 1996). See also Stefan Bollinger and Ulrich van der Heyden (eds.), *Deutsche Einheit und Elitenwechsel in Ostdeutschland* (Berlin, 2002). According to Lothar Mertens, twenty-three historians have been exposed as Stasi informers. See Lothar Mertens, *Lexikon der DDR-Historiker* (Munich, 2006), 23.

2. In a recent book that is based on interviews with GDR professors from Humboldt University, the Dutch researcher Adriaan in 't Groen showed what psychological injuries their final dismissal brought with it. See Adriaan in 't Groen, *Jenseits der Utopie: Ostprofessoren der Humboldt-Universität und der Prozess der deutschen Einigung* (Berlin, 2013).

3. This was, among others, the case for some East German social historians, such as Helga Schultz, Hartmut Zwahr, or, earlier, the historians of the Hanseatic League at the University of Greifswald. Walter Markov and his school interpreted the bourgeois revolutions of the seventeenth and eighteenth centuries in a rather non-dogmatic way. Special attentions deserve the literary historians at the Academy of Sciences.

4. Walter Markov was one of the few East German historians who took psychological factors into account. See his massive *Revolution im Zeugenstand*, 2 vols. (Leipzig, 1982) and *Grand Empire: Sitten und Unsitten der Napoleonzeit* (Leipzig, 1984), English translation: Grand Empire*: Virtues and Vice of the Napoleonic Era* (New York, 1990).

5. Kurt Pätzold, who published since the 1970s substantial works on the history of anti-Semitism and the Holocaust, considered this weakness for his own and his colleagues' research. See his preface to a sourcebook that includes communist and non-communist interpretations of the Fascist mass psychology: Kurt Pätzold (ed.), *Faschismus-Diagnosen* (Berlin, 2015). For a profound overview see Werner Röhr, *Faschismus und Weltkrieg: Problemskizze zur historische Faschismusforschung in der DDR* (Hamburg, 2001).

6. Matthew Stibbe, Review of Lothar Mertens, *Lexikon der DDR-Historiker* (Munich, 2006), H-Net Reviews, July 2008, http://www.h-net.org/reviews/showrev.php?id=14779.

7. See ibid. and Georg G. Iggers (ed.), *Marxist Historiography in Transformation: New Orientation in Recent East German History* (Providence, RI, and Oxford, 1991).

8. See for this aspect Frank Hadler and Georg G. Iggers, "Überlegungen zum Vergleich der DDR-Geschichtswissenschaft mit den 'gespaltenen' Historiographien Ostmitteleuropas nach 1945," Georg G. Iggers et al. (eds.), *Die DDR-Geschichtswissenschaft als Forschungsproblem, Beiheft 27 der Historischen Zeitschrift* (Munich, 1998), 433–44.

9. See also Axel Fair-Schulz, "Tons of Wasted Paper? Jürgen Kuczynski and East German Historiography," Q. Edward Wang and Franz L. Fillafer (eds.), *The*

Many Faces of Clio—Cross-Cultural Approaches to Historiography: Essays in Honor of Georg G. Iggers (New York and Oxford, 2007), 382–401.

10. To mention but two standard works, see Konrad H. Jarausch and Matthias Middell (eds.), *Nach dem Erdbeben: (Re-)Konstruktionen ostdeutscher Geschichte und Geschichtswissenschaft* (Leipzig, 1994); Martin Sabrow, *Das Diktat des Konsenses: Geschichtswissenschaft in der DDR 1949–1969* (Munich, 2001). For Sabrow's stimulating interpretation of the GDR dictatorship as "discourse of rule" (*Herrschaftsdiskurs*), see his essay "Dictatorship as Discourse," in Konrad H. Jarausch (ed.), *Dictatorship as Experience: Towards a Socio-Cultural History of the GDR* (New York and Oxford, 1999), 195–211. See also the dispute between Martin Sabrow and Ralf Possekel on the nature of GDR historiography. Possekel, while appreciating Sabrow's uncompromising rejection of cold-war style condemnation, criticizes him for turning GDR historiography into a "gallery of curious." According to Possekel, Sabrow adopts a viewpoint of an ethnologist who set out to explore an unfamiliar culture. See Martin Sabrow, "Beherrschte Normalwissenschaft: Überlegungen zum Charakter der DDR-Historiographie," *Geschichte und Gesellschaft*, vol. 24 (1998), no. 3, 412–45, and Ralf Possekel, "Kuriositätenkabinett oder Wissenschaftsgeschichte? Zur Historisierung der DDR-Geschichtswissenschaft," Ibid., 446–62. See also Heiko Feldner, "History in the Academy: Objectivity and Partisanship in the Marxist Historiography of the German Democratic Republic," Patrick Major and Jonathan Osmond (eds.), *Communism and Society in East Germany under Ulbricht 1945–71* (Manchester, 2002), 262–78.

11. See, e.g., Nick Hodgin and Caroline Pearce, *The GDR Remembered: Representations of the East German State Since 1989* (Rochester, NY, 2011); Renate Rechtien and Dennis Tate (eds.), *Twenty Years On: Competing Memories of the GDR in Postunification German Culture* (Rochester, NY, 2011); David Clarke and Ute Wölfel (eds.), *Remembering the German Democratic Republic: Divided Memory in a United Germany* (Basingstoke, UK, 2011); Anna Saunders and Debbie Pinfold (eds.), *Remembering and Rethinking the GDR: Multiple Perspectives and Plural Authenticities* (Basingstoke, UK, 2013).

12. See Arnd Bauerkämper (ed.), *Britain and the GDR: Relations and Perceptions in a Divided World* (Berlin and Vienna, 2002); Peter Barker (ed.), *Views from Abroad: Die DDR aus britischer Perspektive* (Munich, 2007); Stefan Berger and Norman LaPorte, *Friendly Enemies: Britain and the GDR, 1949–1990* (Oxford, 2010); Jost Hermand and Marc Silberman (eds.), *Contentious Memories: Looking Back at the GDR*, 2nd ed. (New York, 2000); Mario Kessler, "Die Geschichte der DDR aus der Sicht amerikanischer Forscher," Idem, *Historia magistra vitae? Über Geschichtswissenschaft und politische Bildung* (Berlin, 2010), 121–57.

13. See Mary Fulbrook, *Anatomy of a Dictatorship: Inside the GDR, 1949–1989* (Oxford, 1995); Idem, *A People's State: East German Society from Hitler to Honecker* (New Haven and London, 2005). See also Konrad H. Jarausch's comparative East-West study *After Hitler: Recivilizing Germans, 1945–1995* (New York, 2006). For intellectual trends in both parts of Germany see Sean A. Forner, *German Intellectuals and the Challenge of Democratic Renewal: Culture and Politics After 1945* (Cambridge, 2015).

14. See Ann L. Phillips, *Soviet Policy Towards East Germany Reconsidered: The Postwar Decade* (Westport, CT, and London 1986); Meredith Heiser, *Soviet and East German 'Deutschlandpolitik,' 1968–1973: Leadership's Role in Domestic and Foreign Policy Linkage*, PhD Thesis, Johns Hopkins University School of Advanced International Studies (Washington, DC, 1994); Norman A. Naimark, *The Russians in Germany: A History of the Soviet Zone of Occupation, 1945–1949* (Cambridge, MA 1995). For the cultural transformation of East Germany see David Pike, *The Politics of Culture in Soviet-Occupied Germany,* 1945–1949 (Palo Alto, CA, 1993). For comparative aspects see John Connelly, *Captive University: The Sovietization of East German, Czech and Polish Higher Education, 1945–1956* (Chapel Hill, NC, 2000).

15. Konrad H. Jarausch, *The Rush to German Unity* (New York, 1994); Charles Maier, *Dissolution: The Crisis of Communism and the End of East Germany* (Princeton, NJ, 1997).

16. See Rosalind M. O. Pritchard, *Reconstructing Education: East German Schools and Universities after Unification* (New York and Oxford, 2009); Rosita Munger, *The Transformation Process of the Higher Education System in East Germany After 1989: A Case Study of Leipzig University*, PhD thesis (SUNY at Buffalo, 1998).

17. See Andreas Dorpalen, *German History in Marxist Perspective: The East German Approach* (Detroit, 1985); Georg G. Iggers, "New Directions in Historical Studies in the German Democratic Republic," *History and Theory*, vol. 28 (1989), no. 1, 59–77; idem (ed.), *Marxist Historiography in Transformation.*

18. See Stefan Berger, "Former GDR Historians in the Reunified Germany: An Alternative Historical Culture and its Attempts to Come to Terms with the GDR Past," *Journal of Contemporary History*, vol. 38 (2003), no. 1, 63–83.

19. See Gerhard Fuchs, *Ein Sechsstaatenbürger*, vol. 1: *Jugend in Böhmen*; vol. 2/1: *Erwachsen in Sachsen*; vol. 2/2: *Als deutscher Historiker mit Böhmen verbunden* (Leipzig, 1998–2007); Eckart Mehls, *Unzumutbar: Ein Leben in der DDR* (Schkeuditz, 1998); Günter Benser, *Die DDR: Gedenkt ihrer mit Nachsicht* (Berlin, 2000); Fritz Klein, *Drinnen und Draußen: Ein Historiker in der DDR* (Frankfurt-Main, 2000); Joachim Petzold, *Parteinahme wofür? DDR-Historiker im Spannungsfeld von Politik und Wissenschaft* (Potsdam, 2000); Wolfgang Jacobeit, *Von West nach Ost und zurück: Autobiographisches eines Grenzgängers zwischen Tradition und Innovation* (Münster, 2000); Helmuth Stoecker, *Socialism with Deficits: An academic life in the German Democratic Republic* (Münster, 2000); Helmut Bock, *Wir haben erst den Anfang gesehen: Selbstdokumentation eines DDR-Historikers* (Berlin, 2002); Stefan Doernberg, *Fronteinsatz: Erinnerungen eines Rotarmisten, Historikers und Botschafters* (Berlin, 2004); Peter Hoffmann, *In der hinteren Reihe: Aus dem Leben eines Osteuropa-Historikers in der DDR* (Berlin, 2006); Peter Schäfer, *"Schreiben Sie das auf, Herr Schäfer!": Erinnerungen eines Historikers an seine Universitäten in Berlin und Jena* (Jena, 2007). For Werner Bramke's political experiences see his report *Die Krise der Demokratie: Erfahrungen aus einem ostdeutschen Landtag* (Leipzig, 2006). Between 1994 and 2003 Bramke was deputy for the Party of Democratic Socialism at the parliament of the State of Saxony.

20. See Kurt Pätzold, *Die Geschichte kennt kein Pardon: Erinnerungen eines deutschen Historikers* (Berlin, 2008); Karl Heinz Jahnke, *Gegen das Vergessen: Biographische Notizen. Forschungen zum Widerstand gegen die NS-Diktatur in Deutschland* (Rostock, 2008); Jan Peters, *Menschen und Möglichkeiten: Ein Historikerleben in der DDR und anderen Traumländern* (Stuttgart, 2011); Eckard Müller-Mertens, *Existenz zwischen den Fronten: Analytische Memoiren oder Report zur Weltanschauung und geistig-politischen Einstellung* (Leipzig, 2011). See also Walter Markov's autobiography *Wie viele Leben lebt der Mensch* (Leipzig, 2009) that was published 16 years after the author's death.

21. Werner Röhr, *Abwicklung: Das Ende der Geschichtswissenschaft der DDR*, vol. 1: *Analyse einer Zerstörung* (Berlin, 2011); vol. 2: *Analyse ausgewählter Forschungen, Übersichten, Register* (Berlin, 2012).

22. See Manfred Weissbecker et al. (eds.), *Hoffnungen, Enttäuschungen, neue Erfahrungen: Deutsche Hochschullandschaft in der "Wende." Das Beispiel Friedrich-Schiller-Universität* (Jena, 2007). See also Manfred Weissbecker's and Ludwig Elm's contributions to this volume.

23. See Mario Kessler's contribution to this book.

Appendix

Appeal from University Professors and Former German and Central European Refugees, from *Frankfurter Rundschau*, September 11, 2002

We, the undersigned, university professors concerned with German culture and science, are addressing the government of the Federal Republic of Germany and the German policy-makers in the area of science development, in order to induce them to help as fast as possible the few scholars of the former GDR that are still active in the German academic landscape—on short-term contracts, in independent associations, or as private scholars.

Eleven years after the reunification of the country that was carried out by the state, which was desired by a majority of the population—yet, desired with the hope of an equal basis—the intellectual "infrastructure" of East and West Germany is more different than it ever was during the time of separation. In spite of a restructuring and the new founding of universities and other institutions an intellectual stratum that could support the civil society, is barely noticeable in East Germany.

The reasons are above all to be found in the rigorous removal of East German intellectuals from their pre-1989 professions—a removal that exceeded by far the necessary renewal and the restructuring of the academic landscape made necessary by the reunification.

In spite of commendable efforts on part of some academics that have come to the East, the newly imported West German intellectual leading stratum remains foreign to the majority of the East German population.

However, without East German intellectuals in qualified professions the disappointment that is spreading in the former GDR due to process of an imposition of West German structures and ways of thought, which is experienced as an annexation, and especially due to the economic destructions and the mass unemployment, cannot be overcome. We are especially concerned about the openly appearing animosity of some East Germans, especially of young people, directed against parliamentary democracy, accompanied by right-wing radicalism and chauvinism. Without autochthon intellectuals this challenge cannot be met. The social costs of the removal of highly qualified East German academics almost without exception exceed by far the short-lived benefits of the few who profited from the reunification in this regard.

We appeal to you to become aware of the inherent dangers and to provide the East German academics in the social sciences and the humanities by means of an reintegration program with long-term teaching and research positions, and not only with badly paid, time-limited, and socially barely acknowledged jobs. These academics have achieved and still achieve more than average in the past ten years under the harshest conditions!

We hope to assure through this appeal that a great intellectual potential, whose members knew how to assert themselves against the dominant conventions already in the GDR, does not get lost for German and international science, as well as for Germany's political culture. The measure that we are appealing for also corresponds to the spirit and the letter of the German reunification contract of 1990 that was meant to nurture and protect the academic and cultural substance of the GDR.

We, the undersigned, who left Germany and Central Europe during the time of National Socialism, back then had to rely on support and solidarity. We will now give this support and solidarity to those East German colleagues who need it and who have proven worthy of it through their life and work before and after 1989.

Theodor Bergmann (Stuttgart)
Renate Bridenthal (New York)
Eric J. Hobsbawm (London)
Wilma A. Iggers (Buffalo)
Georg G. Iggers (Buffalo)
Friedrich Katz (Chicago)
David Kettler (Annandale-on-Hudson)
Mikuláš Teich (Cambridge, United Kingdom)
Alice Teichová (Cambridge, United Kingdom)

Translated by Douglass Hansen

Contributors

Marcus P. Aurin, b. 1970, ADB, is a PhD candidate at the University of Chicago and lives currently in Boston. He earned his BA in Anthropology and Political Science at the University of Massachusetts in Boston and his MA in Anthropology from the University of Chicago. He won the 1996 W. H. R. Rivers Undergraduate Prize Essay for his *Chasing the Dragon: The Cultural Metamorphosis of Opium in the United States, 1825–1835* that was published in *Medical Anthropology Quarterly*, 14 (2000), No. 3, pp. 414–441. His MA thesis is titled *From Ideology of Science to Science as Ideology: The Materialization of Socialist Science in the GDR*. Aurin pursues this general topic further with his dissertation project on Science and Cultures: Eastern Germany's Second Scientific Culture.

Stefan Bollinger, b. 1954, Dr. phil. habil., is Senior Lecturer for Political Science at the Free University of Berlin. His book publications include *Dritter Weg zwischen den Blöcken: Prager Frühling* 1968 (1995); *1989: Eine abgebrochene Revolution. Verbaute Wege nicht nur zu einer besseren DDR?* (1999); *Das letzte Jahr der DDR: Zwischen Revolution und Selbstaufgabe* (2004); *1968: Die unverstandene Weichenstellung* (2008); *Weltbrand, "Urkatastrophe" und linke Scheidewege: Fragen an den "Großen Krieg"* (2014). He edited, among other books, *Imperialismustheorien: Historische Grundlagen für eine aktuelle Politik* (2004); *Deutsche Einheit und Elitenwechsel in Ostdeutschland*, with Ulrich van der Heyden (2004); *Ausgrenzung oder Integration? Ostdeutsche Sozialwissenschaftler zwischen Isolierung und Selbstbehauptung*, with Ulrich van der Heyden and Mario Kessler (2004); *Lenin: Träumer und Realist* (2006), and *Linke und Nation: Klassische Texte zu einer brisanten Frage* (2009).

Ludwig Elm, b. 1934, Dr. phil. habil., was Professor of Modern German History and taught, until 1991, at the University of Jena. His doctoral dissertation *Zur Geschichte des Linksliberalismus in der Frühperiode des deutschen Imperialismus* (1964) and his Habilitation *Hochschule und*

Neofaschismus: Zeitgeschichtliche Studien zur Hochschulpolitik in der BRD (1971) foreshadow Elm's lifelong preoccupation with political parties and higher education in Germany. In addition to his scholarly activities, Elm was also a deputy of both the East German and the united German parliament (Volkskammer and Bundestag). His most recent book publications include *Der deutsche Konservatismus nach Auschwitz: Von Adenauer bis Merkel und Stoiber* (2007); *Wenn ich einmal Kanzler wär: Ein Zwischenruf zur deutschen Einheit* (2009); and *Der Mantel der Geschichte und andere deutsche Denkwürdigkeiten* (2011).

Axel Fair-Schulz, b. 1969, PhD, is Associate Professor of European History at the State University of New York at Potsdam, New York. He studied history and anthropology at Brigham Young University and at the State University of New York at Buffalo. After graduating, he was a post-doctoral fellow at the German Historical Institutes in London and Washington, as well as at the Moses Mendelssohn Center for European Jewish Studies in Potsdam, Germany. He is the author of several scholarly articles and book chapters, among them on Robert Havemann, Jürgen Kuczynski, and Stephan Hermlin. His dissertation has been published in 2009 as *Loyal Subversion: East Germany and its Bildungsbürgerlich Marxist Intellectuals*. Together with Mario Kessler he edited *German Scholars in Exile: New Studies in Intellectual History* (2011). He is also on the editorial board of the Collected Works of Rosa Luxemburg, in English, as well as the co-editor, together with William A. Pelz, of Volume Three of this project.

Ulrich van der Heyden, b. 1954, Dr. phil. habil., Dr. rer. pol., PhD, is Senior Lecturer at the Free University of Berlin and Humboldt University of Berlin, specializing in African Studies. His books include *Die Afrikawissenschaften in der DDR: Eine akademische Disziplin zwischen Exotik und Exempel* (1999); *Martinus Sewushan: Nationalhelfer, Missionar und Widersacher der Berliner Missionsgesellschaft im Süden Afrikas* (2004); *Zwischen Solidarität und Wirtschaftsinteressen: Die "geheimen" Beziehungen der DDR zum südafrikanischen Apartheidregime* (2005); *Auf Afrikas Spuren in Berlin: Die Mohrenstraße und andere koloniale Erblasten* (2008). In 2013 he defended his third doctoral dissertation at Rhodes University (Grahamstown, Eastern Cape Province, South Africa) on GDR's international development policy toward South Africa. Among many books he edited are *Orientalische Reise-Beschreibung des brandenburgischen adeligen Pilgers Otto Friedrich von der Gröben* (2013), *Mosambikanische Vertragsarbeiter in der DDR-Wirtschaft* (2014), and *Vom Matrosen zum Künstler* (2015).

Georg G. Iggers, b. 1926, PhD, is Distinguished Professor Emeritus at the State University of New York at Buffalo and holds honorary doctorates from the Technical University of Darmstadt, Germany, University of Richmond, VA, and Philander Smith College, Little Rock, Arkansas. In 1938 he was forced to leave Germany and immigrated to the United States. His book publications include *Deutsche Geschichtswissenschaft: Eine Kritik der traditionellen Geschichtsauffassung von Herder bis zur Gegenwart* (1997); *Historiography in the Twentieth Century: From Scientific Objectivity to Postmodern Challenge* (1997), German ed.: *Geschichtswissenschaft im 20. Jahrhundert: Ein kritischer Überblick im internationalen Zusammenhang* (2007); *Two Lives in Uncertain Times: Facing the Challenges of the 20th Century as Scholars and Citizens*, with Wilma A. Iggers (2006); *Global History of Modern Historiography*, with Edward Wang and Supriya Mukherjee (2008), German edition: *Geschichtskulturen: Weltgeschichte der Historiographie von 1750 bis heute* (2014); *Marxist Historiographies: A Global Perspective*, ed. with Edward Wang (2015).

Konrad H. Jarausch, b. 1941, PhD, is Lurcy Professor for European Civilizations at the University of North Carolina at Chapel Hill and former director of the Center for Contemporary History (ZZF) at Potsdam, Germany, where is now Senior Research Fellow. He is the author of numerous books on modern and contemporary German history, including *The Rush to German Unity* (1994); *Shattered Past: Reconstructing German Histories*, with Michael Geyer (2003); *After Hitler: Recivilizing Germans, 1945–1995* (2006); *Contemporary History as Transatlantic Project: The German Problem, 1960–2010* (2012); *Deutsche Geschichte*, co-author (2014); *Out of Ashes: A New History of Europe in the Twentieth Century* (2015). He edited many books in German and English on modern European history and co-edited the book series *Zeithistorische Studien* at Böhlau Verlag, Cologne, Weimar, and Vienna. He also edited his father's war letters *Reluctant Accomplice: A Wehrmacht Soldier's Letters from the Eastern Front* (2010) and co-authored and co-edited the volume *Gebrochene Wissenschaftskulturen: Universität und Politik im 20. Jahrhundert* (2010).

Mario Kessler, b. 1955, Dr. phil. habil., is Associate Professor at the University of Potsdam, Germany, and Research Fellow at ZZF. He also taught at the University of Massachusetts at Amherst, Columbus State University (Georgia), Yeshiva University (New York), The Hebrew University (Jerusalem), the City College of New York, and Rutgers University (New Brunswick, New Jersey). His most recent books include

Ossip K. Flechtheim (2007); *Von Hippokrates zu Hitler: Über Kommunismus, Faschismus und die Totalitarismus-Debatte* (2008); *Historia magistra vitae? Über Geschichtswissenschaft und politische Bildung* (2010); *Klios Jünger: 100 Historiker-Porträts von Homer bis Hobsbawm*, with Werner Berthold (2011); *Kommunismuskritik im westlichen Nachkriegsdeutschland: Franz Borkenau-Richard Löwenthal-Ossip Flechtheim* (2011); *Ruth Fischer: Ein Leben mit und gegen Kommunisten, 1895–1961* (2013); *Communism—For and Against: The Political Itineraries of Ruth Fischer* (2013); *Moses Hess and Ferdinand Lassalle: Pioneers of Social Emancipation* (2013); *Albert Schreiner: Kommunist mit Lebensbrüchen* (2014); *Grenzgänger des Kommunismus: Zwölf Porträts aus dem Jahrhundert der Katastrophen* (2015); and *Revolution und Konterrevolution: Studien über Gewalt und Humanität aus dem Jahrhundert der Katastrophen* (2016). He edited and co-edited many books, most recently *Reformen und Reformer im Kommunismus*, with Wladislaw Hedeler (2015).

Helmut Meier, b. 1934, Dr. phil. habil., was Professor of Modern History at the Academy for Social Sciences in East Berlin. His book publications include *Leo Stern (1901–1982): Antifaschist, Historiker, Hochschullehrer und Wissenschaftspolitiker*, ed. (2002); *Uneinige Einheit: Der öffentliche Umgang mit Problemen der deutschen Einheit*, ed. (2005); *Unternehmen DDR-Geschichte: Forschungsstand, Defizite, Projekte*, with Stefan Doernberg and Dietrich Staritz (2006). He co-edited the multivolume books series *Gesellschaft-Geschichte-Gegenwart* at Trafo Wissenschaftsverlag, Berlin (since 1995) and was coordinator of the interdisciplinary association *Gesellschaftswissenschaftliches Forum* that organized activities of East German scholars since 1991.

Kurt Pätzold (1930–2016), Dr. phil. habil., was, until 1992, Professor of Modern German History at Humboldt University, Berlin. His main field of research was the extermination of European Jews. Together with Manfred Weissbecker he wrote a history of the Nazi Party and biographies of Adolf Hitler and Rudolf Hess. His most recent books include *Im Rückspiegel: Nürnberg. Der Prozess gegen die deutschen Hauptkriegsverbrecher 1945/46* (2006); *Die Mär vom Antisemitismus* (2010); *Streitfall Geschichte* (2011); *Wahn und Kalkül: Der Antisemitismus mit dem Hakenkreuz* (2012; *Kriegerdenkmale in Deutschland: Eine kritische Untersuchung* (2012); *Der Vergangenheit entgeht niemand: Vergnügen mit Clio?* (2013). *1813: Der Krieg und sein Nachleben* (2013); *Kein Streit um des Führers Bart* (2013); *Zweiter Weltkrieg* (2014); *1914: Das Ereignis und sein Nachleben* (2014); *Faschismus-Diagnosen* (2015); *Der Überfall: Der 22. Juni 1941—Ursachen, Pläne und Folgen* (2016). In 2008 he published his memoirs *Die Geschichte kennt kein*

Pardon: Erinnerungen eines deutschen Historikers. Dr. Pätzold, who died on August 18, 2016, is mourned by his friends and colleagues; we are grateful for his contribution to this book.

William A. Pelz, b. 1946, PhD., is Professor of History at Elgin College (Elgin, Illinois) and director of the Institute of Working Class History in Chicago. Before that he taught at Roosevelt University, Chicago, where he also did research on the German November Revolution and the Workers' and Soldiers' Councils of 1918–1919. His most recent book publications include *Against Capitalism: The European Left on the March* (2008), *Karl Marx: A World to Win* (2012), and *A People's History of Modern Europe* (2016). He edited *Wilhelm Liebknecht and German Social Democracy: A Documentary History* (1994) and *The Eugene V. Debs Reader* (2000). He is editor of the *Encyclopedia of the European Left* (2009). He is on the editorial board of *Left History: An Interdisciplinary Journal of Historical Inquiry and Debate*. He is also on the editorial board of the Collected Works of Rosa Luxemburg, in English, as well as the co-editor, together with Axel Fair-Schulz, of Volume Three of this project.

Jörg Roesler, b. 1940, Dr. oec. habil., was Professor of Economic History at the Institute for Economic History, Academy of Sciences, East Berlin. He also worked at the ZZF and taught at Humboldt University, the University of Fine Arts in Berlin, York University, the University of Toronto, and Portland State University (Oregon). Among his books are *Der Anschluss von Staaten in der modernen Geschichte: Eine Untersuchung aus aktuellem Anlass* (1999); *Die Wirtschaft der DDR* (2002); *Ostdeutsche Wirtschaft im Umbruch, 1970–2000* (2003); *Vom Kombinat zur Aktiengesellschaft*, with Dagmar Semmelmann (2005); *Umweltprobleme und Umweltpolitik in der DDR* (2006); *Momente deutsch-deutscher Wirtschafts- und Sozialgeschichte 1945–1990: Eine Analyse auf gleicher Augenhöhe* (2006); *Kompakte Wirtschaftsgeschichte Lateinamerikas vom 18 bis zum 21. Jahrhundert* (2009); and *Geschichte der DDR* (2012).

Werner Röhr, b. 1941, Dr. phil habil., is Professor Emeritus at the University of Zielona Gora, Poland. Until 1991 he was Senior Research Fellow at the Central Institute of History, Academy of Sciences, East Berlin. He specializes both in the history of philosophy and social and economic history. His book publications include *Europa unterm Hakenkreuz*, Vol. 2: *Die faschistische Okkupationspolitik in Polen 1939–1945* (1989); *Panta rhei: Vorlesungen zur antiken Phil*osophie (2004): *Abwicklung: Das Ende der Geschichtswissenschaft der* DDR, Vol. 1: *Analyse einer Zerstörung* (2011), Vol. 2: *Analyse ausgewählter*

Forschungen, Übersichten, Register (2012); *Faschismusforschung im Spiegel der Kritik* (2014). He also edited the bi-annual *Bulletin für Faschismus- und Weltkriegsforschung* (since 1993).

Rainer Schnoor, b. 1944, Dr. phil. habil., is Senior Lecturer Emeritus for American Cultural Studies at the University of Potsdam, Germany. He has published on writers of the Left, such as Raymond Williams and Studs Terkel, as well as on the theory and practice of American Studies in East Germany. In addition, Schnoor's scholarly interests have focused on immigration, ethnicity, and multiculturalism in the United States. Schnoor wrote his *Habilitation* about the New Left history in the United States (1984) and has edited several volumes, including *Grenzüberschreitungen* (1996); *Amerikanistik in der DDR: Geschichte-Analysen-Zeitzeugenberichte* (1999); and *Against the Grain: Studies in English and American Literature and Literary Theory* (2004).

Manfred Weissbecker, b. 1935, Dr. phil habil., was, until 1992, Professor of Modern German History at the University of Jena, specializing in the history of political parties, especially the Nazi Party. His book publications with Kurt Pätzold include *Adolf Hitler: Eine politische Biographie* (1995); *Rudolf Hess: Der Mann an Hitlers Seite* (1996); *Schlagwörter und Schlachtrufe: Aus zwei Jahrhunderten deutscher Geschichte*, 2 vols., eds. (2002); *Geschichte der NSDAP 1920–1945*, 3rd ed. (2008). He edited, under the auspices of the Rosa Luxemburg Foundation Thuringia, several books on the history of East German social sciences. He also co-edited *Lexikon zur Parteiengeschichte 1789–1945*, with Dieter Fricke et al. (1983–1986, CD-Rom edition 2014). His most recent book publications are *Das Firmenschild "Nationaler Sozialismus": Der deutsche Faschismus und seine Partei* (2011) and *Weimarer Republik* (2015).

Index of Names